Knowledge Management and Organization

Knowledge Management and Organization

Healthcare Quality in Montenegro

Ivan Radević

LEXINGTON BOOKS
Lanham • Boulder • New York • London

Published by Lexington Books
An imprint of The Rowman & Littlefield Publishing Group, Inc.
4501 Forbes Boulevard, Suite 200, Lanham, Maryland 20706
www.rowman.com

6 Tinworth Street, London SE11 5AL, United Kingdom

British Library Cataloguing in Publication Information Available

Library of Congress Cataloging-in-Publication Data

Library of Congress Control Number: 2021934276

ISBN 978-1-7936-4102-1 (cloth)
ISBN 978-1-7936-4103-8 (electronic)

Contents

List of Figures

List of Tables

Acknowledgments

This book is the result of a seven-year long research (2013–2020)—doctoral and postdoctoral researches. To thank everyone who contributed to the quality of this research and the successful completion of this book during that period is not possible. So I choose to mention five important insights that emerged as a derivative of my work on this book.

1. *Knowledge is important.* And where you get it is important too. Being a part of the oldest education institution in Montenegro was a privilege, because of knowledge and skills and because of many friends and contacts I made. I am grateful to the entire staff of the Faculty of Economics of the University of Montenegro and to my past and current students, because each in their own way motivated me during my work on this book. I would also like to thank my teachers and friends from the Elementary School "Savo Pejanović," the School of Economics "Mirko Vešović," and the Faculty of State and European Studies in Podgorica. The knowledge I acquired and many life lessons from the entire period of my education were a defining factor in choosing my further professional orientation.

2. *Management is simple.* And so are the solutions even for the most complex challenges when you have the right support. I owe a debt of gratitude to Professor Vlado Dimovski (Faculty of Economics, University of Ljubljana, Slovenia), my mentor during my work on my doctoral dissertation, which is the foundation of this book. Also, I owe gratitude to Professor Anđelko Lojpur and Professor Božo Mihailović from the Faculty of Economics, University of Montenegro, who were members of the commission for the defense of my doctoral thesis. Their experience, knowledge, time, and availability for consultation, criticism, support, and friendly advice

were a stable support in the writing of this book. I am also very grateful for support in the research to professors who were kind and willing to share their knowledge and experience with me: Simona Kukovič (Faculty of Social Sciences, University of Ljubljana, Slovenia), Charles Snow (Pennsylvania State University, USA), Børge Obel (School of Business and Social Sciences, Aarhus University, Denmark), Jasmina Ćetković (Faculty of Economics, University of Montenegro), Đorđije Blažić (Faculty of Administrative and European Studies, Podgorica, Montenegro), Dorthe Døjbak Håkonsson (Aarhus University, Denmark), Richard M. Burton (Duke University, USA), Božidar Popović (Faculty of Science and Mathematics, University of Montenegro), Sandra Penger (Faculty of Economics, University of Ljubljana, Slovenia), Milenko Popović (Faculty of Administrative and European Studies, Podgorica, Montenegro), and academician, Professor Radovan Radonjić (Montenegro).

3. *Organization is a system.* Support of the system to this research came from the Ministry of Health of Montenegro, and the Union of Doctors of Medicine, who delegated respondents from health institutions, and I am very grateful to all of them. Also, not only for the special gratitude for the time they invested but also for their support, I owe to all healthcare professionals and the citizens of Montenegro who took part in this research.

4. *Quality is important.* And it matters who you spend your time with. Even though I did not have as much time for my family or friends as I wanted while I was working on this book, I am grateful to my friends who were very understanding and found the time and energy to contribute to the quality of this book. Special thanks to my class from 2005, from the Faculty of Economics, as well as to my friends from the Alumni Club of the School of Rhetoric and the Sports and Recreational Association of Students of Economics and Management "Ekomen." Spending time with them would always boost my energy and they were all a great motivation.

5. *Health is happiness.* And the greatest happiness is to have a family that gives you abundance of support, motivation, and understanding.

Podgorica, January 2021
Ivan Radević

Introduction

The rapid progress of information and communication technologies has led to the wide-ranging availability and presence of technology in life. Along with this phenomenon, there is a problem of the human ability to use all the prospects that technology provides organizationally and anthropologically. However, this may be achieved through knowledge management and with adequate organizational design.

Knowledge management, although known for decades, has been in the focus of scientists and professionals, together with the development of information and communication technologies that have contributed to the accelerated spread of knowledge everywhere. It represents a new dimension of the management approach and a major research challenge to the management theory and practice. Its important determinant is that it chooses the proactive approach instead of acting after the change occurs. Also, knowledge management dictates a greater learning ability of the company and affects the organization by initiating changes in order to improve its performance.

In a turbulent environment and constantly changing circumstances, where the organizational and nontechnological innovations have to be ahead of technological innovations to be able to control processes and know how to use all the best advantages of technology, knowledge management becomes ever more relevant. In addition to adequate (re)configuration of the system through organizational design, knowledge management should provide adequate knowledge-based application and the function of execution, in accordance with the structural components of organizational design and all with an overarching purpose of achieving organizational goals.

Therefore, the main topic of this book covers knowledge management and organizational design and treats them as factors of quality of health system's services. There were three reasons to choose the health sector as the topic of analysis: first, because health is among of the most responsible and demanding social activities, as any change within the health system affects the quality of life; second, because health organizations are constantly facing the problem of growing demand due to an aging population, increased number of different types of diseases, accelerated pace of life and lifestyle, which often (unreasonably) makes work and earnings a priority over health; and third, because Montenegro ranks twenty-third out of thirty-five listed European countries according to the European Health Consumer Index—EHCI (Björnberg and Phang, 2019), which takes us to the conclusion that there are multiple reserves and opportunities to increase the quality of health system in Montenegro.

Management-related sciences identify modern competitive environment through concepts such as change, speed, risk, uncertainty, insecurity, instability, and problems. In such a complex environment, knowledge management occurs as a response to these organizational challenges, combining knowledge management, innovation, flexibility, networking, speed, and proactivity as critical success factors of modern organizations.

For these reasons, the author made a final decision to use the following topic for this book "Knowledge Management and Organization: Healthcare Quality in Montenegro."

THE GOAL AND UNDERLYING RESEARCH QUESTIONS OF THE BOOK

The goal of the book is to provide insight into the prospects of improving the quality of health care on the basis of complex theoretical and empirical material and by applying the knowledge management model, followed by a multi-contingency approach to organizational design.

In particular, the book tackles the relationship between knowledge management and the quality of services of health organizations, as well as the impact of elements of organizational design and their various combinations on the quality of health services. Furthermore, it addresses the mutual relation between knowledge management and organizational design, all with the purpose of creating a thorough insight into their effect on the efficiency and effectiveness in providing services by health organizations.

In addition to the above, the book offers guidelines for improving the health system, which is dimensioned through the following analyses: first, the level of representation and quality of application of knowledge management in health organizations in Montenegro; second, the quality of harmonization of elements of organizational design of health organizations in Montenegro; and third, the quality of services of health organizations in Montenegro. Due to the geographical dispersion of health organizations as units of analysis, this book will present differences between health organizations from different regions and between private and public health organizations, based on selected aspects.

Accordingly, the reader will be able to find answers to the following research questions:

1. *How can knowledge management and organizational design improve the quality of services of health organizations?*
2. *What is the relationship between knowledge management and organizational design in order to improve the quality of services of health organizations?*
3. *To what extent is knowledge management represented in health organizations in Montenegro?*
4. *What are the possibilities for improving the macro and micro organization of health system in Montenegro?*
5. *What is the level of quality of services of health organizations in Montenegro?*
6. *Is enough attention given to permanent internal and external harmonization of the elements of organizational design and transformation in health organizations in Montenegro in order to increase the quality of health services?*
7. *How can reconfiguration of the organizational model cause increased quality of services of health organizations?*

The basic research problem addressed by this book is based on three basic constructs: knowledge management, organizational design, and quality of health services. Therefore, the following section will briefly present the used methodology.

RESEARCH DESIGN

This study is exploratory (research), descriptive (illustrative), and explicative (explanatory). The research design included a combination of quantitative and qualitative research methods.

In addition to a rich set of secondary data that are based on a detailed review of contemporary literature and multiple documents dealing with health care, knowledge management, and organization, this book offers numerous analysis and conclusions that are based on a rich set of primary data.

The research design involved the use of three questionnaires. One of them concerned knowledge management and organizational design and was distributed to employees of health organizations in Montenegro, as part of a field research. The other two questionnaires predominantly covered the area of health care and the quality of health services, and as such were distributed to the citizens of Montenegro—users of health institutions—one of them was distributed through the field research and the other online. Furthermore, following a quantitative analysis of the data, the author began working on qualitative research through interviews and focus groups in order to increase the validity of conclusions, as described below.

QUESTIONNAIRES

The first questionnaire, adapted to quantitative research, consisted of two segments of questions: the adapted version of the questionnaire used by Downes (2014) was used for the first segment of questions on knowledge management, while the second segment that addressed organizational design, used the questionnaire of a group of authors: Burton, Lauridsen, Obel, and Hakonsson (Burton, Lauridsen and Obel, 2003; Burton, Obel and Hakonsson, 2015). The questionnaire contains a total of 190 questions. In addition to the demographic characteristics of respondents, the key variables covered by the questionnaire are the following: level of knowledge management application, knowledge management effectiveness, organizational culture, organizational structure, organizational infrastructure, leadership, management style, organizational climate, environment, technology, strategy, complexity, formalization, centralization, and others. This questionnaire was used to collect data from employees in health institutions, that is, from three members: member of the administration, medical doctor, and medical technician. After that, independently, the same questionnaire was used to collect data from other doctors, members of the Union of Medical Doctors.

The second questionnaire referred to the quality of health services. To develop it, the author used several different questionnaires from the field of quality of evaluation of health services. A group of authors: Choi, Cho, Lee, S., Lee, H., Kim, Delene, Bunda and Kim (Choi, Cho, Lee, S., Lee, H., and Kim, 2004; Lee, Delene, Bunda and Kim, 2000) developed the basic structure of the second questionnaire. A set of questions regarding the perception of corruption in health care was used from the questionnaire of the Center for Monitoring and Research Podgorica, which they used in 2012 for their project "Fight against corruption in the health system of Montenegro" that was implemented with the support of German Embassy in Podgorica. These models of questionnaires underwent incremental adjustments in accordance with the nature of the studied problem, and the final version contained a total of 163 questions. In addition to basic information about respondents, the questionnaire measured different categories, such as waiting time for an examination, quality of services, financial motivation of doctors, quality of nutrition, physical activity, self-medication, corruption in health care, autonomy of health system, health problems, differences between private and public health institutions, among others. Even though the Ministry of Health of Montenegro adopted the "Rulebook on detailed instructions for monitoring and establishing the evaluation process, with indicators and criteria used to monitor and evaluate the quality of health care" (Official Gazette of Montenegro 17/15), it is not used in practice (or only partially and not in a form that can be used, or, in other words, the ministry does not have data that would be usable for the analysis). Therefore, the author measured the dimensions of quality of health care based on the perception of health care users (citizens of Montenegro) through the above-mentioned questionnaire.

The third questionnaire is a combination of the above two, with the addition of a set of questions regarding the COVID-19 pandemic. It contains as many as 184 questions, and it was filled in by users of health care services in Montenegro, that is, citizens of Montenegro.

INTERVIEWS

A set of individual, personal, semistructured in-depth interviews were conducted in accordance with the sequential design of the mixed research method, following the preliminary processing of quantitative data in order to deepen the analysis and provide additional explanations on certain matters. That helped identify the topics that need to be researched in more detail, and based on that, define questions for semistructured interviews, as one of the most common approaches to interviewing in qualitative research.

SAMPLE—SELECTION OF UNITS OF ANALYSIS

When it comes to filling out the first questionnaire (which concerned knowledge management and organizational design), health institutions in Montenegro were selected as research units. In each health institution covered by the research, one member of the administration (usually the director), one medical doctor, and one medical technician each answered the questionnaire that measured the categories of knowledge management and organizational design. This approach is in line with the method of triangulation, which increases the validity of results.

Practically, to collect data from employees from public health institutions implied conducting a kind of a census, and for private health institutions, the author used a combination of a convenient sample and a snowball sample. The convenient sample belongs to the category of nonrandom samples that imply selection of members of the population who are available at a specific time. A snowball sample is a type of nonrandom sampling, in which respondents help the researcher in identifying other respondents and establishing cooperation with them.

The research was conducted on a sample of the following forty-five health institutions:

1. Health centers (eighteen institutions) in Andrijevica, Bar, Berane, Bijelo Polje, Budva, Cetinje, Danilovgrad, Herceg Novi, Kolašin, Kotor, Mojkovac, Nikšić, Plav, Pljevlja, Podgorica, Rožaje, Tivat, and Ulcinj.
2. General hospitals (seven institutions) in Bar, Berane, Bijelo Polje, Cetinje, Kotor, Nikšić, and Pljevlja.
3. Special hospitals (three institutions) in Brezovik, Dobrota, and Risan.
4. Institute of Public Health in Podgorica, Clinical Center of Montenegro in Podgorica, Institute of Emergency Medical Services in Podgorica, and Institute of Physical Medicine, Rehabilitation and Rheumatology "Dr Simo Milošević" AD Igalo.
5. Private health institutions (thirteen institutions): Biochemical and microbiological laboratory "In Vitro" in Podgorica, Codra Hospital in Podgorica, Krapović Medical in Budva, Milmedika Nikšić, Eye clinic "Borović" in Podgorica, Eye clinic "Dr Lutovac" in Berane, Polyclinic Hippocrates in Podgorica, Polyclinic Mercur Nera in Podgorica, Spa Medica Podgorica, Specialist hospital of internal medicine "Dr Masoničić" in Bar, Special hospital "Dr MedTim" in Podgorica, Dental practice "Mušura" in Budva, Tesla Medical in Berane.

It is worth noting that public health institutions involved all health centers and all general and specialized hospitals in Montenegro, as well as the Clinical Center of Montenegro and the Institute of Public Health. That adds to the quality of results and helps drawing general conclusions about Montenegrin public health system as a whole. Furthermore, the author chose to include the most important and most representative private health institutions and made sure that institutions from all three regions are represented in private health institutions[1] (center, north and south). In addition to the above, sixteen medical doctors, members of the Union, filled in the questionnaire. The purpose of additional examination was to identify if the respondents from the basic sample were biased and to point out the likelihood of needs for the internal harmonization of elements of organizational design. The identification of bias in this particular case was performed by comparing the ratings obtained by members of the Union and the ratings of employees in health institutions, who were delegated by the Ministry of Health to take part in the research. Data from this part of the research (basic sample) were collected during the period from May 16 to 30, 2019. The additional sample, which involved doctors who are members of the Union, was conducted in the period from August 7 to 13, 2019.

In the case of the second questionnaire, which was used in the field survey that was conducted among citizens, the author used the voter list of Montenegro as a sampling frame. A stratified simple random sample was drawn from it, with the planned size of 1,800 respondents (in reality 1,769 took part), whose strata were the North, Center, and South, and the Capital Podgorica. The allocation of the sample is proportional to the size of polling stations (measured by the number of adults). The sample was implemented at 180 polling stations. Given the fact that each polling station has a large number of adults, the author had to make sure that the interviewers had strict rules to follow, in order to respect the principles of probability, rather than choosing respondents according to their own preferences. In this regard, the interviewers had to interview ten people in each polling station area. Households were selected by applying the method of a random direction from a given place, and the respondents from a particular household were selected on the basis of household members' birthday date that was closest to the day of interview. For the stated sample size, confidence interval of 95 percent with an incidence of 50 percent is ± 2.33 percent. Data from this segment of research were collected in the period from May 24 to June 15, 2019.

Data collection through the third questionnaire, unlike the previous two, was implemented online due to the COVID-19 pandemic, from April 30 to May 4, 2020. In this case, the survey included a total of 11,359 respondents, and a more detailed structure of this sample is presented in chapter 10.

After obtaining preliminary results based on quantitative analysis, the author started conducting interviews with managers of health institutions and organizations, prominent experts in the field of management and health, and with several patients too in order to verify the results and reach better conclusions. The author organized a total of ten semistructured interviews. In addition to the above, five focus groups were organized too (two with seven, two with six, and one of five members). The focus groups included doctors, medical technicians, and employees of the Ministry of Health, experts in the field of management and organization, as well as patients. Interviews and focus groups were conducted on two occasions, in September 2019 and September 2020.

METHODS USED

The text of the book excludes a more detailed explanation of the methods used in order to make it more appealing to a wider readership. Therefore, the author will list only the methods that were used to analyze the data and results. In addition to descriptive statistics, tests of normal distribution (*Kolmogorov–Smirnov test*), scale reliability analysis (*Cronbach Alpha*) and factor analyzes, both parametric and nonparametric methods and techniques were applied, such as *t*-test, ANOVA, Mann–Whitney U test, Kruskal–Wallis test, and chi-squared test. Descriptive statistics included absolute and relative frequencies, measures of central tendency, and measures of variation. The Pearson and Spearman correlation coefficients were used to determine the relationship between the dependent and independent variables. To check the factor structure of the set of variables, the author used the analysis of main components (*PCA—Principal Component Analysis*) and confirmatory factor analysis (*CFA*). Since the correlation cannot determine the cause-and-effect relationship between the variables, but only their relationship, the author applied the Structural Equation Modeling (SEM) analysis through the use of structural equations. The author used regression analysis to identify factors that significantly contribute to the prediction of dependent variables and the magnitude of the effect of each independent variable on the dependent one, as well as to estimate the unique contribution of each independent variable to the dependent variable. In addition to the above, the qualitative part of the analysis included the following methods: CRAAP test, bibliometrics, SPELIT analysis, case study, semistructured interview, focus groups, and the method of grounded theory.

BOOK STRUCTURE

In addition to the introduction and conclusion, this book consists of ten interrelated chapters.

The first three chapters provide a theoretical background and an overview of contemporary literature in this area, while the next seven chapters logically rely on the first three and discuss the topic of the book from the standpoint of empiricism and primary data.

The first chapter focuses on knowledge management. It defines the role and importance of knowledge management in modern business and lists different approaches to defining knowledge management and addresses the basic causes of the development of this concept. Then, it continues with the basic components and phases of knowledge management, and points out to the measurability of the impact of knowledge on the success of the organization.

The second chapter addresses the organizational design. This section presents different approaches to defining organizational design. Then, it points out to external and internal factors that are vital for configuring the organization of the health system. In particular, this section presents an overview of internal factors such as organization size, technology, goals, strategy, organizational culture, leadership style, and organizational climate. Moreover, it tackles structural components such as formalization, centralization, and complexity, as well as the concept of organizational structure. At the very end, one will find a presentation of a modern—multi-contingency approach to organizational design.

The third chapter presents a theoretical relational triangle between knowledge management, organizational design, and healthcare. The interrelationship between knowledge management and organizational design is in the focus as a precondition for positive business results. Then, the author elaborates on the notion of organization from the standpoint of building shared values as a prerequisite for its sustainability. Finally, this part views the health system from the standpoint of modern scientific literature and from the angle of knowledge management and organizational design.

The fourth chapter offers a comparative analysis of macroeconomic indicators related to knowledge management and organizational design with health systems of other European countries. This section provides information on the health and education budget of Montenegro, number of employees in education and health, and the share of these categories in the gross domestic product. This part discusses the average income of health workers and addresses the motivation of young people to commit to knowledge, science, and healthcare.

The fifth chapter is a detailed presentation of results of knowledge management in the health system of Montenegro. A special part is dedicated to the quality of application of knowledge management and its effectiveness that significantly determines the quality of health services. This chapter also addresses the organizational culture, organizational infrastructure, and leadership in Montenegrin health institutions, evaluating them as special segments of knowledge management. Each segment of the analysis is presented both at the level of the entire system and by regions, that is, the territorial criterion. Furthermore, it presents the results of the analysis for public and private health institutions.

The sixth chapter portrays the organizational and legal aspect and management context of the health system of Montenegro. This part analyzes the challenges of the decentralization process. Special attention was given to the possibility of greater involvement of local self-government units in the provision of health services. This part addresses key problems in the process of decentralization of the health system too and gives specific recommendations for improving the organizational and legal dimension of the health system of Montenegro.

The seventh chapter gives an overview of the state of four important organizational determinants of the health system of Montenegro. Organizational strategy is viewed through its focus on efficiency and effectiveness. The author analyzed the organizational structure from the standpoint of the degree to which it supports the application of the knowledge management model, while the organizational culture was used to measure the representation of four basic types of organizational culture. Finally, the organizational climate is viewed from the angle of the organization's readiness for change and the levels of tension in the organization. All results are presented aggregately at the level of the system as a whole, by regions and type of ownership.

The eighth chapter indicates in detail the level of quality of health services in Montenegro, measured by the perception of users of health services, that is, citizens of Montenegro. Based on the results of field research on a representative sample of respondents, this chapter gives an overview of the quality of health services in relation to different criteria (geographical, ownership, etc.). Respondents assessed the commitment and knowledge of doctors, waiting time for an examination, the kindness of nurses, the equipment of health institutions with technology, and the price and quality of service. This part defines the key environmental determinants of the health system of Montenegro with special reference to corruption in health care. In the end, this chapter identifies the key factors influencing the growing health problems.

The ninth chapter, based on empirical data, makes specific conclusions about the interdependence of knowledge management and organizational design in the function of improving the quality of health services. In addition, by introducing an additional sample of respondents from the Union, this chapter compares the perception of the management of health institutions with one of the members of the Union. This chapter presents a detailed analysis of internal elements of organizational design and the possibilities of reconfiguration of Montenegrin health organizations. Also, special attention is given to the analysis of external harmonization of organizational design, which includes the need to be oriented to market, that is, to monitor patients' needs better.

The tenth chapter focuses on the response of Montenegrin health system to the challenges of the COVID-19 pandemic. Special attention was paid to the quality of decisions and procedures made during the pandemic, from the aspect of the organization of health system and the application of knowledge management. This part presents in detail the problem of organizational bifurcation, with a special analysis of specific circumstances that further complicate not only the application of knowledge management, but also the functioning and response of the health system to current and future challenges too.

The conclusion offers a sublimation of all result. It closes with the overview of literature used, index, as well as the biography of the author.

MONTENEGRO IN A NUTSHELL

Given that key aspects of this analysis are focused on Montenegro, this section will provide background information on a country that little is known about in the world. The information that follows is given for the purpose of a better understanding of this book and ambient factors of the system that was observed.

History of Montenegro

Montenegro regained its independence on May 21, 2006, and in that context, it earned the status of one of the world's youngest countries. However, this small country in Southeast Europe has a rich state-building tradition and culture that goes back three millennia into the past.

Montenegro is the smallest Slavic nation, but with a multilayered culture, defined by its geographical position. Located in the Balkans, a region that represents a bridge between Europe and Asia, the area of Montenegro has always been influenced by different cultures: Illyrians and Celts, Greeks and Romans, Western-Catholic, Eastern-Orthodox Christianity, and finally Islam. The earliest human communities on the territory of Montenegro date back to the Middle Paleolithic. In that sense, Montenegro has often been a crossroad of history and culture of many civilizations.

Tracing the roots of its statehood from the first Slavic principalities and kingdoms in early Middle Ages, contemporary Montenegro emerged in the turbulent wars for independence that Montenegrins fought in the eighteenth and nineteenth centuries. The century-long struggle was completed when on July 13, 1878, the principality of Montenegro received its international recognition. During the twentieth century, Montenegro was part of several forms of now-former state called Yugoslavia, but following its military tradition participated in both wars on the side of the Allies.

The diversity of culture and turbulent political past has created Montenegro as a multiethnic and multireligious nation. What binds all the citizens of Montenegro is the sentiment of common belonging to the ideals of preserving the achieved independence, peace, and tolerance.

According to the data of the Ministry of Foreign Affairs of Montenegro, Montenegrin diplomatic activity began in 1711 when the first relations with Russia were established, and later with Austria. After gaining official international recognition at the Berlin Congress (July 13, 1878), Montenegro established its official diplomatic relations with many countries. First with Russia and France (1878), then with Great Britain, Austria-Hungary, Italy, and the Ottoman Empire in 1879, Greece in 1881, Serbia in 1897, while official diplomatic relations with the United States were established in 1905, and with Germany in 1906.

Montenegro Today

Montenegro belongs to the so-called "Western Balkan" countries. It borders with Serbia, Kosovo, Croatia, Bosnia and Herzegovina, Albania, and across the sea—with Italy. Montenegro's coastline is 293.5 km long. According to the data of the Statistical Office of Montenegro (Monstat, 2020), the country covers an area of 13,888 km^2, and its population is 622,028, according to the latest estimate from 2019.

The economy of Montenegro predominantly relies on service activities, specifically tourism. The economic structure of Montenegro (according to the data of the Tax Administration from April 2020) consists of 35,870 business entities, of which 99.06 percent is entrepreneurs, micro, and small enterprises (Montenegrin Employers Federation, 2020). According to Eurostat (2020), Montenegro's GDP per capita, according to the buying power amounted to 50 percent of the European Union average in 2019, while this indicator for countries in the region is Croatia 65 percent, Serbia 41 percent, North Macedonia 38 percent, Bosnia and Herzegovina 32 percent, and Albania 31 percent. As of November 2020, according to the Statistical Office—Monstat (2020), the average gross salary in Montenegro amounted to 784 euros, or 525 euros net.

Somewhat slower development of Montenegrin economic system and the longer transition to a market economy are a result of country's history (turbulent past of the Balkans) which was pervaded by wars and frequent changes in the country's legal status.

On a referendum on state legal status, on May 21, 2006, Montenegro voted for independence and regained its independence and full international legal personality. Today, Montenegro is defined by its Constitution as a civil, democratic, ecological, and the state of social justice that adheres to the rule of law.

After the restoration of its independence, Montenegro began its official relations with NATO, through the Partnership for Peace program (November 29, 2006), and on June 5, 2017, it officially became a member of NATO. Montenegro submitted its application for membership in the European Union on December 15, 2008, and two years later on December 17, 2010, the country was given the status of a candidate country. The ongoing accession negotiations officially started on June 29, 2012.

Nature of Montenegro

When the famous English poet George Gordon Byron, described Montenegrin pearls of nature—the Montenegrin coast and the Bay of Kotor, he used the words "at the moment of the creation of our planet, the most beautiful merging of land and sea occurred at the Montenegrin seaside" (Montenegro Travel, 2021).

Montenegro is a country of exceptional natural resources and amazing contrasts, and the diversity of its climate and terrain, as well as the position of Montenegro on the Balkan Peninsula and the Adriatic Sea creates conditions for the formation of biological diversity with very high values, that puts Montenegro among biological "hot-spots" of European and world biodiversity (United Nations, 2020). The ecosystem of Montenegro is made up of the sea, coastline, through saltpans, freshwater lakes, canyons, caves, dense forests, mountain plateaus, to high mountain peaks. As much as 13.41 percent of the country's land area is protected as national, regional and nature parks, nature reserves, and the like.

Interesting Facts about Montenegro

What follows is the presentation of several interesting historical facts that speak in favor of rich Montenegrin historical and cultural heritage.

1. Money was minted in the second century BC (in Risan, 168 BC) on the territory of today's Montenegro. The Korčula Statute from 1424 mentions foreign currencies on that island (Croatia), and brings up Balšić's coin with a wolf, which means that Montenegro (then Zeta) had a convertible currency at that time (Novaković, 2012: 50).
2. During the Crnojević dynasty, at the end of the fifteenth century (1493), Montenegro had its own printing house in Cetinje. That was the first printing house among the South Slavs.
3. The well-known German scholar Karl Neumeyer stated in his work from 1987 that Montenegrins were the only Slavs who had their own, authentic law—since the Russians used German, the Poles French, the Serbs Austrian, and the Bulgarians Byzantine and Italian. (Košutić, 2002: 27). The General Property Code for the principality of Montenegro, authored by Valtazar Bogišić in 1888, revealed to the world the fascinating political and legal culture of Montenegro. In just three to four years, it was translated into many world languages and accepted as a model to redefine and supplement civil codes of Japan, India, Germany, and France. (Radonjić, 2011).
4. Montenegrins were the first people to raise a mass uprising against fascism in Europe during World War II (July 13, 1941). The famous French philosopher Jean-Paul Sartre described this "Thirteenth of July Uprising" as the most amazing and magnificent event in the entire European revolutionary history of the twentieth century (Stanišić, 2005: 88). Hungarian academician Jozef Bajza describes Montenegrin history as "a symbol of

freedom, a beacon of state ideas and a metaphor for the survival of small states and people" (Bajza, 2006: 17).

5. The nature of Montenegro includes five national parks (one is under the protection of UNESCO as part of the world natural heritage) and diverse flora and fauna, one of the two European rainforests, the largest lake in the Balkans, the river (Tara) with the deepest canyon in Europe, among others. About 3,600 plant species have been registered in Montenegro so far, and 66 percent of the European ornithofauna. In order to protect natural resources and preserve identity of its unique space, Montenegro adopted the Declaration on the Ecological State (September 20, 1991), which was validated by the Constitution.

NOTE

1. Speaking strictly formally, Montenegro does not have regions as territorial units, and hereinafter this term will be understood as separate parts of the country in accordance with the geographical criterion.

Chapter 1

Knowledge Management

This section discusses knowledge management from the standpoint of understanding the role and importance of knowledge management in an organization, analysis of different approaches to defining knowledge management and identification of basic causes for development of the concept itself. Basic components and basic stages of knowledge management will be analyzed too.

ROLE AND IMPORTANCE OF KNOWLEDGE MANAGEMENT IN MODERN BUSINESS

Information is the currency of the knowledge economy (HR Magazine, 2009), and the value of such a company currency predominantly depends on the knowledge of an organization, how it uses its knowledge, and how quickly it is ready and able to learn something new. In the past, competitiveness was determined on the amount of capital available to the company, but today, knowledge is the foundation of competitiveness.

The last decade of the twentieth century was marked by the concept of knowledge management. Quite a few authors perceived this concept as a trend that would be abandoned soon. As literature suggested, this modern syntagm would be used to impress rather than to research this area in pursuit of useful and usable knowledge management (Scarbrough and Swan, 2001; Ponzi and Koenig, 2002; Hislop, 2010; Serenko, Bontis, Booker, Sadeddin, and Hardie, 2010; Oluikpe, 2012). However, at the end of the twentieth century, there was an exponential growth of the literature on knowledge management, and there are no signs that growing trend of interest in this area would end. Thus, initial assumptions that knowledge management was just a fashion were rejected. What is obvious today is that knowledge management as an exceptionally important category is associated with all organizations regardless of the sector they belong to—private or public, for-profit or nonprofit, labor-intensive or capital-intensive, production or service.

In modern business environment where knowledge makes the fundamental resource for development, effective knowledge exploitation is impossible without an appropriate setting up of knowledge management as one of the prerequisites for achievement of goals of modern organizations. Ensuring success of an organization in the long run means creating a coherent organizational system that connects people, processes and technology in order to increase the knowledge of its members and the organization as a whole. Therefore, knowledge management is recognized as a critical factor in achieving strategic competitive advantage of modern organizations (Omotayo, 2015). Furthermore, it is perceived as a basis for sizing organizational performance, competitiveness, and profitability.

As a rule, organizations that create and use knowledge in the right way are more innovative and function better than those with inadequately developed knowledge management (Riege, 2007; Omotayo, 2015). In addition, knowledge management is one of the basic determinants of sustainability and prosperity of the organization (Teece, Pisano, and Shuen, 1997; Cegarra-Navarro and Cepeda-Carrión, 2010; Kamhawi, 2012; Cavicchi, 2017), and a crucial driver of organizational performances too (Bosua and Venkitachalam, 2013). A higher degree of knowledge management in the organization requires a higher degree of productivity and greater flexibility of the organization (Martensson, 2000). Therefore, even from the macroeconomic standpoint, knowledge in modern business conditions is perceived as the basis for growth of gross domestic product across national economies.

Globalization and development of information and communication technologies, which have contributed to the enormous speed of information, are among the causes that affect the growing importance and significance of knowledge management in the modern business environment (Greiner, Böhmann, and Krcmar, 2007). Consequently, globalization and the development of information and communication technology, as complementary processes, have contributed to the multiplication of knowledge by sharing information, and due to the increasing availability of knowledge and the speed of information flow, information and knowledge become obsolete at great speed. This means that knowledge management requires permanent focus.

DIFFERENT APPROACHES TO DEFINING KNOWLEDGE MANAGEMENT

Formally speaking, there are many different preferences regarding the definition of knowledge management. This is largely due to the fact that knowledge management requires interdisciplinarity, so researchers in this field come from different disciplines. Still, in spite of many definitions in literature, complementarity of definitions is evident. First, knowledge management is treated as a process of coordination and exploitation of organizational knowledge resources with the purpose of creating competitive advantages (Drucker, 1999). Second, knowledge management is defined as a process of comprehensive changes that is based on exploitation of knowledge in an organization and a continuous improvement of organizational performance by strengthening elements of organizational design and their mutual connections (Forcadell and Guadamillas, 2002). Third, knowledge management can be presented as a systematized and organized process that makes the knowledge in an organization available to all individuals or groups of people (employees), in order to improve organizational and business performance (Đorđević-Boljanović, 2009). Fourth, many authors describe it as a multiphased process that most often include knowledge creation, knowledge acquisition, knowledge storage, knowledge sharing, and knowledge application (Sydänmaanlakka, 2002). Fifth, knowledge management has many positive effects, such as improving performance and strengthening the competitive position of an organization in the first year (North and Hornung, 2002). Furthermore, positive correlation of knowledge management with innovation of an organization has been confirmed too (Akgül and Tunca, 2016).

BASIC CAUSES OF THE DEVELOPMENT OF KNOWLEDGE MANAGEMENT CONCEPT

Organizational survival, competitiveness, globalization, and aging of labor force are most commonly cited factors that cause the creation and strengthening of knowledge management systems (Omotayo, 2015). The globalization and development of information and communication technologies have contributed to the following:

a) Information and communication technologies expose organizations to competition worldwide and require from their management to make extra efforts and achieve new knowledge and practices to be able to remain competitive across the world.

b) Greater competition means a harder way for organizations to stand out, which may be possible only through a strategy that combines new knowledge, proactivity, and creativity.
c) As the supply becomes more complex, the demand becomes complex too, which means the customers will be more demanding when choosing a company to trust.
d) In addition to the aging labor force, there is an increasing turnover of employees between countries, which, in absence of an adequate knowledge management system, can lead to the waste of knowledge in an organization, repetition of past mistakes, and unfavorable circumstances for the company.

Many authors have identified the need to align the strategies of knowledge management and organization as a critical factor to the success of an organization (Gao, Li, and Clarke, 2008; Oluikpe, 2012). As first, it is necessary to provide a system for recording and sharing organizational knowledge and best practices, and the knowledge management strategy will affect the innovation of the organization too.

BASIC COMPONENTS OF KNOWLEDGE MANAGEMENT

Knowledge is the only resource that guarantees the creation of a sustainable competitive advantage of an organization (Groènhaug and Nordhaug, 1992; Davenport and Prusak, 1998; Jasimuddin, 2008). Storing, development, organization, and use of employees' knowledge require appropriate positioning of knowledge management within the organization. Regardless of the diversity of definitions in scientific literature, it is typically based on four components: knowledge, people, technology, and processes (Desouza, 2011; Omotayo, 2015).

Knowledge

Many authors focused their attention to knowledge, and as a result, there are many ways of defining it. Knowledge is a basic part of knowledge management that represents a collection of information from theories, processes, and systems—expressed as opinions, ideas, and studies. While information give answers to questions—*who, what, where, and when*, knowledge provides answers to questions *how* and *why*? Knowledge is based on the quality of information that includes ideas, facts, and expertise that altogether have a crucial influence on individuals, team, and organizational performance (Wang and Noe, 2010). Also, it can be seen as a fluid mix framed by experience, values, contextual, and expert insight that provides a framework for evaluating and creating new information and experiences (Davenport and Prusak, 1998; Omotayo, 2015). Knowledge is perceived through the ability, awareness, understanding, and pragmatism of members of an organization. It can also be defined as an invisible or intangible asset, whose acquisition includes complex cognitive observations, shaped by the processes of learning, perception, understanding, communication, and logical reasoning (Epetimehin and Ekundayo, 2011). Knowledge provides an opportunity to create a new perspective based on information that is combined with experience, context, contemplation, and interpretation (Davenport, De Long, and Beers, 1998; Omotayo, 2015) and provide a new level of understanding and approach to organizational problems. Knowledge is not found only in documents, books, and databases, but also in organizational routines, processes, customs, habits, values, norms, and organizational culture as a whole.

Just as there are different definitions of knowledge, there are many options to categorize various forms of knowledge. The first typology of knowledge generates a division into explicit and implicit (tacit) knowledge (Polanyi, 1966, 1967; Nonaka, 1994; Blackler, 1995; Nonaka and Takeuchi, 1995).

Explicit knowledge is coded, documented, formal, and systematized and, as a rule, can be collected, stored, and transferred. Usually, it includes data, information, policies, procedures, algorithms, software, among others. Explicit knowledge can be shared through information and communication technologies. Knowledge coding means shaping it into certain documented, structured, fixed contents such as books, manuals, guidelines, plans, specifications, scientific formulas, databases, projects, among others. People, as a rule, know more than they can say or show. For this reason, explicit knowledge is treated as a part of implicit knowledge, that is,. the one that can be formalized, documented and articulated, or expressed in words or numbers (Polanyi, 1966; Nonaka and Takeuchi, 1995). The aspiration of knowledge management is to code implicit, individual knowledge as adequately as possible, which is intangible and document and translate it into explicit, documented knowledge, which should be made available to members of the organization.

Implicit knowledge is conditioned predominantly by entire intellectual habitus of an employee. It is located in the employee's mind, behavior, reactions to different situations, and is developed through practice and specific actions. Unlike explicit, implicit knowledge is personal, subjective, often informal, and difficult to document. It arises in the domain of cognitive and experimental learning and depends on the circumstances in which it manifests itself and does not have to be analogous to formal education and typical coded patterns of behavior, which makes its transfer to other members of the organization difficult. Implicit knowledge is deeply grounded in action, procedures, commitment, values, and can only be accessed indirectly (Baloh, Desouza, and Paquette, 2011). Implicit knowledge sharing is possible through networking of employees and their joint activities, but members of the organization have to be willing to act proactively and to "steal knowledge," to use this popular catchphrase as an illustration, or to show interest and ability to learn through watching. Implicit knowledge is the basis for creating a sustainable competitive advantage, taking into account the fact that competitors have a hard time documenting it (Omotayo, 2015) and applying it through an appropriate benchmarking strategy.

People

People are the source of knowledge (Omotayo, 2015). Their ability to think creatively, and their talents and experiences make them the foundation of any knowledge management process. Employees in the organization are required to not only search for knowledge, experiment with it, learn from it but also strive for innovation with other members, that is, to share and create new knowledge (Drucker, 1999). Human resources management, which focuses on the selection of proper staff, is highly important for proper implementation of the knowledge management strategy. The main task of human resource management in the selection of staff must be the selection of personnel whose values are complementary to the organizational culture and who are ready to work in a team and share knowledge (Robertson and Swan, 2003; Swart and Kinnie, 2003). Human resources management provides for the employee satisfaction and their greater loyalty, which contributes to greater motivation of employees to share knowledge, and to lower turnover rate in the company and less loss of knowledge in such cases. In this sense, the role of communication in an organization is crucial for the implementation of knowledge management strategy. In addition, an adequate knowledge management strategy must be supported by appropriate incentives and motivation of people who use and share their knowledge with other members, or, in other words, complementary to the overall organizational culture (Hansen, Nohria and Tierney, 1999; Cabrera E. and Cabrera, A., 2005; Olatokun and Nwafor, 2012; Omotayo, 2015). The essence of the knowledge management strategy is to stimulate initiatives and activities through the use of organizational knowledge (implicit and explicit), expertise, experience, processes, documents, and intellectual assets in the form of culture, informal networks, and trust, where all these are based on information and communication technologies and the appropriate organizational structure of the company (Dalkir, 2005).

Technology

Technology is an indispensable segment of any knowledge management strategy. The application of the concept of knowledge management has been significantly facilitated by the development of information and communication technologies that enable communication between people and teams, regardless of their geographical dispersion. The process of acquiring and applying knowledge is often facilitated by the use of modern software solutions. Technology makes the process of knowledge sharing within the organization simpler and faster, and thus the process of knowledge management depends heavily on the degree of people's trust in technology, as well as on the scope of their knowledge of possibilities that technology offers in better sizing of organizational functionality.

Processes

Processes are logical systems of rules, procedures, and operations that are created in advance and implemented to perform tasks in an organization. Knowledge management must recognize the importance of the component of processes as a critical factor in the efficiency of an organization in most cases. Processes involve humans and machines. Process mapping creates a systematic overview of events and tasks solving in the organization, which helps in the analysis of process rationalization that should be permanent, as in Japanese *kaizen* methodology, which altogether results in increased efficiency and effectiveness of the organization. Continuous focus on processes is necessary due to the danger that excessive introduction of *smart* technologies might jeopardize development of employees, who rely on technology even more than on their own power of reasoning and critical thinking. In this sense, processes must be designed in such a way as to result in synergistic effects of combining people and technology, that is, technology should be a "wind at one's back" in the development of cognitive abilities of employees, not vice versa.

PHASES OF KNOWLEDGE MANAGEMENT

The process of knowledge management is usually presented in four phases:

1. Knowledge creation
2. Knowledge storage
3. Knowledge sharing
4. Knowledge application

The process of knowledge management begins with the identification and collection of knowledge, with the goal of enabling knowledge sharing within the organization and creating opportunities to generate new knowledge. Having shared their knowledge, employees can use new knowledge in their business activities, and consequently increase efficiency of their organization.

The process of creating new knowledge is vital for the survival, growth, and development of any organization. Creating new knowledge enables sustainability and the creation of a competitive advantage based on knowledge, which is of great importance for any organization that wants to survive in complex and changing market conditions (Hislop, 2013; Omotayo, 2015). Knowledge creation is possible through daily activities, communication with colleagues, formal training, taking part in projects, and through the use of software systems of artificial intelligence. However, although technology can make the creation of new knowledge easier, it cannot replace people.

Consolidation of organizational knowledge makes a special part of the knowledge management process, with the aim of enabling its more efficient distribution among all members of the organization. In the case of implicit, individual knowledge of employees, the knowledge management process is difficult, especially due to turnover of employees. If an employee leaves the organization, the organization loses ideas, experience, contacts, relationships, thoughts of the employee, among others. Therefore, it is important to find a way to document implicit knowledge in a timely manner and translate it into explicit. So in case of high employee turnover, the organization could ensure continuity and further development of new knowledge, without setbacks. In this sense, knowledge sharing is a critical success factor of knowledge management (Lee and Choi, 2003; Rabiu, 2009; Gururajan and Fink, 2010; Epetimehin and Ekundayo, 2011; Olatokun and Nwafor, 2012; Oluikpe, 2012; Amayah, 2013; Omotayo, 2015). Knowledge without its use or sharing with other members of the organization does not contribute to the organizational goals.

MEASURABILITY OF THE IMPACT OF KNOWLEDGE MANAGEMENT ON THE SUCCESS OF THE ORGANIZATION

Measuring the impact of knowledge management is a major challenge in creating and implementing strategies and policies of knowledge management because measuring something that has not happened cannot be easy. Knowledge management prevents the loss of money, time, and human resources. It is difficult to quantify the time spent in finding the right information or the cost of creating knowledge in one organizational sector of a company, even though it already exists in another sector (Dumitriu, 2016). It is equally difficult to calculate the cost of time lost using obsolete knowledge, rather than the latest knowledge that guarantees a higher level of productivity, or the cost of investing in technology without a quality assessment of its competency to improve knowledge availability in the organization. Even in the profit sector, where indicators such as profit, revenue, or number of clients can be used to gauge the organization's performance, measuring the impact of knowledge management activities on business results is difficult to quantify and can only be measured indirectly (Resatsch and Faisst, 2004; Dumitriu, 2016). The option of measuring business results based on knowledge management is a topic that is still the subject of scientific research of many authors; however, there are several conclusions that can be singled out from the literature on practical ways to understand and measure the effectiveness of knowledge management activities in private and public sector organizations (Hoss and Schlussel, 2009; Dumitriu, 2016).

Benefits of knowledge management may not come directly or quickly, but it is a fact that they exist and are long-standing. Although the savings coming from the prevention of errors and losses of a company based on knowledge management are invisible at least from the accounting standpoint, there are indicators that can measure the excessive waste of time and human resources.

Benefits of knowledge management can be identified through (Dumitriu, 2016):

1. improved organizational efficiency that is in harmony with the development of information and communication technologies and with professional experience of employees;
2. cost reduction by optimizing the performance of daily routines, error reduction and, if necessary, making a complementary team who will raise organizational efficiency to the maximum;
3. strengthened intellectual and specific knowledge of employees, through network business connections too.

Measuring the quality of knowledge management is not easy, but it is not impossible. Some of ways to do this are (Dumitriu, 2016):

1. existence of a strategic document that regulate direct knowledge management;
2. alignment of vision, mission, and goals with specific documents and guidelines on knowledge management;

3. addressing responsibility for the level and quality of knowledge management in the organization by appointing knowledge management manager;
4. incentive activities and measures for the purpose of lifelong learning and improvement of knowledge;
5. existence of a significant correlation of knowledge management with the business success of the organization.

In spite of the fact that appropriate measures of quality of knowledge management cannot be defined in simple terms, it does not mean one should avoid measuring knowledge management in an organization. As Peter Drucker once said, "You can't manage what you don't measure," it is necessary to take continuous care of knowledge in any organization and develop measuring instruments. Even though it is difficult to conclude which business results we owe to the concept of knowledge management, if knowledge is not a key resource for development in an organization and an underlying reference to move forward, that becomes evident in modern business and in many cases leads to disappearance of organizations.

Chapter 2

Organizational Design

An organization is a system of behavior of people who interact with each other. The goal of organization's existence is to integrate its members' efforts in order to achieve efficient system performance that will allow for top performance of a particular task, that is often divided into several subsystems (Lawrence and Lorsch, 1967). An organization is a social entity that is goal-oriented and entails coordination, management, and control (Snow, 2016; Beans, 2016). Key elements of any organization are its people and their relationships. From the point of view of theory, it can be viewed as a subsystem of the environment in which it functions. Mutual relations of the organization's members are very important, as well as the organization's connection and interaction with the environment.

The allocation of organizational resources in accordance with its tasks is done on the basis of an internal pattern of authority, communication and relations, also known as the organizational structure (Koufteros, Nahm, Cheng, and Lai, 2007; Daft, 2013; Grah 2016). Organizational design implies structuring organizational tasks and designing relationships that are used as basis for their performance. This notion will be explained in more detail below.

DIFFERENT APPROACHES TO THE DEFINITION OF ORGANIZATIONAL DESIGN

Organizational design is a matter that has long been on the agenda of researchers both on a theoretical and practical level. Moreover, organizational design is the best illustration of the fact that theory and empirical research are complementary activities. They contribute to the development of modern approaches to management phenomena and to improved organizational performance only when they support each other. Therefore, there is an extensive number of works of management theorists and management practitioners in scientific literature that discuss the problem of organizational design.

According to Herbert Simon, organizational design can be defined as a management activity that deals with the choice of a goal, strategy, and model of organizational structure with a contingency approach and decision-making system (Rumelt, 1974). Second, it is seen as a process that plans how relations between different elements will be regulated to best fulfill a certain purpose, and also as the outcome of shaping and harmonizing all components of the organization in accomplishing its mission (Stanford, 2007). Third, researches shows that the ability of an organization, as seen from the standpoint of its efficiency, is largely due to the coherence between different elements of organizational design (Obel, 1993; Dotty, Glick, and Huber, 1993; Volberda, Van der Weerdt, Verwaal, Stienstra, and Verdu, 2012; Burton, Obel, and Hakonsson, 2015). Fourth, organizational design represents managerial decisions and the enforcement of decisions on how employees should perform their tasks and activities, including decisions on how to execute tasks and activities, define competencies and responsibilities, and how to conduct the process of departmentalization (Dimovski, Penger and Škerlavaj, 2007). Fifth, organizational design is portrayed as a special form of solving human problems whose basic task is to direct more individuals with different knowledge and interests toward collective accomplishments, which they would not be able to accomplish otherwise (Puranam, 2012). Sixth, organizational design, as a tool, can enable managers to create a productive, pleasant work environment to accomplish new goals that will serve individual and collective interests (Snow, Fjeldstad, Lettl, and Miles, 2010). Seventh, organizational design is a decision-making process that includes two main topics: first, the distribution of the overall task of the organization to smaller parts and units; and second, the coordination of smaller units and parts to fit together, in order to accomplish larger task, that is, organizational goals (Lojpur and Kuljak, 2005; Burton, Obel, and Hakonsson, 2015).

As you will find on the following pages, this researcher will attempt to explain the concept of organizational design from the standpoint of its important internal and external factors that are the underlying elements of organizational design's essence.

EXTERNAL FACTORS

No system exists in a vacuum. Every system is part of a larger system. An employee is part of a company. The company is part of a market. A country is part of the global economy. Therefore, every organization should be viewed as an open system that interacts with its environment at all times. Therefore, a comprehensive analysis of the performance of the organization is necessary, especially from the standpoint of the organization's relationship with the environment, which is in line with the system (integrative) theory of management. Given the fast-changing environment and the number of its elements, connections and interactions that exist within it, it is necessary to review every change within the organization and in the environment, from the standpoint of its impact on business performance. However, maintaining the system's internal stability and adapting to the environment are two conflicting goals. Excessive focus toward internal stability can lead to a weakening of the connection with the environment (market), while a constant focus on the external environment (market changes) requires the organization to change and adjust itself, and that may jeopardize the stability of relationships within the organizational system. In that sense, to work continuously on the organizational design and harmonization of its elements in relation to external factors is the only way to create a sustainable organizational system, as organizations are man-made systems that strive to entropy. The organizational design should be aligned with external factors on the basis of theory of general systems and cybernetics, as a separate science that studies management of complex dynamic systems.

External factors imply all elements outside the organization that directly or indirectly affect its functioning. Organizational design through alignment with external factors creates organizational effectiveness, that is, it provides products or services that are in demand at the market. The organizational design is critical to organization's flexibility in relation to the changes in the environment. High degree of specialization, followed by formalization and centralization, works well in organizations that exist in stable environments, while decentralization and lower formalization are recommended for organizations operating in a dynamic environment (Dimovski, Penger, and Škerlavaj, 2007). Event prediction is important for organizational design, and requires decision-makers to be vigilant at all times, and to apply contingency approach, which implies different scenarios for different situations. External factors can be divided into several categories (e.g., general and specific environment), depending on how they affect the organization—directly or indirectly. The general environment most often includes the social, political, economic, legal, intercultural and technological dimensions of the environment. An important thing to point is that elements of the general environment have indirect impact on the company. The specific environment, unlike the general one, directly affects performance of the organization. In this sense, it consists of customers, competitors and suppliers. Porter's model of five forces is most often used to analyze specific environment (Porter, 2008; Grah, 2016), and helps in shaping the company's strategy (intensity of rivalry among competitors, bargaining power of suppliers and customers, presence of substitute products, barriers to entry). For this reason, it is necessary to take into account environmental factors in organizational design as stronger focus to this segment contributes to greater confidence in business performance and sustainability of the organization.

INTERNAL FACTORS

Internal or inner factors are the ones that are under control of the organization (Burton, 2013). In this paper, internal factors include: size of the organization, technology, goals and strategy, organizational culture, organizational climate and leadership style.

The organization should take into account the alignment of internal factors with organizational structure, and the organization as a whole should be harmonized with its environment (Carmeli, Gelbard, and Gefen, 2010).

Size of the Organization

Size of the organization is an important element of organizational design, and shows substantial inter-conditionality in relation to other elements. The choice of indicators that are used to make difference by size is a subject of broad and current interest across different markets. This is natural, because something that is considered big in Montenegro (e.g., number of employees) does not have to be big at another market (e.g., China). The most precise answer to the question regarding the size of an organization is—it depends on what we measure it against. Organizations can be classified in different categories according to their size: micro, small, medium, and large enterprises. In accordance with the Law on Accounting (2016), size of an organization in Montenegro is determined on the basis of average number of its employees, total assets and total annual income. Size of the organization is closely linked to the organizational design. As a rule, small organizations are more flexible and faster (in terms of decision-making) than larger ones, which allows them to be more innovative than larger (rigid) systems. As a rule, the scale of formalization and specialization is low in small organizations. Also, one of the basic characteristics of small organizations is their impossibility to use the effect of economies of scale, due to their small production capacities that imply higher unit costs. Communication in a small organization is more direct and personal, and in most cases, employees are motivated to do the job. The so-called economic definition of small organizations say that small firms are those with a relatively small market share, whose owner is the manager at the same time and that are not part of a larger company (Deakins and Freel,

2012). On the other hand, large organizations can be more efficient through the economies of scale based on mass production (average costs of production of products and/or services are lower). The level of specialization and complexity of the organization are higher, as well as the formalization that should respond to issues of coordination and control, which is present in large organizations, unlike in small ones. Therefore, organizational design has the tendency to be configured in such a way as to take advantage of small systems too, for example, flexibility and quality of communication, and economies of scale from larger ones. For this purpose, decentralization of decision-making is widely used, as well as a *flat* organizational structure with as few organizational levels as possible that is based on network business connections.

Technology

Technology involves the information, equipment, techniques, and processes needed to transform inputs into outputs, hence it is crucial to the process of organizational design (Burton and Obel, 1998). Depending on the predominant technology of production of products or services (i.e., the share of a specific type of cost in the structure of total costs), organizations can be divided into "labor-intensive," "capital-intensive," "technology-intensive," "knowledge-intensive," and so on (Peneder, 2002). Technologies can be classified into routine and specific. In routine technologies, the method of production is well known in advance, there are few exceptional circumstances and problems that are usually easily solvable (Burton, Lauridsen, and Obel, 2003). On the other hand, specific technologies imply many exceptions, adaptability, flexibility and continuous learning. The choice of technology is crucial to the organizational design, and routine technologies are not recommended for a changing environment, or specific technologies for stable environment. Also, production technology in production and service systems is different, which largely affects the configuration of other elements of organizational design.

Goals and Strategy

The process of setting goals usually starts with the vision of the organization. The vision is a description of what the organization hopes to become in the future. The statement about what we hope to become needs to be focused, flexible, pictorial, achievable, desirable and easy to remember. The mission is a concretization of the vision. Mission statement explains the organization's purpose by answering questions—*what the organization needs to do, who the organization function for, and how it seeks to respond to market needs.* Company goals represent the state or level of business performance that the organization aspires to achieve. It is very important that the goals are mutually harmonized and compatible with the vision and mission. In addition, definitions of goals should comply with basic principles: goals are specific and unambiguous, measurable, attainable, realistic and time-bound. The function of goals is to motivate and direct the organization toward achievement and to enable the control function to review what has been achieved and planned.

Goals can be seen from different angles. One of the basic approaches to goals is whether they are aimed at efficiency or effectiveness. Efficiency focuses on the optimal use of resources with the aim to reduce production costs, while efficiency looks at the final product or service as a key requirement. In other words, it focuses on the placement of products and services on the market in order to generate as much revenue as possible. From this standpoint, there are four characteristic situations that can be distinguished in relation to the goals of the organization (Burton, Obel and Hakonsson, 2015):

a) Low effectiveness and low efficiency
b) High effectiveness and low efficiency
c) Low efficiency and high effectiveness
d) High efficiency and high effectiveness

Each of these possibilities calls for a different approach in the further creation of organizational design. Once the vision, mission and goals are defined, it is time to start formulating the strategy. To put it simply, strategy is a way of achieving goals of the organization. Organizational strategies design the path to achieving organizational goals while improving company's performance and adhering to the vision, mission and strategic goals of the organization. Integrating knowledge management strategies with overall organizational strategies contributes to multiplicative positive effects, with an emphasis on knowledge as an important organizational resource (Dumitriu, 2016). It is highly important to design specific roles and responsibilities of staff in order to translate the knowledge management strategy into concrete initiatives and activities. The strategy can be dimensioned through the above-mentioned model of Porter's five forces (Porter, 2008). Marketing strategy can be defined based on four basic elements of a marketing mix—product, placement, promotion and price (Kotler, 2000). The typology of Miles and Snow (1978) is widely accepted as one of the most popular ones and it is dimensioned through the prism of exploration and action (exploitation). Exploration involves the study of new technologies, innovation, risk-taking, and greater flexibility. Action (exploitation) implies efficiency and specific action, that is, application. In relation to these two dimensions of strategy, the following typology can be conducted (Burton, Obel and Hakonsson, 2015: 32–33): Reactor, Defender, Prospector, and Analyzer. These strategies can be explained as follows:

1. Reactive strategy is based on a passive approach and could not be considered effective or efficient. Organizations that have reactive strategy operate without a focus on exploration and action. Typically, these organizations try to adapt to change after it happens. Therefore, they often miss opportunities that changes bring, that is, they react after the possibilities brought about by the changes have been absorbed by their competitors. In the long run, such a strategy is not sustainable.
2. Defensive strategy is based on the exploitation of resources. It does not focus on exploring new market opportunities or developing new products. This strategy primarily takes into account efficiency, improvement of existing products and services and better use of resources in order to reduce costs, and with the purpose of maintaining competitive position and preventing the entry of new competitors into the market. Defensive strategy can produce results for some time, but in the long run it can be problematic when market preferences change or when new competitors with stronger focus on innovation emerge.
3. Prospective strategy is focused on exploration, effectiveness, change, and introduction of new products. This strategy implies a continuous focus on the market. Organizations with a prospective strategy constantly experiment with new ideas, technologies, and processes, neglecting efficiency (production costs are high). The idea behind is that organizations will be the ones to dictate the situation on the market, and based on high innovation of their products and services, they can position themselves with high prices too (until the substitute products and services of competitors emerge on the market).
4. Analytical strategy without innovation is a strategy similar to the defensive one, but with a passive innovation strategy. Organizations with this strategy, in addition to their focus on efficiency, try to imitate products and services of their competitors and thus effect some changes without taking on too much risk. They try to build their position using benchmarking methods, that is, after a new products or services are launched on the market, they attempt to offer something very similar, or even more advanced, especially in terms of costs and diversify their offer.
5. Analytical strategy with innovation focuses on both efficiency and effectiveness at the same time. On the one hand, costs are minimized and the organization positions itself in the market while developing new products and services. Similarly to the prospective one, this strategy dictates the market dynamics by introducing new products and services (and not imitating others). In addition, organizations practicing this strategy are committed to cost efficiency. This is the best strategy, but the most demanding one too that must be supported by a flexible organizational design.

Strategy is nothing else but the application of knowledge, and changes in knowledge are the cause of changes in existing strategies and the application of new ones. In this sense, during different phases of the organization's life cycle, it is natural to have changes in the domain of organizational knowledge and in strategy, in accordance with the multi-contingency approach to organizational design.

Organizational Culture

Organizational culture is recognized as an internal factor of organizational design. It constitutes unique characteristics of each organization that are based on symbols, rituals, values, and assumptions about reality and the organization itself, which have developed through interaction and exposure to specific problems and challenges (Schedlitzki and Edwards, 2018). Awareness about common values within the organization contributes to simpler and more efficient coordination and communication. In that sense, it is much easier to manage organizations whose organizational culture is developed.

Understanding and knowing organizational culture is an important prerequisite for good organizational management, and organizational changes too (Alsoulami, Banjar, and Mahran, 2018). OCAI instrument (Organizational Culture Assessment Instrument) is used often to assess the dominant type of organizational culture, which is based on competitive values framework. Competitive values imply specific patterns of organizational culture too. The organizational culture of each organization is made up of four basic types.

Through the assessment of six key dimensions of organizational culture (dominant characteristics of the organization, organizational leadership, management style, source of loyalty to the organization, strategic direction and success criteria) a simple algorithm brings us to four basic types of organizational culture.

The four quadrants are dimensioned based on two criteria—"stability and control or flexibility and freedom" and "internal focus and integration or external focus and differentiation" (Quinn and Rohrbaugh, 1983; Cameron and Quinn, 2011). It is worth pointing out that there is no general consent on the best model of organizational culture, but according to the theory of contingency, each of them can be best in a certain context.

These four basic (mutually opposed) types of organizational culture include (Quinn and Rohrbaugh, 1983; Cameron and Quinn, 2011; OCAI Online, 2019):

1. *Family culture* (model of interpersonal relationships). Organizations of this type look like happy families (Pilav and Jatić, 2017). Collectiveness, teamwork, as well as loyalty to the organization are conspicuous.

Interpersonal relationships and the quality of communication are at the highest level. Success is determined by caring for people (employees and customers). Special attention is paid to the development of members of the organization, their empowerment and encouragement to take active part for the purpose of effectiveness. The leader of such an organization has the role of mentor too.

2. *Adhocracy culture* (open system model). Organizations of this type are dynamic, creative and show entrepreneurial reasoning. All members of the organization show openness to innovation and willingness to accept risks (Idris, 2017; Santti, Eskelinen, Rajahonka, Willman, and Happonen, 2017). Organizations encourage experimentation and search for new products and/or services for the purpose of system flexibility. Special attention is paid to constant improvements based on the *kaizen* methodology, causing customers' excitement and creating new standards in a given field of activity. Success is defined through leadership in innovation. As a rule, leaders of such organizations are visionaries and innovators.
3. *Hierarchical culture* (model of internal processes). The organization is a very formal entity. Business continuity is important and so is respect for formal rules and policies (Mandal, 2017). Control function is crucial to accuracy, consistency and efficiency. Success is defined by low costs and secure (stable and continuous) delivery of standardized products and/or services (Bremer, 2008). Usually, leaders of this type of organizations are good coordinators and organizers who strive for efficiency.
4. *Market culture* (model of rational goals). The organization is result-oriented. People are competitive. Market-leading position is an aspiration. Customer preferences and network business connections are crucial for creating a positive image. Success and the drive to win at all times make a strong integrator of members of the organization. Success is defined by competitiveness, that is, market share and profitability (Anning-Dorson, 2017). The leader of such an organization is competitively oriented.

These types of organizational culture exist almost in every organization, and OCAI instrument measures level of each type of organizational culture and identifies dominant type. This paper will identify basic patterns of organizational culture in healthcare organizations in Montenegro in chapter 7 that will cover data analysis and results.

Leadership Style

The growing complexity of organizations from all fields of social activity demands an increasingly adequate connection and coordination of different entities within the system, which is impossible without the role of a mediator and/or leader taken by prominent individuals or groups (Radević, 2018:13–14). There is a wide variety of definitions of leadership, and it is often heard that there are almost as many definitions of leadership in the literature as there are authors who have tried to define it (Stogdill, 1974). However, as most definitions suggest, leadership is the process in which a leader exerts influence on a particular group with the purpose of achieving a common goal.

Leadership rests on an understanding of organizational culture. Given that organizational culture is a changeable category, it means that it can and should be managed. Therefore, leaders have the key role of change agents in the process of shaping the culture of their organization, as their purpose is to improve functioning of the system they lead (Schein, 2004). Unlike managers, whose role is to act within the existing culture, leader is the one who designs and identifies new organizational patterns. Hence, the leader influences the behavior, through emotions, words and by personal example (Radević, 2018).

Leadership style is the way of managing employees by a leader. Leadership styles can be divided into two basic categories, depending on whether the leader is predominantly task-oriented or relation-oriented. The first category takes the end result as the basic measure of success, and insists on the execution of tasks, even at the cost of neglecting (disrupting) interpersonal functioning. The second category focuses on building good relationships among members of the organization, even at the cost of neglecting the execution of tasks (Northouse, 2008). Relation-oriented leadership has the greatest impact on social capital in health organizations (Strömgren, Eriksson, Ahlstrom, Bergman and Dellve, 2017). However, a successful leader needs to find a "middle solution," that is, create an organizational climate that will nurture good, relaxed and flexible relations between employees, but not in a way that can harm the timely execution of tasks.

Douglas McGregor developed two theories that can be used to choose a leadership style (Mašić, Babić, Đorđević-Boljanović, Dobrijević, and Veselinović, 2010). The so-called *X theory* assumes that members of an organization are lazy, dislike work, avoid work and responsibility, oppose change and have no ambition. For this reason, they need supervision at all times, along with a hierarchical structure and a narrow range of control at all levels. According to this theory, this situation requires an authoritative leadership style that is predominantly task-oriented. *Theory Y* implies a participatory (democratic) leadership style. Employees are allowed a high degree of autonomy, they are encouraged to work as a team and be creative. This theory assumes that members of the organization are ready to take responsibility and commit to the goals of the organization and have a high potential for development. According to this theory, leadership style is predominantly relationship-oriented.

One of widely accepted divisions of leadership styles refers to the preferences for delegation and avoiding uncertainty. Delegation preferences imply the willingness of top management to encourage lower-level managers to make decisions independently. Uncertainty avoidance is the extent to which top management avoids high-risk actions. Based on these two dimensions, there are four basic styles of leadership (Burton, Obel, and Hakonsson, 2015: 161–162): Maestro, Manager, Leader and Producer. Basic characteristics of these styles are as follows:

1. Maestro has weak preferences for delegation and does not avoid uncertainty. This style can make leaders overwhelmed with responsibilities. The leader does not focus on efficiency or effectiveness. Research has shown that this leadership style corresponds with the reactive strategy.
2. Manager has weak preferences for delegation and avoids uncertainty. The main characteristic of this style is that it is predominantly focused on efficiency and short-term decisions, while very little attention is paid to effectiveness and strategic management. This leadership style best fits a defensive strategy of the organization.
3. Producer has high preferences for delegation and avoids uncertainty. In this case, the leader is focused on both efficiency and effectiveness. Also, Producer looks after the balance between conflicting short-term and long-term goals. Therefore, this style is suited for the analytical strategy.
4. Leader has strong preferences for delegation and does not avoid uncertainty. Delegation allows more time for market research and long-term thinking. He trusts his employees and encourages them to become more involved and suggest new initiatives. He is focused on effectiveness and is willing to take risks by making strategic decisions. This leadership style corresponds to the prospective strategy.

Each of these styles may be appropriate in a given situation, but analysis of the suitability of a particular style should be done in accordance with the multi-contingency approach to organizational design, which is explained in more detail on the following pages.

Organizational Climate

The organizational climate explains the sentiment that members of the organization share, which is a product of dominant organizational culture. In short, it is the perception of organizational culture from the standpoint of members of the organization. Unlike the organizational culture that is observed at the organizational level, the organizational climate may differ in different parts of the organization.

While leadership style refers to top management, organizational climate pertains to all members of the organization. The organizational climate can be measured by analyzing trust, conflict, system of rewards, resistance to changes within the organization and so on.

Burton, Obel, and Hakonsson (2015: 166–173) established two dimensions to distinguish between four types of organizational climate. The two dimensions refer to the level of tension within the organization and the willingness to change. Above authors describe the tension as a "psychological edge" in the work atmosphere, that is, the stress level among members in the organization. The level of tension is determined by the mutual trust and respect of the members of the organization, credibility of leaders, ethical and moral principles, number of conflicts, and the system of responsibility, reward, and sanctions. High tension usually means a low level of trust, large number of conflicts, unfair reward system, low level of trust of team members in the leader and so on. However, sometimes conflicts can be positive and cause greater energy and commitment to problem-solving. Readiness to change is measured by the degree to which members of the organization are willing to accept change (methods of work, markets, etc.).

Accordingly, the four basic types of organizational climate are group climate, climate of internal processes, development climate and climate of rational goals:

1. The group climate has a low level of tension and a low level of readiness for changes. Organizations that nurture this type of climate are perceived as peaceful places. The employees feel pleasant and nice and there are no conflicts. The sense of attachment to the organization is strong. The level of trust is high, as is the credibility of leaders. This climate can be stressful for leaders, who may encounter problems when initiating change.
2. The climate of internal process has a high level of tension and low readiness for changes. In this type of climate employees are usually disappointed, tired, and unhappy. The atmosphere is not pleasant for work, number of conflicts is large and the motivation of team members is low.
3. The development climate has a low level of tension and a high level of readiness for changes. This type of organizational climate is similar to the group climate in terms of the atmosphere. Team members are motivated, trust each other and feel comfortable. It focuses on the growth and development of team members and the growth and development of the organization. Team members are flexible, optimistic, happy and enthusiastic about changes.

4. The climate of rational goals has a high degree of tension and high degree of readiness for changes. Team members are motivated for changes. The tension is high, but it does not compromise the organization's performance. The goal is to retain qualified and valuable team members and not worry if employees at lower hierarchical levels are unhappy and decide to leave the organization.

Regardless of the organization, organizational climate is crucial to its performance, efficiency and effectiveness. In this field too, it is necessary to analyze repeatedly the concordance of the type of organizational climate with other determinants of organizational design.

STRUCTURAL COMPONENTS

This part of the paper will discuss three basic components that may determine the organizational structure: (Pertusa-Ortega, Zaragoza-Sáez, and Claver-Cortés, 2010): formalization, centralization, and complexity.

Formalization

Formalization implies organizational rules, policy papers and formal procedures that allow people and sectors that engage in different tasks to coordinate their activities adequately. Authors have contradicting opinions about the impact of formalization on knowledge creation. Some argue that excessive formalities complicate and curtail the application of knowledge management (López, Peón, and Ordás, 2006), while some studies show that formalization is a prerequisite for the creation and application of knowledge (Kern, 2006). Difference should be made between routine and formalization. Routines imply implicit knowledge, while formalization implies explicit and codified knowledge (Reynaud, 2005). Routines and formalization can be the antithesis of system flexibility (Pertusa-Ortega, Zaragoza-Sáez, and Claver-Cortés, 2010). Excessive formalization, manifested through too many rules and regulations, in most cases makes the organization sluggish and has negative effect on the motivation of employees. However, without an adequately formalized organizational structure, the efforts of members to achieve set goals may prove ineffective. Formalization should allow for the codification of best practices (accordingly, practical knowledge gained in this way can be used in the future), reduce uncertainty and ambiguity in the functioning of the organization, and create a mode of operation that would improve business performance by adhering to appropriate quality standards.

Centralization

Centralization is the degree of concentration of authority and the power of decision-making at the top of the organization (Lojpur and Kuljak, 2005), while decentralization implies distribution of authority to team members at different (lower) organizational levels. Accordingly, decentralization involves a larger number of members in the process of strategic planning and contributes to greater knowledge creation (naturally, more people will have more ideas). The autonomy of the individual, provided by decentralization, encourages members of the organization to create and apply new knowledge (Nonaka, Toyama and Konno, 2000; Pertusa-Ortega, Zaragoza-Sáez and Claver-Cortés, 2010). On the other hand, centralization can have a negative effect on the interpersonal communication, quality of relationships in the organization, and development of new ideas and knowledge accordingly. Let us mention a few disadvantages of a centralized decision-making system: lower motivation of team members, overburdened managers, and inability to react quickly. When it comes to advantages, the control system is simple, in some cases even more cost-effective than the centralization, conflicts are rare, and so on. Constantly, changing modern business environment dictates the dominant use of network structures and decentralized systems (Certo, SC and Certo, ST, 2011), while centralized systems can operate in a stable environment.

Complexity

As a structural component, complexity refers to the degree of differentiation within an organization. There are three types of differentiation: horizontal, vertical, and spatial differentiation. Horizontal differentiation means the number of various positions at the same level of the organization. In other words, horizontal differentiation means the degree of specialization within an organization. Vertical differentiation refers to the number of hierarchical levels in the organization, while spatial differentiation means the geographical dispersion of organizational units.

Horizontal differentiation is considered more important for knowledge creation than the vertical and spatial differentiation (Damanpour and Schneider, 2006). This is because specialization allows for greater commitment to a specific task, greater degree of efficiency (Mintzberg, 1980), in-depth research of a specific problem and improvement in task performance.

Organizational complexity contributes to the development of knowledge management. A high level of complexity implies a high degree of specialization and heterogeneity of knowledge. However, regardless of the organization's complexity, it is necessary to make sure that its members engage in constant communication as it is the basis for the creation, sharing, and application of knowledge management.

ORGANIZATIONAL STRUCTURE

Organizational structure can be defined as a system of connections and relationships between elements in the organization that is designed to last for longer periods of time (Lojpur and Kuljak, 2005), illustrated by the organizational scheme and formally shaped by the acts of the organization. The organizational structure defines the schedule of tasks, authorities, and responsibilities of team members in order to achieve organizational goals.

There are two basic types of organizational structure—formal and informal. Formal organizational structure is predetermined (planned) by acts of the organization and is non-flexible, while informal includes all relations and types of communication between members of the organization, regardless of hierarchical level and flow of information that is regulated by acts, and is created to compensate for rigidity and inflexibility of formal organizational structure.

The organizational structure follows strategy (Chandler, 1962). Therefore, any change in strategy implies a change in the organizational structure (Pertusa-Ortega, López-Gamero, Pereira-Moliner, Tarí, and Molina-Azorín, 2018). However, the organizational structure is not a mere instrument of strategy, but also a kind of framework for the adoption and implementation of new strategies for growth and development of the organization too (Ivanović, 2007).

In terms of the arrangement of structural components, organizational structure can be divided into mechanistic and organic. The mechanistic structure shows a high degree of centralization, formalization, and standardization. Hierarchy is crucial to simpler coordination. Given all these features, mechanistic structure is referred to often as classic or bureaucratic structure. The organic structure has a high degree of flexibility and a low degree of centralization, formalization, and standardization. Also, close cooperation between team members and informal communication are typical for the organic structure, while decision-making is decentralized. The literature often describes it as entrepreneurial or behavioral. Mechanistic organizational structure is recommended for stable environments, while organizational structure is better suited for uncertain and dynamic environment.

Mintzberg's typology (Mintzberg, 1980) includes five basic models of organizational configuration: simple (entrepreneurial), machine (bureaucratic), professional, divisional and adhocracy (innovative). The simple structural configuration relies on high centralization and leader (top management) who supervises directly other members of the organization. Formalization is low and communication is mostly informal. It often occurs in smaller (and newly established) organizations. It is desirable in dynamic environments and during crises. The mechanistic organizational configuration predominantly relies on high specialization and formalization. Horizontal decentralization is limited, and authority is concentrated at the top of the organizational pyramid. It can produce good results in a stable environment, in larger (and older) organizations that are characterized by mass production. Recently, mechanistic is being replaced by adhocracy (innovative) organization. Professional configuration of the organization relies on team members' expertise, standardization of skills, high specialization, minimal formalization, and great autonomy of team members. Both vertical and horizontal decentralization are articulate. It is characteristic of complex but stable environments. Professional configuration of the organization is typical for the health and education sectors (Šunje, 2003). The divisional model implies a delegation of authority to organizational units in the middle line (limited vertical decentralization) in order to standardize results and develop an appropriate system of control of organizational performance. It is typical for large (and mature) organizations operating in different markets. Adhocracy (innovative) organizational configuration implies specialization, low level of formalization, inclusion of all members and it encourages lifelong learning. Innovation is a key source of competitive advantage in this type of organizational configuration. Therefore, since every innovation is an act of creativity of team members, human factor is extremely important in this type of configuration.

The range of controls makes an important aspect of the organizational structure, that is, the number of subordinates that a manager can manage. The larger the scope of control, the larger horizontal differentiation, while a narrower scope of control usually implies a larger vertical differentiation, that is, a larger number of hierarchical levels.

There are two basic dimensions that can be used to classify models of organizational structure—market orientation and functional specialization. Market orientation means external focus of the organization, such as when organizational units are tied to a specific product or service, or a specific market. Functional specialization indicates the level of division of labor, that is, grouping of specialized activities of the organization into separate organizational units. For example, when a company establishes marketing, finances, or production as separate organizational units that are the internal orientation of the organization.

Four basic models of the organizational structure determine the above-mentioned dimensions: simple, functional, divisional, and matrix model. It is important to note that each of basic models of organizational structure can be combined with other types, depending on other factors of organizational design. Mixed models most often occur in practice, making a combination of these basic models. Common features of these four basic models of organizational structure are, as follows (Burton, Obel and Hakonsson, 2015: 69–87):

1. Simple model—low level of market orientation and low level of functional specialization. This model is typical of small organizations consisting of an owner (manager) and several employees. Specialization is very low and so is efficiency. Since all decisions are made by the owner (manager), he is often overburdened and unable to respond adequately to all the challenges related to efficiency and effectiveness.
2. Functional model—low level of market orientation and high level of functional specialization. In this model of organization, activities are grouped through separate organizational units. Each organizational unit has its own manager. Specialization results in high efficiency. What may be a problem here is lower flexibility and the likelihood of conflicts between various functional parts of the organization. Quality coordination between organizational units based on unbroken communication is crucial to better decision-making.
3. Divisional model—high level of market orientation and low level of functional specialization. This model of organizational structure forms special organizational units (divisions) or "strategic business units," as they are often called, that focus on a specific product, customer or market. Therefore, the orientation is of the external type (effectiveness). The goal of this model is to create divisions with minimal interdependence. For that reason, autonomy of organizational units is greater—divisions can make their own decisions to adapt to market requirements. This model is more flexible than the functional one; however, efficiency is the problem with this model. Often, organizations cannot avoid parallel establishment of same functional units, which significantly increases costs.
4. Matrix model—high level of market orientation and high level of functional specialization. The matrix organizational structure focuses on achieving organizational efficiency and effectiveness at the same time. It is designed so as to take advantage of a functional and divisional model. A matrix model can have two or more dimensions (e.g., three-dimensional matrices include function, product, and the country or continent where the products are sold). As an illustration, one employee may be positioned in the accounting department (function). In it, the employee performs administrative tasks in the field of accounting for entire organization while being included (delegated to) in the team that works on the development of a specific product for a certain market. This model of organizational structure is recommended for complex and dynamic environment. It is typical of large systems. Strong horizontal and vertical differentiation make the communication process complex, and management is required to commit to harmonizing the entire organization and its elements that are established according to this model.

There are many other forms of organizational structures in the literature. However, each of them somehow relies on the above four models and makes their combination. Burton, Obel and Hakonsson (2015) categorize organizations based on their geographical location. They state that the organization can be close to the resources that will allow them the highest degree of efficiency or close to the market where they will place majority of their products. On the other hand, members of the organization can be physically present at a market that the organization intends to penetrate, or not. These authors also list specific features of organizational design regarding company's independence, measured by a number of formal and informal contracts (e.g., for premises, equipment, raw materials, human resources, etc.). Each specific situation requires a contingency approach.

Global business environment with rapid and sudden changes in all societal segments, requires an organic approach to organizational design, with low formalization and centralization, high interdependence, coordination and integration of different parts of the system. In this sense, creation of mutual trust and respect resulting in the motivation of members of the organization and synergy is a fundamental assumption of the quality of organizational structure (Miles, RE, Miles, G. and Snow, 2005; Snow, 2015; Beans, 2016). It is necessary to create a structure that makes the organization flexible enough to conclude strategic partnerships based on network business connections and common interests. In creating an organizational design, it is necessary to take into account the aspects of trust, respect, and motivation, not only at the level of organization (between its members) but between organizations too (those that are interconnected and located in the same production and transport chain and between competitors). Communication, motivation, cooperation and knowledge sharing are becoming increasingly important (Anand and Daft, 2007; Dimovski, Penger, Škerlavaj and Žnidaršić, 2005; Eklof and Ahlborg, 2016), hence, the organizational structure should be supportive toward these essential determinants of knowledge management, as opposed to traditional hierarchical approaches.

MULTI-CONTINGENCY APPROACH TO ORGANIZATIONAL DESIGN

The basic principle in designing an organization is that the organizational structure should follow the function, that is, enable an efficient achievement of goals. The process of designing would be simple if organizations were isolated systems functioning in stable environments. However, reality is different, which is why organizational design is a very complex and increasingly relevant area for theorists and practitioners alike. The basic task of organizational design is to create preconditions for achieving strategic goals through the harmonization of elements of the organization, based on delegating tasks to its members. The elements considered most often in the process of organizational design are (Hinrichs, 2009):

1. people—members of the organization and their development,
2. processes—that enable creation of value,
3. systems—information, knowledge, communication, financing and control,
4. structure—the way how organizational elements are configured and connections between them, and
5. culture—shared values that are the integrating factor of members of the organization, and facing the environment.

In contrast to the mechanistic model of the organization, whose features are a high degree of centralization, hierarchy, stability, and the pursuit of efficiency, the organic approach becomes dominant in modern business. Its characteristics are adaptation to the environment and the intensity of changes in it, proactive approach and decentralization. It is important to understand that stability and change, competition and cooperation, the individual and collective—are not opposing and mutually exclusive tendencies in absolute terms (Hinrichs, 2009). The organic approach to modeling of organizational structure is the one that insists on integration and elimination of dominantly perceived antagonism between the above elements. This means that in a turbulent environment, only appropriate degree of flexibility that will imply frequent changes can guarantee long-term stability. Also, even though the competition becomes stronger, the cooperation between competitors is even more intense owing to their common interests (Bierbooms, Van Oers, Rijkers and Bongers, 2016) and network business connection (Pouwels and Koster, 2017) that is based on specialization and pursuit to provide products and services of top quality. In addition, only an organization in which each person feels happy and free can count on having a harmonious and strong team that is based on synergy and enjoy all positive benefits it generates.

The multi-contingency approach in the process of organizational design points to the need for adequate configuration of elements of organizational design in terms of their mutual harmonization. This approach is consistent with the organizational design models of Leavitt (1964) and Galbraith (1995). Therefore, the environment, strategy, and organizational structure are basic elements of organizational design that need to be harmonized (Miles and Snow, 1978). Burton, Obel, and Hakonsson (Burton and Obel, 2002; Burton, Obel, and Hakonsson, 2015) enriched this approach by developing a multi-contingency model, that takes into account the size of an organization, organizational climate, management style, the environment, technology, and strategy as situational dimensions of organizational design, organizational structure, complexity, formalization and centralization as organizational elements, all with the purpose of creating an efficient and effective organization. So, it is important to harmonize organizational factors with situational ones. Internal inconsistency of organizational design elements is identified through theoretical and empirical evidence of its significant negative impact on organizational performance. For example, if the organization set efficiency as its goal, defensive strategy would be the best strategy to achieve that goal, while the best structure that follows the chosen strategy in this case is functional. Compatible with the above elements is the leadership style that shows weak preferences for delegation, avoids uncertainty, and internal-process organizational climate is preferable. On the other hand, if the goal is effectiveness, then a prospective strategy is the best choice, with an accompanying divisional structure. Development organizational climate is most compatible with a given set of elements of organizational design, and leadership style that shows strong preferences for delegation and does not avoid uncertainty.

The multi-contingency model is based on "if-then" rules, that is, on determining the suitability and consistency of elements of organizational design, which determines the quality of configuration of organizational design's elements and their internal consistency. Discrepancy between two or more elements of organizational design affects the poorer performance of the organization, but it is also a signal for change, that is, it affects the need for organizational transformation too. This model insists that the change of one variable of the model causes the need to adapt others, which is why it is necessary to monitor all relevant dimensions of organizational design at all times. A change of goals of the organization, which is a result of changes in the environment, will result in a change in strategy. A changed strategy will result in a change in organizational structure. The new organizational structure will change the organizational climate and motivation system, and will require a new leadership style. In that sense, the company's management must analyze each change and harmonize organizational elements continuously in order to achieve maximum performance of the organization.

Chapter 3

Relational Triangle

Knowledge Management, Organizational Design, and Health Services

KNOWLEDGE MANAGEMENT AND ORGANIZATIONAL DESIGN IN THE FUNCTION OF BUSINESS PERFORMANCES

The literature offers three basic approaches to knowledge. The first one defines knowledge as a mechanism for reduction of uncertainty (Galbraith, 1974; Bensaou and Venkatraman, 1995). The other speaks of knowledge as a resource that reduces transaction costs in decision-making (Monteverde and Teece, 1982; Pisano, 1989; Subramani and Venkatraman, 2003). And the third assigns knowledge the status of a key resource for creating a competitive advantage of the organization and its differentiation in the market (Nelson and Winter, 1982; Nonaka, 1994; Dierickx and Cool, 1989; Farjoun, 1994; Venkatraman and Tanriverdi, 2004; Ketchen and Bergh, 2004). In this sense, the evolution of theoretical approaches to knowledge as an organizational resource openly indicates its connection with organizational design and modeling of organizational structure.

Although the organizational structure alone does not guarantee learning and knowledge sharing in an organization, the wrong choice of organizational structure may jeopardize these processes. This is due to the fact that organizational learning depends on the flow of information among members of the organization (Wang, Zeng, Arntzen, Kim and Liu, 2017), and the algorithm of information flow is conditioned by the organizational structure. Also, autonomy and flexibility, greater decentralization and lower formalization are cited as drivers of organizational learning (Kim, 1993; Hodge, Anthony and Gales, 2003; Espinosa and Lindahl, 2016).

The possibility of improvement within the existing resources of the organization is an important dimension of knowledge management. Almost every organization has latent reserves of insufficiently used knowledge of its employees which, if activated, could result in better efficiency of the organization. Given that effective knowledge management depends not only on technology but also predominantly on the human and managerial resources of the organization, it is important to empower employees and motivate them to be proactive and participatory in creating, sharing, and using knowledge. Therefore, successful knowledge management is one that is based on a sound vision and has an appropriate organizational culture that nurtures the creation, dissemination, and use of organizational knowledge (Dumitriu, 2016).

Organizational design is one of the factors that greatly affects the quality of application of knowledge management (Claver-Cortés, Zaragoza-Sáez, and Pertusa-Ortega, 2007). There are vast possibilities to improve the process and save money, which a survey of 1,200 large European companies confirmed (Arevuo, 2002). More than 70 percent of companies improved their business results owing to knowledge management.

Organizations are complex, dynamic, nonlinear, diverse living systems that do not evolve in a steady or predictable way (De Toni, Biotto and Battistella, 2012). Instead of traditional centralized management systems, the modern business environment requires the design of models that will enable bottom-up processes. This can be achieved through greater use of new technologies, based on networking, information exchange, and collective problem-solving. In addition, an important aspect of business models is the strengthening of organizational flexibility and creativity (Dimovski, Penger, Peterlin, Grah, Černe and Klepec, 2017) as critical success factors in an increasingly changing environment.

In addition to improving relations between members of the organization, organizational culture influences the choice of appropriate management style (Andish, Yousefipour, Shahsavaripour, and Ghorbanipour, 2013). In addition, organizational culture affects the organizational strategy and organizational structure (Alsoulami, Banjar, and Mahran, 2018), exerting a positive impact on the management of organizational changes (Al-Otaibi, 2014).

Furthermore, studies suggest that quality of organizational culture is crucial to financial performance of the organization (Andish, Yousefipour, Shahsavaripour, and Ghorbanipour, 2013).

ORGANIZATION IN THE FUNCTION OF CREATION OF COMMON VALUES

McKinsey 7S model of organization was developed in 1980 by managers of the McKinsey company. This model indicates that organizational effectiveness depends on the interrelationship of seven key elements of the model:

structure, strategy, system (hard variables), knowledge and skills, people, management style, and shared values (soft variables). At that time, one of the basic ideas of the model was to point out the importance of the so-called soft variables, which were overshadowed by strategy, structure, and system. The model had wide application in the fields of organizational change and organizational transformation. Shared values are this model's foundations, as segments of organizational culture. In that sense, this model connects different components of knowledge management and organizational design and indicates their interrelationship. Changing one component of the model requires adjustment of other elements, which is why flexibility and constant reconfiguration of elements are crucial to organizational design in accordance with integrative management theories, which include theories of contingency and system management (Mašić, Babić, Đorđević-Boljanović, Dobrijević, and Veselinović, 2010). For example, a change in the level of knowledge results in a new strategy, and a change in strategy demands a change in organizational structure. A new organizational structure may need new people. Different number of people in an organization requires different management styles, different systems, and different processes that are pervaded by the building of shared values as fundamentals of success. The management of successful organizations pays close attention to the system of values within the organization and aspires that all employees should take part in its creation (Šunje, 2003). Therefore, staff interaction and involvement are encouraged, which results in the organizational system of shared values of all employees and ensures the homogeneity of the organization in terms of its values as a prerequisite for the success and sustainability of the organization in the long run.

Also, Ichak Adizes underlines the importance of shared values. Namely, he defines business success through the function of external integration and internal disintegration (Adizes, 2015). The quotient of these two quantities (the denominator is internal disintegration and the numerator is external integration) will result in a prediction of the organization's business success, be it is on the level of an individual, organization, or the economy as a whole. External integration refers primarily to the marketing dimension of the organization and to approach that is based on monitoring of changes in the environment. The essence of marketing concept is in the adequate use of the organization's capabilities in order to exploit emerging opportunities at the market. In other words, the goal is to identify and meet needs of customers. Internal disintegration represents various setbacks within the company (mistrust, disrespect, conflicts, hatred, vanity, etc.). Internal disintegration measures "the level of mutual trust and respect in organizational culture, if any" (Adizes, 2018). Furthermore, Adizes explains that each system has a constant amount of energy, which, as a rule, is always directed to internal disintegration, while only excess energy may be directed to external integration. To illustrate this on a personal example, a man neglecting his health will not have the energy for any business venture until his health gets better. Therefore, entire energy will be directed to finding the solution of internal disintegration. Take an organization as an example, this means that excessive disintegration consumes all the energy of the organization through resolving internal conflicts and disputes (e.g., conflicts between the management and Union members), so nothing (or very little) remains for the organization's clients. An organizational culture based on trust and respect, where conflicts between team members can be resolved in a constructive way, will reduce the denominator of the fraction from the abovementioned success formula to the lowest level. On the one hand, this will mean that organizations are able to dedicate more time to clients and the market, and on the other hand, mathematically, business success will be higher due to an increase in numerators and/or a decrease in denominators. And since changes are very frequent, and each new change can result in internal disintegration of the system, the balance of the system and the harmonization of elements of organizational design have to be in the focus at all times. In that sense, Adizes also draws an interesting parallel between a man and an organization. A man has twenty-four hours at his disposal, and one part of that time has to be spent sleeping. During his rest and sleep, he experiences inner integration and inner peace, which enables him to be ready to focus adequately on the circumstances in the environment. Likewise, the organization needs inner harmony and peace. The management of the organization must find time to focus continuously on the process of internal integration of members and building an organizational culture, which will recognize a happy team member as a critical success factor in any business in the long run.

The aspiration in organizational design is to provide the organization with dual properties, that is, to make sure it is both stable and dynamic (O'Reilly and Tushman, 2004; Petković and Lukić, 2013), which is significantly facilitated by the use of information and communication technologies. Many strategies, such as diversification, outsourcing, networking, and strategic partnerships would not be possible without information and communication technologies. Impact of network technologies on leadership style and employee behavior was confirmed too (Hedman and Kalling, 2002; Petković and Lukić, 2013). The explosion and revolution of data, based on Internet technologies in the digital economy, have called for the need to develop new models for efficient data storage, manipulation, and analysis (Tisen, Andriesen, and Depre, 2006). Owing to the so-called *Big Data* models that enable the processing of large amounts of structured and unstructured data, today, it is possible to predict social behavior and act proactively. These models include quick management and systems, that is "business intelligence systems and expert systems equipped with the smartest models of economic science and management and decision-making theory" (Lazović and Đuričković, 2018). Social physics is a field of science that studies human behavior using the *Big Data* model. Unlike elementary particles, units of analysis in social physics are people, who are by nature complex, unique, and unpredictable. However, human behavior is determined by social context as much as by rational thinking (Pentland, 2014). In this sense, social physics is defined as a quantitative social science that mathematically determines the links between the flow of information between individuals (in the real and virtual world) and human behavior—moves, productivity, and creativity (Epstein, 2013; Pentland, 2014; Perc, 2019). This clearly shows that knowledge management based on the use of most sophisticated software solutions determines the process of organizational design. However, what must be remembered is that organizational diversification and business networking rest on mutual trust, respect, and shared values as much as on information and communication technologies.

HEALTH SYSTEM FROM THE STANDPOINT OF KNOWLEDGE MANAGEMENT AND ORGANIZATIONAL DESIGN

Global challenges of modern organizations boil down to three categories—increased quality, reduced costs, and being flexible (Cegarra-Navarro, Soto-Acosta, and Wensley, 2016). Each of these challenges is essentially determined by organizational configuration through the process of organizational design. Mutual trust and respect are crucial to the quality of management and organization in almost any field, but health and education are exceptionally important.

Health care systems across the globe face similar problems, such as staffing, funding, access to health care services, privatization processes, the use of information and communication technologies, constant need to improve services, and the development of information systems (Almalki, Fitzgerald and Clark, 2011; Alsoulami, Banjar, and Mahran, 2018).

In recent years, user participation in the process of improving health care services has become an increasingly important factor in the competitiveness of health care organizations (Philips, 2004). A large number of health care organizations enable the creation of virtual communities of health care users through a number of information and communication solutions (Nambisan and Nambisan, 2009; Zhao, Wang and Fan, 2015). This is in line with the theoretical concept of knowledge management, that is based on networking and synergistic effects of knowledge creation (Sawhney and Prandelli, 2000;

Gohary and Hamzel, 2016), as well as with the stakeholder management theory (Reed, 1999). The application of stakeholder management theory contributes to sustainability of the organization's system (Uribe, Ortiz-Marcos, and Uruburu, 2018; Porter and Kramer, 2019), through the sizing of organizational strategy that will prevent or avoid the risk of failure (Azim, Gale, Lawlor-Wright, Kirkham, Khan, and Alam, 2010; Muriana and Vizzini, 2017), all based on a proactive management approach. This theory is based on the permeation of rhetorical skills and emotional intelligence as basic tools for stakeholder management (De Carvalho and Rabechini, 2015). In this sense, the need for a holistic marketing approach in health care organizations is necessary, which indicates the need to monitor the perception of health care users and to manage these perceptions for quality market positioning (Fields, 2007). Reduction of patient dissatisfaction and reduction of negative campaigns' effects ("word of mouth") affect the financial stability and sustainability of health care institutions (Jandavath and Byram, 2016).

In addition, the result of health care services is conditioned by the cooperation between medical doctors and patients, so in order to increase the quality of health care services, strong attention should be paid to this relationship, building mutual trust and active role of patients in the process of providing health care services (Peters, Löbler, Brodie, Breidbach, Hollebeek, Smith, Sörhammar, and Varey, 2014; Ostrom, Parasuraman, Bowen, Patrício, and Voss, 2015). Patients have ever more information through network technologies, which significantly changes the system of direct interaction between physicians and patient (Osei-Frimpong, Wilson, and Owusu-Frimpong, 2015) and requires an additional flexibility of service providers in communication (Myllärniemi, Laihonen, Karppinen, and Seppänen, 2012), in order to find the most adequate solution for the patient's health issues. In parallel with better information quality, which is made possible by Internet, people tend to replace the reactive approach with proactive, that is, they become interested in disease prevention and health promotion, instead of a passive approach—treatment after the disease occur (Oh, Ghose, Chung, Ryu and Han, 2014). This imposes a higher level of application of knowledge management, which will contribute to the quality and quantity of interaction (Gohary and Hamzel, 2016), due to the fact that services are increasingly being viewed from the standpoint of user experience at time the service is being provided (including the period with preventive activities), based on direct interaction with the service provider (McColl-Kennedy, Cheung, and Ferrier, 2015), instead of assessing service quality solely based on treatment outcomes.

According to recent research, organizational culture and organizational climate are significantly correlated with the health of members of the organization. When it comes to maintaining health, there are three most prominent factors: regular physical activity, quality nutrition, and adequate rest time. An important point that is omitted in these approaches is the dimension of the quality of social interaction, that is, the way individuals behave among each other (World Economic Forum, 2019).

Studies show that love, friendship, community, purpose of life, and the environment can have a greater impact on health than anything that may happen at the doctor's. The roots of this study date back to 1978, when Dr. Robert Nerem made an experiment to establish a link between blood cholesterol levels and heart condition in rabbits. However, the experiment showed that connection with others is a hidden health factor. Acts of kindness have been found to affect health to a great extent. Recent studies have shown that positive relationships reduce cortisol and stress, have positive effect on blood pressure and strengthen immunity.

According to a study of Dr. Harding of Columbia University, "chronic loneliness can be as damaging to health as smoking 15 cigarettes a day or consuming large amounts of alcohol," while having a motivating goal has a positive effect on the health (Harding, 2019a). Empathy, kindness, and human interaction have a positive effect on health. In particular, relationships in family, school, neighborhood, at workplace, and the wider community are crucial to an individual's health. Harding (2019b) rightfully underline that having a good doctor is important, but it is equally important to have a good manager, who will develop an appropriate climate of trust, mutual respect, kindness, and synergy within the organization (Harding, 2019b).

Under the circumstances of frequent occurrence of new diseases, and the need to work on solutions for their treatment and find new and better treatment methods for already known diseases, continuous search for the latest knowledge is a key factor in health system success. In order to properly search for knowledge, appropriate knowledge management and organizational design are needed to support these concepts. In addition, it is not only necessary to find new knowledge based on scientific research, but it is also necessary, especially in the case of the emergence of new viruses (such as COVID-19), to build the trust of health care users in the system, taking into account the fact that people are usually very sensitive and cautious when it comes to applying new and unknown methods. In this context, appropriate organizational design is an important link so that knowledge management could fully realize its performance potential.

Chapter 4

Macroeconomic Context of Knowledge and Health in Montenegro

MACROECONOMIC CONTEXT OF KNOWLEDGE IN MONTENEGRO

Montenegro, one of the smallest countries in Europe, declared its independence on May 21, 2006 and has faced a number of challenges in institutionalizing its system ever since. Montenegro's gross domestic product (GDP) is lower than in EU member states or Western Balkan countries (Eurostat, 2020) as they may be the next EU member states after Croatia's accession. The countries of the Western Balkans are surrounded by EU member states so they are often referred to as the so-called Balkan Ring (Đurović, 2017), and all of them set integration into the EU as one of their key foreign policy priorities.

Small Economy—An Advantage or Not?

If we compare GDP of Montenegro to the one of Luxembourg (i.e., another small country), we see that Luxembourg's GDP in 2019 is approximately thirteen times higher than Montenegro's. Therefore, it is evident that the size of a country may be a drawback in some cases, but an advantage too. For a small economy such as Montenegro's with all its vast resources, knowledge has to be one of key development factors for the country to reach or exceed the level of quality of life and economic standard of developed European countries in the future. In particular, strong focus on knowledge, future, and integrations are crucial given the turbulent and complex political-historical context and all negative events that took place in the Balkans over the past few decades. In this sense, Montenegro, being oriented toward knowledge and the future, must take advantage of small systems, such as flexibility and the ability to react quickly to change, in order to make its current rates of growth and development even stronger and faster. The forecast of the International Monetary Fund from 2019 indicated that Montenegro's GDP was expected to grow continuously in the following five years, with a real growth rate of 3.4 percent in 2020. However, COVID-19 pandemic has made dramatic changes in public finances and caused problems in many countries. According to the forecasts of the International Monetary Fund from 2020, Montenegro is projected to see an economic decline of 12 percent (International Monetary Fund, 2020), which is the largest decline along with Croatia (9%) and Albania (7.5%), and it is caused by the factual reliance of economies of these three countries to the sector of tourism.

Investment into Knowledge as a Factor for Growth and Development

As presented in table 4.1, Montenegro's budget (in absolute amounts) for education has seen a steady growth over the past five years, and the number of employees in the sector of education grew too, which is an indicator that education is recognized as one of the major factors of development of national economy. Also, the country had plans to increase the budget for education for 16.51 million euro in 2020.

Table 4.1 Overview of Basic Macroeconomic Aggregates in the Field of Education in Montenegro 2009–2020

Year	*Total GDP of Montenegro (in current prices)*	*Sector of education in GDP (in current prices)*	*Number of employees in the sector of education*	*Budget of Montenegro*[1]	*Budget of education*
2009	2,993,886,000	125,891,000	12,992	1,623,684,943.65	149,383,608.50
2010	3,125,090,000	147,563,000	12,282	1,425,963,634.38	132,710,312.27
2011	3,264,781,000	151,824,000	12,223	1,400,606,987.97	131,114,278.24
2012	3,181,477,000	157,603,000	13,101	1,378,561,776.66	132,958,692.08
2013	3,362,481,000	153,822,000	13,250	1,375,793,668.99	138,028,699.64
2014	3,457,922,000	152,076,000	13,363	1,509,031,975.30	154,100,301.62
2015	3,654,512,000	158,759,000	13,575	1,963,260,900.49	155,901,807.03
2016	3,954,212,000	168,434,000	13,759	2,125,615,876.83	165,009,559.88
2017	4,299,091,000	172,485,000	14,165	2,005,790,487.10	169,353,606.29
2018	4,663,130,000	178,297,000	14,494	2,004,134,964.15	172,455,311.56
2019	4,950,717,000	181,352,000	14,770	2,384,016,305.99	183,070,000.00
2020	-	-	-	2,578,920,533.32	199,580,000.00

Source: Monstat, November 22, 2020
Law on the Budget of Montenegro (2009–2019)
Bill of the law on budget of Montenegro for 2020
Ministry of Finance of Montenegro - Explanation of the current budget, reserves, and budget by functional classification (2009-2019), November 23, 2019

In relative indicators, budget for education saw a declining trend during the period 2014–2018, that is, it went down from 4.5 percent of GDP in 2014 to 3.7 percent in 2018. As one of the world's leading economies, China allocated 4.11 percent of its GDP for education in 2018 (Xinhua, 2019). In 2017, according to the World Bank data, Serbia allocated 3.95 percent of its GDP to education. In the same year, Montenegro's budget for education accounted for 3.94 percent of GDP. Given the evident high rate of economic decline in 2020, high share of public debt in GDP (before the COVID-19 pandemic it amounted to 80%), as well as the turbulent social and political circumstances in Montenegro, the country's policymakers are expected to face many challenges in the coming period. Under such circumstances, knowledge is undeniably the only factor of stabilization and further growth and development.

Knowledge is Still Underestimated

According to results of the 2020 survey that was conducted on a sample of 12,359 citizens of Montenegro, as many as 52 percent of respondents disagree with the statement that knowledge is a key condition for individual career advancement in that country. Also, based on interviews and focus groups with employees in the health sector, one gets the impression that knowledge in Montenegro is not valued as it should be, as the respondents mentioned family ties, friends, and/or political connections and references as more important than knowledge. Employees in the education sector are not happy with their income, in spite of some positive but incremental changes in that field. Education system, as the cornerstone of every society and the source of knowledge of every profession, must be built in such a way so as to value the status of its teachers and health workers. If not, best talents will be avoiding careers in education and seek more financially viable engagements in private companies or abroad. That may have permanent negative systemic consequences.

At times when all social aspects are prone to quick and unpredictable changes, knowledge (in terms of lifelong learning) should be in the focus of decision-makers and recognized as a basic prerequisite for competitiveness of the national economy. Therefore, systemic flexibility, sustainability, and resilience to changes in the environment should be built in such a way to recognize knowledge and professional training as key references for progress in all areas of life. Only in that case, young people will choose quality over quantity in the long run, and knowledge rather than grades, activation, and interest instead of indolence.

MACROECONOMIC CONTEXT OF HEALTH CARE IN MONTENEGRO

Risk of Migration of Montenegrin Health Workers

The lack of doctors is a problem that many European countries share, and according to a study by the European Journalism Network that is based on data analysis (European Data Journalism Network) Europe will face a shortage of 230,000 doctors in 2020. The European Commission highlighted this problem in 2012 and dimensioned it for the territory of the European Union. The situation is not different in America, where the growth in demand for doctors continues to grow faster than supply, and by 2032, the shortage of doctors in America is expected to be between 46,900 and 121,900 (Heiser, 2019). Many doctors from less-developed countries of the European Union choose Germany, Scandinavian countries, and Great Britain as their destinations (Berthier, 2018).

The causes of doctors' shortage are their age structure, growing, and aging population, doctor's lack of interest to work in rural areas or in less-developed countries, and extremely low salaries. It is important to emphasize that Scandinavian countries, Great Britain, France, Estonia, Slovakia, and Hungary face the problem of shortage and uneven number of medical doctors in relation to their population size. In Slovakia and Hungary, the number of doctors in urban areas per 1,000 inhabitants is twice as high than in rural areas. On the other hand, the number of doctors aged fifty-five years or above is most evident in Italy (55%), Estonia (48%), and France (47%), which indicates the need to create young qualified staff (Berthier, 2018).

Although Montenegro is not part of the European Union yet, it has not been spared from the problem of insufficient number of doctors or from the likelihood of their international migration. Low salaries and long working hours (including overtime) make doctors unable to have a balance between their private and professional life, which makes them feel unhappy, stressed, and susceptible to the idea to leave the country. Romania registered the largest international migration of doctors as their health system has lost over 5,000 doctors in the past twenty years. Following the migration of doctors, Romania reacted and made a significant increase in salaries for health care workers (a threefold increase). However, that did not result in prompt return of doctors, indicating that care for the standard of doctors must be continued and acted upon proactively (before the problem occurred) rather than reactively (after).

Table 4.2 Overview of Basic Macroeconomic Aggregates in the Health System of Montenegro 2009–2020

Year	*Total GDP of Montenegro (in current prices)*	*Health and social care sector in GDP (in current prices)*	*Number of employees in the health and social care sector*[2]	*Budget of Montenegro*	*Health budget*
2009	2,993,886,000	117,221,000	12,238	1,623,684,943.65	161,245,610.31
2010	3,125,090,000	120,149,000	10,945	1,425,963,634.38	175,211,784.80
2011	3,264,781,000	121,681,000	10,565	1,400,606,987.97	168,508,804.28
2012	3,181,477,000	125,684,000	10,869	1,378,561,776.66	173,504,551.60
2013	3,362,481,000	130,704,000	11,001	1,375,793,668.99	166,635,992.10
2014	3,457,922,000	130,500,000	11,288	1,509,031,975.30	169,348,750.44
2015	3,654,512,000	138,571,000	11,482	1,963,260,900.49	172,088,746.51
2016	3,954,212,000	151,933,000	11,695	2,125,615,876.83	183,295,942.29[3]
2017	4,299,091,000	159,493,000	12,124	2,005,790,487.10	198,271,859.13
2018	4,663,130,000	165,503,000	12,526[4]	2,004,134,964.15	207,945,018.68[5]
2019	4,950,717,000	166,613,000	12,715	2,384,016,305.99	241,590,000.00
2020	-	-	-	2,578,920,533.32	285,160,000.00

Source: Monstat, November 22, 2020
Law on the Budget of Montenegro (2009–2019)
Bill of the law on budget of Montenegro for 2020
Ministry of Finance of Montenegro—Explanation of the current budget, reserves, and budget by functional classification (2009-2019), November 23, 2019.

Growing Investments into Health Care

The need for continuous improvement within the health system and the growing expectations of health care users imply the need for rising investments. Table 4.2 shows how Montenegro's health budget has grown since 2013 (in absolute amounts), as well as the number of health employees.

In relative indicators, health budget saw a decline from 4.9 percent of GDP in 2014 to 4.5 percent in 2018, as measured in relation to GDP. In 2016, according to the available data of the World Bank, the United States allocated the most (17.07%), while Switzerland allocated the most of European countries (12.24%). In 2017, the European Union allocated a total of 9.6 percent of its GDP to health (OECD, 2018), which is almost the same as in two previous years, due to the same increase in health expenditures and overall economic growth. In 2017, seven EU member states spent 10 percent or more of their GDP on health care: France, Germany, Sweden, Austria, Denmark, the Netherlands, and Belgium. According to Eurostat data, Montenegro spent 5.9 percent in the same year,[6] while Serbia, Slovenia, Croatia, and Macedonia spent 9.4 percent, 8.0 percent, 7.5 percent and 6.1 percent, respectively (WHO, 2018; Eurostat, 2019). In 2017, Turkey and Romania recorded a lower share of health expenditures in GDP in comparison to Montenegro, that is, 4.2 percent and 5.2

percent, respectively. Globally, total health spending is growing faster than GDP, especially in low- and middle-income countries (Xu et al, 2018).

Health Workers Are Not Happy with Their Salaries

Based on interviews and focus groups with employees in the health sector, employees stated inadequate salaries of health workers as the biggest reason for their dissatisfaction. Dissatisfaction is so strong that the Union of Medical Doctors pointed out that "most doctors are learning German," alluding that many health workers and future ones (medical students) are considering to leave Montenegro. Furthermore, continuous increase of health budget in the previous five years has not affected employees' salaries, they say. Average salary of general practitioners and junior doctors in Montenegro is 550 euros, specialists have 670 euros, and subspecialists around 750 euros, highlighted the Union. Although working overtime means extra income, members of the Union point out that overtime work is paid much less than the work during standard working hours. Assuming that time is the most limited resource, then overtime work means more opportunity costs for doctors (as they lack time for private life and rest) than working within standard working hours, which is why the overtime should be paid more.

The fact is that doctors receive much lower salaries than their peers in other regional countries that are also facing the problem of likely or actual problem of migration of doctors, so the Union is trying to accentuate this problem and fight for a better position of health workers in Montenegro. For that reason, intensive negotiations are underway between the Union of Medical Doctors and the Government of Montenegro on improving the status of health workers. Unhappy with measures of the Government of Montenegro and the announced increase of 9 percent for 2020 (which is significantly lower than the originally requested amount of 300 euros), doctors have launched a petition to increase the coefficient of salaries for doctors, specialists, and subspecialists to be no lower than 14, 18, and 20, respectively, compared to the current 8.25, 10.25 and 11.00 (Petition to increase doctors' salaries, 2019). For these reasons, the matter of financial motivation of employees in the health system (in the system of education too) must be treated with care, yet, taking into account the budget structure. À propos the thesis that knowledge makes the best investment, one can make equally important conclusion that saving at the expense of people who have the required knowledge is the most expensive saving in the long run. The relationship between supply and demand is an illustration of the fact that prices increase once demand is higher than supply. In other words, things that exist in insufficient quantities have a greater value. It is especially worth noting that people are the basis of any system and substituting work with technology is more difficult in health and education than in all other sectors and, as a rule, limited. The motivational aspect of employees is certainly not financial only. But as long as employees in the health sector have to care about their existential needs, one may not expect any significant improvements in the health sector (or in any other). Even though the number of medicines covered by health insurance in Montenegro is increasing, as is the budget for health care, the question of priorities and purpose of budget spending is open. For example, the effectiveness of budget spending for medicines may be questioned, assuming the likely shortage of staff that will prescribe therapies and appropriate treatment to patients (due to staff shortages, or delays in examination, or losing focus due to overtime). In particular, from the point of view of system sustainability and in the long run, the question is whether young people will be sufficiently motivated to go to school (the average training time for a medical doctor is seven to fifteen years) and work for a salary that is not sufficient for a decent life in their country. So it is likely to expect an increased need for the number of trained young doctors, and the growing problem of motivating young people to become medical doctors. The potential problem of migration must be addressed in several ways and in a timely manner. One of the solutions could and should be to build the public health system to attract patients from developed countries to Montenegro, that is, foreign health institutions to outsource their deficient health services through Montenegrin health system, instead of having doctors migrate. Ultimately, that would contribute to the development of tourism, as the most important industry in Montenegro.

NOTES

1. In this segment, the planned amounts of funds for the specific time-frame were treated on the basis of the Law on Budget due to the lack of data for the observed period after the final budget account (the amounts would be partly different, for example, due to the budget amendments, if the analysis would be done on the Law on Annual Statement on Budget).
2. This column summarizes employees in the health and social care sectors. Of the presented number, 81–85 percent are employees in the health sector (depending on the year), while employees in the field of social care make between 15 percent and 19 percent.
3. According to the Health Insurance Fund, the realized budget for health care this year differs significantly from the planned one, and amounts to 228,571,270.84 euros.
4. Health care amounts to 10.571 (84%) and social care 1.955 (16%).
5. According to the Health Insurance Fund, the budget for health care this year was 230,408,527.56 euro, which is the largest difference in the data in the observed years (along with 2016, as previously indicated).
6. Data from official statistics often differ depending on the methodology.

Chapter 5

Knowledge Management in Health System of Montenegro

This chapter will focus on data analysis and results of the level of application and effectiveness of knowledge management in Montenegrin health institutions. First, the chapter will provide information about the sample, that is, the structure of respondents, followed by concrete results about the level of application of knowledge management, effectiveness of knowledge management, organizational culture, organizational infrastructure, and leadership in the health system of Montenegro. In addition to a detailed explanation about the assessments of basic determinants of knowledge management, this chapter will shed light on the existence of statistically significant differences in determinants between health institutions from different parts of the country, as well as between private and public health institutions (Kruskal–Wallis test, Mann–Whitney U test, and ANOVA).

SAMPLE STRUCTURE

The research was conducted on a sample of 135 respondents from forty-five Montenegrin health institutions, thirty-two public, and thirteen private ones. A total of three persons were interviewed in each of forty-five institutions—one member of the administration, one medical doctor, and one health associate (e.g., medical technician). All respondents have been working in the field of health for more than five years.

When it comes to sex structure, the sample consisted of fifty-five men and eighty women (40.7% and 59.3%, respectively). The average age of the respondents is forty-nine. On average, respondents have worked in the health sector for twenty-four years and seventeen years in health institutions, they represented and spoke about.

The research covered health institutions from all parts of the country thus facilitating comparisons by region. Majority of health institutions covered by this survey are located in the central part of Montenegro (40.0%), while the number of institutions from the southern and northern part is smaller and amounts to 31.1 percent and 28.9 percent, respectively.

The sample of institutions is diverse even from the aspect of ownership, so the survey included both public and private health institutions. There were thirty-nine (thirteen institutions) or 28.9 percent respondents from private health institutions, while ninety-six (thirty-two institutions) or 71.1 percent respondents came from public health institutions.

By applying the Kolmogorov–Smirnov test for evaluation of normality of the data series, the distribution proved to be asymmetric (Sig. <0.05). For that reason, the author used nonparametric method to analyze the data of a research conducted among employees in health institutions. Nonparametric methods are used in case when we do not have a normal distribution, work with small samples or use ordinal data only. Lower accuracy of these methods in comparison to parametric methods is one of disadvantages of these methods. However, the use of nonparametric techniques in this particular case will not show a fundamentally different picture compared to parametric methods, as this is the perception of employees in health institutions in question, and their attitudes and opinions.

LEVEL OF APPLICATION OF KNOWLEDGE MANAGEMENT IN HEALTH INSTITUTIONS IN MONTENEGRO

The research (on a sample of 135 health workers) showed the average assessment of the level of application of knowledge management in health institutions in Montenegro stands at 4.02 (measured by the Likert five-point scale). When it comes to regions, the highest score was recorded in the central part of the country (4.17), followed by the northern (4.11) and the southern (3.76) that had the lowest score. However, the analysis showed no statistically significant differences between these figures.

Based on the respondents' answers, one can draw a parallel in the level of application of knowledge management in Montenegrin health institutions, from the aspect of ownership—according to the type of ownership. The level of application of knowledge management was rated 4.06 in public health institutions, while in private health institutions, the score was 3.94. These are statistically significant differences in the level of application of knowledge management. Measured by the median, the level of application of knowledge management stands at 4.21 in public institutions, while in private institutions it is 3.94.

Special attention was given to the analysis of the level of representation of knowledge management per phase. This analysis did not find any major differences in evaluation of separate phases of knowledge management. An average score of 3.90 was given to knowledge creation, 4.01 to knowledge retention, 4.12 to knowledge sharing, and 4.06 to knowledge application (on scale from 1 to 5).

Furthermore, the application of knowledge management in Montenegrin health institutions by regions was analyzed as well. Based on the research, the northern region is in the lead when it comes to knowledge creation, while in terms of storage, sharing, and application of knowledge, health institutions from the central part of Montenegro ranked as first. Health institutions from the southern region, through all four phases, had weaker results than institutions from the northern and central region.

Statistically significant difference was identified in the levels of quality of knowledge storage and knowledge application in relation to the region where health institutions are located. The author found a statistically significant difference in knowledge storage and knowledge application between the southern and central regions, while there are no such differences between the southern and northern, or between the northern and central regions.

When it comes to analysis by type of ownership, public health institutions rank better than the private ones in all four phases of knowledge management. Statistically significant differences were found between public and private health institutions in the quality of knowledge creation and knowledge sharing. Also, although not statistically significant, the levels of quality of knowledge storage and knowledge application are at a higher level in public (median is 4.0 and 4.25, respectively) than in private institutions (3.8 and 4.0, respectively).

EFFECTIVENESS OF KNOWLEDGE MANAGEMENT IN HEALTH INSTITUTIONS IN MONTENEGRO

Effectiveness is defined as "doing the right things" (Drucker, 2007). The real thing in the context of organizations that provide health services is to produce the desired outcome in the treatment of patients. In that sense, effectiveness of knowledge management in this research treats the quality of health services.

Effectiveness unlike efficiency ("doing things right") is an external feature of the organization, that is, it provides an answer to the question of whether an organization function in the way that produces the desired market response to their products and services.

In accordance with the well-known statement of one of the world's greatest authorities in the field of management, Peter Drucker, "What cannot be measured, does not exist," this research emphasizes the dimensions of quality that can be measured. Therefore, in this particular case, the effectiveness of knowledge management implies a positive reflection on the quality of health services through improved cooperation and communication, higher level of flexibility, willingness to learn, and improved organizational skills.

Total average score of the effectiveness of knowledge management in institutions in Montenegro (on a sample of 135 respondents) is 4.09. By region, the highest score in terms of effectiveness of knowledge management was assigned to the northern region (4.16), while scores are almost the same in the south and central regions (4.07 and 4.06, respectively). There are no statistically significant differences in these scores.

When it comes to the aspect of ownership, the analysis showed the effectiveness of knowledge management is higher in public than in private health institutions. Effectiveness of knowledge in private health institutions scored 4.01, while in public health institutions, it stood at 4.12, and even in this case, the differences are not statistically significant.

When it comes to individual features of the effectiveness of knowledge management, the greatest effectiveness of knowledge management was measured through a higher level of flexibility of the organization (4.15). Improvement in communication was rated at 4.13, improved cooperation at 4.09, while improvement in organizational performance was rated at 3.99.

Also, features of effectiveness of knowledge management in three regions were ranked. Cooperation, communication, and flexibility are best ranked in health institutions of the northern region, while institutions in the central region show best organizational performance. However, these differences are not statistically significant when observed by region.

Finally, levels of effectiveness of knowledge management in private and public health institutions were compared. The analysis showed that the differences were not statistically significant, but in terms of quantity, all four characteristics of knowledge management effectiveness were rated better in public than in private health institutions.

ORGANIZATIONAL CULTURE IN THE FUNCTION OF KNOWLEDGE MANAGEMENT

Quantitatively speaking, the quality of organizational culture based on the questionnaire from the introduction, was given an average score of 4.07. Scores of organizational culture are almost identical in different regions and amount to 4.07 for the central and northern region, and 4.06 for the southern.

When it comes to differentiation of health institutions according to the type of ownership, organizational culture is at a higher level in public health institutions (4.10) than in private ones (4.00), as the results suggest. Nevertheless, this difference is not statistically significant.

The analysis includes special features of organizational culture too. Organizational learning was rated at 4.13, while trust, cooperation, and mutual respect had a similar score (4.12). Creativity and innovation were rated at 4.07, while commitment to mission had the lowest score (3.96).

Some differences in the quality of features of the organizational culture in different regions were noted too. Thus, commitment to the mission was best rated in health institutions of the northern region. Trust, cooperation, and mutual respect are greatest in the southern region, while organizational learning, creativity, and innovation are strongest in health institutions in the central part of Montenegro. A statistically significant difference between the central and northern regions was found in mission commitment. There were no significant differences in the levels of organizational learning, trust, cooperation and respect, creativity, and innovation in health institutions in different regions.

When it comes to ranking of features of organizational culture by type of ownership, three of the four observed characteristics of organizational culture are ranked better in private health institutions: organizational learning, trust, cooperation and respect, creativity, and innovation (differences are not statistically significant). On the other hand, commitment to the mission was rated better in public health institutions (with statistical significance of the difference in mission commitment). The level of mission commitment measured by the median in public institutions is 4.00, while in private ones, it is 3.67.

ORGANIZATIONAL INFRASTRUCTURE

Average score of the quality of organizational infrastructure of health institutions in Montenegro is 3.82. By region, central part of Montenegro has the best organizational infrastructure (3.97), followed by the slightly weaker one in the northern part (3.78), and the southern part earned the weakest rate (3.68). A statistically significant difference in organizational infrastructure was confirmed in institutions from the central and southern regions, unlike in institutions in the central and northern, or southern and northern region.

Comparative analysis of organizational infrastructure according to the ownership type showed that the organizational infrastructure is of better quality in public than in private health institutions. In this aspect, public health institutions were rated with an average score of 3.84, while the average score for the quality of organizational infrastructure in private institutions was 3.78. Still, there are no statistically significant differences in this case.

Individual scores of features of organizational infrastructure in Montenegrin health institutions were analyzed too. The quality and adequacy of available resources received the highest score (4.08), followed by the suitability of technology (3.82) and human resource management as support to the knowledge management (3.81). Measurement of organizational performance, as well as the knowledge management process, were rated at 3.79, while the chances of acquiring, sharing knowledge and support related to information technology were rated slightly lower, at 3.75 and 3.71, respectively.

These features of the organizational infrastructure were analyzed according to the presence of health institutions in a certain region. Above all, six out of seven features of organizational infrastructure were rated best in the central region. The exception is the suitability of the technology, which was best rated in the northern region. The process of knowledge management, human resource management as support to knowledge management, measurement of organizational performance, and suitability of technology are worst in health institutions in the south, while the quality and adequacy of available resources, information technology support, and opportunities for knowledge acquisition and sharing were worst rated in the northern region. The knowledge management process differs statistically significantly between institutions in the southern and central region, while support and training in the field of information technology differs statistically significantly in institutions from the northern and central, and in institutions from the southern and central region.

The ranking of features of organizational infrastructure by type of ownership showed that four of seven features were better in public and three in private health care institutions. In particular, the following characteristics had better scores in public health institutions: quality and adequacy of available resources, knowledge management process, human resource management as support to knowledge management, and measurement of organizational performances. On the other hand, it turned out that the adequacy of technology, support, and training in the field of information technology, as well as the chances of acquiring and sharing knowledge were at a higher level in private than in public health institutions. In spite of the identified differences, the only statistically significant differences were identified in the domain of measuring organizational performance. The average score in the measurement of organizational performances by public health institutions is 3.91, while in private institutions it is 3.51.

LEADERSHIP

Average score of the quality of leadership in health institutions in Montenegro is 3.53. By region, the highest quality of leadership is in the central region (rated with an average score of 3.62). In the northern region, the leadership score is 3.54 and the lowest is in health institutions of the southern region (3.42). Statistically significant differences in the quality of leadership in the regions were registered between the southern and central regions, while there are no such significant differences between the central and northern, or northern and southern regions.

Also, statistically significant differences are evident in the leadership of public and private health institutions. Leadership in state health institutions was rated at 3.58, while a slightly lower score was assigned to private health institutions that is, 3.41. The median as an indicator of leadership quality in public health institutions is 3.57, while in private institutions it is lower and amounts to 3.43.

Individual features of leadership were taken into consideration as well. Support by management and employee empowerment was rated higher than other features, that is, 4.22 and 4.02, respectively. This is followed by the control system by top management (3.98), employee involvement (3.91), and knowledge management within strategic planning (3.71). Significantly, lower scores were given to status, formality, and internal policies (2.77), as well as the preference of action (work) over management (delegation) by the management (2.12).

A comparison of health institutions from different regions show that knowledge management within the framework of strategic planning, employee involvement, employee empowerment, and the control system by top management are of highest quality in institutions from the central region. Management support, status, formality, and policies, as well as the preference of action over management by the management, were best rated in health facilities from the northern region. When it comes to features of leadership process, health institutions from the southern region received the lowest scores in five of the seven categories (knowledge management within strategic planning, management support, employee involvement, employee empowerment, status, formality, and policies).

Even though some differences have been found, they are statistically significant only in the domain of knowledge management within strategic planning between the southern and central regions, while there are no such differences in this field between the southern and northern, and central and northern regions.

From the standpoint of the leadership process, public health institutions were rated better than private ones in all seven categories. In this area, statistically significant differences were found in management support and employee empowerment. The average score of management support in public health institutions is 4.28, while in private, it is 4.05, and the empowerment of employees in public institutions is rated on average at 4.11, while in private ones, the average score is 3.79.

Chapter 6

Organizational-Legal and Management Context of the Health System of Montenegro

Organizational design is a social invention that helps decision-makers to manage an organization (Clark, 1975). Importance of organizational design is mirrored in the creation of an organizational structure that is able to respond to growing uncertainties in its inner and outer environment and properly integrate basic elements of organizational design.

Organizational design of health system of Montenegro will be discussed in more details on the following pages.

CHALLENGES IN THE PROCESS OF DECENTRALIZATION OF HEALTH SYSTEM IN MONTENEGRO—ORGANIZATIONAL AND LEGAL CONTEXT

This section aims to evaluate the organizational design of Montenegro's public health care system from the organizational and legal standpoint. Furthermore, it aims to evaluate the likelihood of system decentralization through an inclusion of local self-governments with the goal to increase the quality of health care. This analysis is based on the method of case study. The research covered Montenegrin legislation and Montenegrin and European regulations and strategic documents that refer to local self-governments and health care systems. Individual and group interviews were carried out with selected individuals, from the range of top executives and managers in the Ministry of Health of Montenegro, Health Insurance Fund of Montenegro, Ministry of Public Administration, with professional experience of more than five years.

This paper attempts to answer the following core questions:

1. Is the health system of Montenegro centralized or decentralized?
2. Is Montenegrin health legislation prodecentralization of the public administration system?
3. To what extent are the local self-governments involved in health care system?
4. How can local self-governments become more involved in order to increase the quality of health system?

This chapter aims to determine which legal and organizational factors affect the quality of organizational design and the decentralization of health care system, and based on that to identify possibilities for improvement of the health care quality.

DECENTRALIZATION TRENDS IN ADMINISTRATIVE SYSTEMS

Some of the features of modern management of public administration are the following: modernization of administration systems based on development of public services and public regulatory bodies, professionalization of administration, and decentralization that is based on cooperation of public administration entities. Global trends and modern society require a service-oriented state and administration that sees its citizens as clients and partners, while "'modern administration bases its legitimacy on actual support of its citizens to measures and regulations of the administration" (Radević and Haček, 2019: 472).

Local authorities have a centuries-old tradition in Europe. Stoker (1991) even claims that local administration is a key element of the political system of European liberal democracy, an accomplishment of civilization, and a theoretical and practical component of all modern democratic political systems. The simplest definition of a local authority is that it is a level of authority that is closest to citizens, whose task is to represent the interest and opinions of local community. Activities of local administration is a demanding task, which relates primarily to the division of powers between the state and local communities (Haček, Kukovič, and Brezovšek, 2017: 113; Kukovič, 2018: 86). There are three basic normative elements that the local governments in Europe rest on autonomy, democracy, and efficiency (Greer, Murphy, and Ogard, 2005). Autonomy is the degree of decision-making power between the central and local authorities. Decision-making at the local level prevents the concentration of political power at the central level and allows for different political choices in different local communities. Democracy is an element that local authorities use to present a political platform for citizens' participation in management of local activities. Efficiency is an important element, since local authorities are more efficient than the central ones in providing public services and finding solutions for local problems and adapting their measures to local environment.

The European Charter on Local Self-Government of the Council of Europe contributed to the development of local governments and local democracies. It was adopted on October 15, 1985, in Strasbourg, and entered into force on September 1, 1988, when it was ratified by the first four Council of Europe member states, while Montenegro ratified it in September 2008. The countries that have adopted the Charter committed to adhering to the principles and rules of the Charter, aligning their legislation frameworks so as to include local self-governments in national legislations, and defining the field of activity of local self-governments, methods and criteria for delegation of competences. Local authorities must have a certain degree of autonomy, protection of borders, and restriction of control over local community. It is necessary to ensure "democratic election process, freedom of expression and association and adequate participation of citizens in all forms of local democracy" (Brezovšek and Kukovič, 2015: 218–219). In addition, local authorities are entitled to appropriate financial resources (originating from local taxes and fees) to use them within their own competences. The goal is to create an efficient local self-government that is close to its citizens, in line with principles of democracy and decentralization, while strengthening ties with other municipalities and cross-border cooperation.

In addition to the decentralization of administrative systems by strengthening local self-governments, the notion of public services is important too. It was developed in France, with the key contribution by Léon Duguit. Like most French authors of that time, Duguit sought the criteria for "delineation between judicial and administrative control" (Pečarič and Bugarič, 2011, 20). Duguit's concept of public service, management of public law principles implies every activity that is necessary for the existence and development of a society as a whole. It must be ensured, regulated, and controlled by those who rule, and any delay in these activities may lead to disorder and stagnation in the society. The role of the government and its administrative bodies, according to Duguit, is to regard the state as a community, that is, a network of public services, and different functions of the state are different ways to establish and implement public service (Rakočević 1994: 137). Many years later, Rivero (1971: 397) argued that public service is "a form of administrative activity through which public entities ensure the public interests are met." In modern English administrative theory, the concept of public services is very broad, as public services are "all public sector organizations that provide public goods to citizens, including state and local governments, health, education and police" (Fahrham and Horton, 1996: 7–8). Public services mean providing public goods, in the following ways (Brezovšek, Haček and Kukovič, 2015): first, it has to be in the public interest; second, the state or local self-government should be responsible for continuous provision of services; third, public services should be made available to everyone and under equal terms; fourth, price of public services should be regulated; fifth, provision of public services should be implemented in line with a special regime of public law, due to the need to ensure balance between the public interest and the market principles of functioning.

Public interest should prevail over private interest in public services, even though private entities may carry out activities of public services. However, in such cases, a quality regulation of ties between the state and private sector should be made.

Laws of the European Union have relatively few provisions directly applicable to public services, but it is possible to find a common string of duties of public services that member states have to provide (Grafenauer and Brezovnik, 2006): first, a duty of service providers to provide at least a minimum level of services to all users in a territory of the state for the purpose of exercising public interest; second, services must be provided continuously; third, all standards of quality must be adhered to; fourth, public services should be provided at affordable prices.

Public services can be divided into national and local services. However, different countries generated other forms with the purpose of a more efficient functioning, and they can be systematized in three basic forms (Pečarič and Bugarič, 2011):

- the state or local communities carry out public services themselves;
- independent organizations owned by the state or local communities; and
- individuals or private companies that are granted the exclusive right to perform public service activities by the state or local community.

COMPLEXITY OF THE PROCESS OF DECENTRALIZATION OF HEALTH SYSTEMS

The quality of decentralization of public administration is largely dictated by a country's legal framework. In it, legal arrangements of the state and nonstate administration play an especially important role. Non-state public administration, which in theory encompasses both the local self-government and public services (in a wider sense of the word, public services include local public agencies, public bodies, special organizations, etc.) gained momentum in overtaking a growing number of state and administrative functions from classic state bodies, on the grounds of entrusted public powers by the state.

Therefore, we are witnesses to a flourishing decentralizations of administrative systems, which brings benefits, but calls for caution too. Some of the benefits are a stronger motivation and involvement of citizens in administrative activities, which results in a higher degree of trust between the citizens and the administration, more solutions, which altogether results in a higher satisfaction with the quality of administrative affairs. However, "strategy of decentralization is incremental and is implemented in parallel with development of administrative and other capacities" (Kassak, Ali, Tauk, and Abdallah, 2007, 447). Otherwise, excessive, fast decentralization of the system that is not sufficiently based on laws or organization, results in weakening relations between the elements of the system and in poor decisions.

Health system is among the most complex and financially challenging systems to manage (Dickinson and Pierre, 2016). To plan and coordinate such a system requires a delegation of roles and responsibilities to all parties within the health system, with the purpose to provide an adequate response to growing expectations of citizens in terms of quality and accessibility of health care. In addition to this, intersectoral cooperation is important and so is the decentralization of the system by modeling an organizational design of the public health system in accordance with the initiative of the World Health Organization—Health in all Policies—that Montenegro joined too. Importance of cooperation of all entities with the purpose of improvement of the health system is best described by the emerging term "health ecosystem," that refers to multifaceted and interdependent elements of health system (Albers, 2014).

Human factor is crucial for the quality of health care in health institutions, but it is clear that a high-quality health care does not depend on brilliance of individuals, but rather on the quality of the organization of all elements that are necessary to satisfy the needs of patients (Allen, 2018).

Decision-makers carry a tremendous amount of responsibility on their shoulders along with the evident need for a continuous improvement of efficiency due to growing health care-related costs (Baumol, 1993; Praag and Ferrer-i-Carbonell, 2004; Watcharasriroj and Tang, 2004; Hammad, Jusoh, and Ghozali, 2013).

An important part of the organization and functioning of the health care system is the connection of system on all levels, its territorial distribution, decentralized management, and a coordinated course of action of all entities. On the other hand, in spite of the need for decentralization, health care system must develop a system of intersectoral communication, and the ability for centralized management in case of emergency.

LEGAL ASPECTS OF LOCAL SELF-GOVERNMENTS AND PUBLIC SERVICES IN MONTENEGRO

Legal and Systemic Framework of Local Self-Government in Montenegro

To define terms from the standpoint of the governing law is vital for functioning of the system, or, in other words, it is an important prerequisite for quality of practical implementation of specific legal norms about the public administration's affairs and organization. The Constitution of Montenegro guarantees the right to local self-government, which is in accordance with the European Charter of Local Self-Government (Article 22). Furthermore, it defines that some duties of state administration may be delegated by law or government regulation to the local self-government or to another legal entity (Article 112). In case that certain state administration affairs are conferred (by law) or entrusted (by government regulation) to the local self-government, such laws or regulations define the method of their financing too. Beforehand, as a prerequisite, it is essential to have a feasibility study on entrusting the state administration affairs, which, in accordance with Article 37 of the Law on State Administration, contains "(1) justification to entrust the affairs; (2) detailed list of the affairs to be entrusted; (3) views and opinions of state administration bodies from the domain of which the affairs are entrusted, about the possibilities and conditions for the performance of entrusted affairs in the local self-government; (4) existence of conditions for performance of the entrusted affairs in relation to the organizational, technical, financial, material matters, and to human resources; (5) manners and conditions of funding of the entrusted affairs." Competent ministries control the conferred and entrusted affairs of the local self-government, and in case the local self-government fails to act upon its recommendations or fails to undertake appropriate measures for performance of affairs in terms of quality, "may propose to the Government to withdraw the conferred and/or entrusted affairs" (more details in Article 39–40 of the Law on State Administration).

Pursuant to Article 113 paragraph 1 of the Constitution of Montenegro and to Article 6 paragraph 1 of the Law on Local Self-Government, it is regulated that "in the local self-government the decisions shall be made directly and through the freely elected representatives." Also, Article 113 paragraph 2, defines the local self-government as "the right of citizens and local self-government bodies to regulate and manage certain public and other affairs, in their own responsibility and in the interest of the local population," which fully corresponds to the European Charter of Local Self-Government (Article 3 paragraphs 1 and 2).

Article 16 paragraph 1 of the Constitution of Montenegro defines that a special law has to regulate the system of local self-government and competences of local self-governments in execution of public affairs that are in interest of local population. However, demarcation between the state affairs and local self-government affairs has not been defined thoroughly, unlike the following items: manner of decision-making, form and bodies of local self-government, and property-related powers, independence, and financing of local self-governments (Articles 113–117).

The Law on Local Self-Government governs the affairs of the local self-government that are of direct and common interest to the local population, that are performed through the bodies of local self-government, bodies of local community and self-government, and public services, all in accordance with the law, statute, and other regulations (Articles 4 and 5). Bodies of local self-government are secretariats, administrations, and directorates (Article 69 paragraph 1); while specialized services can be established for performance of some professional affairs (Article 69 paragraph 2). And special services are established to perform specific affairs within the local self-government, such as the communal police, protection and rescue services and other services, in accordance with Article 69 paragraph 3 of the Law.

As per the Law on Local Self-Government, public services are the following: "institutions, legal entities and other forms of establishment with the purpose of providing public services" (Article 29 paragraph 1 item 2). In addition, any establishment of public services is allowed in cases when "performance of affairs is an indispensable requirement for life and work of the local population, or if the needs of citizens in such fields are not addressed in a high-quality and economical manner by means of a private initiative or in any other manner" (Article 29 paragraph 2).

Bodies of local self-government supervise legality of regulations passed by public services, and legality, appropriateness of their work and inspection control (Article 72). "Any conflict of competences between the bodies of local self-government is resolved by the chief administrator, while any such conflict arising among the bodies of local self-government, local public services and legal entities, to whom the assembly has decided to delegate certain affairs, are resolved by the mayor" (Article 87).

Municipalities finance their own affairs from the following sources: (1) municipal revenues, (2) public revenues established by the law, (3) equalization fund, (4) budget of Montenegro, and (5) other sources in accordance with the law (Article 150).

The Law on Local Self-Government provides for the participation of citizens in their exercise of local self-government, and it regulates the relations between the bodies of local self-government and public services established by the state. Pursuant to the Law (Article 157), a municipality "creates conditions, stimulates and assists the participation of the local population in their exercise of local self-government," whereas "the local population takes part in bodies of public services and in other legal entities that exercise public powers and provide services to citizens, for the purpose of addressing their needs in the fields of culture, sport, education, health, information and other." Article 175 regulates the cooperation of bodies of local self-government with public services and other legal entities founded by the state, through participation of bodies of local self-government in the procedure of design and implementation of plans of development, in making proposals, giving suggestions and opinions concerning the carrying out activities on the territory of the municipality. Furthermore, public services are under obligation to provide the local self-government with plans and programs of development from their jurisdictions on the territory of the municipality, and to report about the implementation of plans and programs.

Affairs of the local self-government typically refer to development and regulation of communal activities, municipal roads, local transport, urban development land, entrepreneurial actions and agricultural production, protection of environment, protection of consumers, water supply, housing, and development of culture, tourism and sport.

In accordance with Article 27 (paragraph 1 items 12, 15, 20, and 21), the following items are listed among the affairs of local self-government: "(1) in accordance with the possibilities, participation in the provision of conditions and improvement of sectors of health protection, education, social and children welfare, employment, and other sectors of interest for the local population, and carrying out rights and duties of a founder of institutions that are established within these sectors by the municipality, in accordance with the law; (2) providing of conditions for protection and rescue of population, material and cultural goods and environment in the area of municipality, from natural disasters, technical-technological, and other accidents; (3) organization and implementation of measures for protection of citizens against infectious diseases; (4) regulation, providing and taking care of the tourist development, and development of services which contribute to the development of tourism." Within its own jurisdiction, the municipality, among other things "determines the public interest for the expropriation of real estates to meet local needs, in accordance with law" (Article 28 paragraph 1 item 5).

Heterogeneity of Montenegrin Administration

Montenegrin administration has a fairly heterogeneous composition. Pursuant to the Law on State Administration, the government establishes state administration bodies by means of its act (Article 27), which is controversial from the standpoint of Montenegrin Constitution. That is, Article 16 paragraph 1 item 3 which defines that a separate law, in accordance with the Constitution, regulates the manner of establishment, organization, and competences of the bodies of authorities and the procedure before those authorities, if so required for their affairs. In this context, it seems necessary to regulate the organization of state administration by the law on ministries and state administration bodies, similarly to how the countries from the region and beyond have done. Also, the government determines administrative fields for which state administration bodies are established, and the organization and method of operation of state administration too. In accordance to the Law on State Administration, state administration affairs are performed by the ministries and other state administration bodies (Article 2 paragraph 1). Pursuant to the regulation on organization and manner of work of the state administration (2018), there are seventeen ministries (Article 2), with twenty-nine administrative bodies (Article 20). Similarly, the regulation defines in more detail the fields of operation for each body. Holders of public powers are state agencies, state funds, and other holders of public powers established by the law (Article 42). The ministry controls the affairs of state institutions that are founded by the state (Article 78 paragraph 1).

The Law on State Administration in Article 12 lists the affairs of the state administration as follows: "(1) proposals of interior and foreign policies; (2) legislative activities; (3) enforcement of laws and other regulations; (4) decision-making and undertaking of administrative activities in administrative matters, in accordance with the law; (5) administrative supervision; (6) performance of affairs of public interest; (7) other affairs of state administration as defined by the law and other regulations."

Administration for Inspection Affairs is body of state administration too. Legality and expedience of the administration and legality of administrative regulations for some administrative areas from the administration's field of competence shall be supervised by ministries that are competent for certain administrative area, while the government shall supervise the coordinated activities of the administration through the Ministry of Public Administration (Article 51 paragraph 4).

In addition to state administration, complexity of the system of public administration in Montenegro is further aggravated by a number of non-state entities that are holders of public powers, to the point that oftentimes the status or form of such entities cannot be said for sure. Although the public service can be considered as any activity of social, economic, and cultural significance for the local community, that is, addressing the needs of citizens that are in the public interest; however, from the legal standpoint, a public service exists only if it is regulated by special legal acts which govern their regular and constant functioning. The Constitution mentions the notion "public service" only twice (Articles 66 and 79), and the notion "organizations exercising public authority" are mentioned twice too (Articles 51 and 57). Without clear and systemic definitions of notions "public powers," "public services," "non-state administration," there is room for different interpretations of public services in Montenegrin legislation.

In such situations, according to Professor Blažić (2009: 129), non-state entities, as holders of public powers in Montenegro, depending on their form of organization and public functions, can be divided into several categories:

1. local self-government (capital city, Old Royal Capital, and municipalities);
2. public services (funds, institutions, public companies, concession public services, and other public services);
3. public agencies and public bodies (committees, associations, commissions, etc.);
4. Independent—specialized organizations (e.g., Central bank, National Security Agency, etc.);
5. regulatory bodies (Securities Commission, Agency for Electronic Communications, and Postal Services, etc.);
6. professional and other associations (e.g., Chamber of Commerce etc.);
7. natural persons (e.g., public notaries); and
8. other forms (committees, institutions and offices).

Legal and Systemic Framework of Public Services in Montenegro

Establishment of public services in Montenegro is regulated by so-called sectoral laws (Law on Health Care, General Law on Education, Law on Social, and Child Protection, among others). Unlike Serbia, for example, Montenegro failed to adopt the law on social services,[1] although its adoption had been defined in the Public Administration Reform Strategy of Montenegro 2002–2009, and in the Strategy of Public Administration Reform in Montenegro 2011–2016. The Public Administration Reform Strategy 2016–2020 encompasses the system of state administration, local self-government, and organizations with public powers (organizations with their own legal personality that perform certain administrative tasks pursuant to powers conferred upon them by the law or pursuant to the law). However, the Strategy in question "does not refer to the wider public sector, i.e., public health, education, social welfare, culture etc" (Public Administration Reform Strategy 2016–2020: 10). Yet, the Ministry of Public Administration of Montenegro has recognized the fact that "from the standpoint of consistency of the system of public administration, a special problem is the position of organizations with public powers (public agencies, public funds and public institutions)" (Public Administration Reform

Strategy, 2016-2020: 14). This is due to great diversity in their status and functioning and to insufficient possibilities for supervision of legality and appropriateness of their work.

Problem of Consistency of Administrative and Legal System

Many entities in Montenegrin administrative system have the same name (e.g., agencies), that are entirely different in terms of their status, organization, and function. Intertwining of some of the public services leads to a confusion when one attempts to understand their various forms, even when professionals try to do that, let alone the lay users of public services. And while Montenegro has failed to adopt the law on public agencies, any attempt to regulate that field by means of sectoral laws results in public services that have no defined legal status. So the analyses of definitions of legal status show that the Montenegrin Investment Promotion Agency is a public institution, Administration for Protection of Competition is a body, Agency for Electronic Communications is a regulatory body, Agency for Pharmaceuticals and Medical Devices lacks a status, Agency for Amicable Settlement of Labor Disputes is a special organization, National Security Agency is an independent service, Agency for Prevention of Corruption is an independent state institution, among others.

One of the prerequisites for a proper response to the need to regulate the system of public administration in Montenegro is the establishment of the Ministry of Public Administration that began operating in November 2016. With that move and within the context of the need to strengthen the administrative and systemic capacities and, in parallel, within the context of accession to the European Union, the Government of Montenegro demonstrated its determination to improve the systemic prerequisites for an efficient functioning of the public administration. To that effect, one of the most important laws for efficiency of administrative procedures and for provision of services was adopted—the Law on Administrative Procedures that came into force on July 1, 2017. However, adjustments of the legal framework are still underway. The Law on Public and Private Partnership was adopted in 2019 and its adoption meant an elimination of one of legal and systemic drawbacks.

The new Law on Administrative Procedures provides for a possibility of entering into legal agreements with the purpose to establish a public and private partnership (Article 27–30). However, to enter into such an agreement, it is necessary to align and elaborate the contents of administrative agreements from the standpoint of substantive laws. Due to the fact that substantive laws do not support that kind of obligation, this could mean that public bodies cannot enter into administrative agreements, although there is such need in almost every field of public interest.

Perhaps one of the best indicators of an insufficiently consistent legal system, and perhaps of a lack of responsibility in the area of governing, is presented in the Administrative Court's statistics. It shows that "more than a half of a total number of decisions of ministries that were brought to the Administrative Court were annulled in 2016" (Milošević 2018: 14).

Pursuant to Article 84 of the Law on State Administration, "the Government resolves the conflicts of competences among (1) ministries, (2) administration bodies, (3) ministries and administration bodies, (4) ministries and holders of public powers, and (5) administration bodies and holders of public powers." Efforts will be made in future to insist on a better communication among bodies of public administration, as an assumption of a successful model of decentralization. This is for the reason that systemic deficiencies are noted in the area of development and coordination of policies, "especially between the central and local levels" (Milošević 2018: 27–28).

The lack of a systematic regulation of public services and definitions of their position through regulations from different areas of social life result in risks of having legal gaps, in collision of regulations, and in disorder of these segments of the system. Consequences of such legal framework of insufficient quality result in lack of trust of citizens in institutions of the system, which has a negative effect on all social activities including the health system too. Chambers (2012: 6) explained that well by pointing out that there is no sustainable health system if there are no following elements that are interdependent "high trust—high challenge—high motivation and engagement."

CENTRALIZATION VERSUS DECENTRALIZATION

Until the beginning of 1990s, the centralization was a predominant feature of the political system in Montenegro. However, although things gradually started moving toward the decentralization at the end of twentieth century, Montenegrin administrative system is still prevalently perceived as a centralized one. Globally, one can say that a "traditional, vertical-hierarchical or homogenous-systemic perception of the social structure gives way to the notion of network-wise perception of structures of the society" (Radević 2103: 19).

Centralism is a system of state organization where decision-making and control of their implementation is mostly or entirely in hands of central bodies (Blažić, 2011). Centralistic tendencies are directed to strengthening of the role and powers from central bodies to noncentral ones. Central bodies are entitled to appoint and dismiss officials and officers of noncentral bodies, and to make substitution of affairs from their field of competencies too. That is an indicator of a subordinated position and of a lack of independence of noncentral bodies that have to act upon the orders of the central point (Eisenmann, 1988; Blažić, 2011).

Decentralization represents the process of weakening of influence of the organizational system's center to individual parts of that system (Pusić, 1989; Larson and Ribot, 2004; Coaffee and Johnston, 2005; Kojo Sakyi, Awoonor-Williams, and Adzei, 2011). The organizational design of modern organizations implies a mandatory and desirable decentralization of the system, with fewer hierarchical levels, greater autonomy entrusted to smaller organizational units, but with their stronger communication and networking. Trust, human relations modeled through an adequate organizational culture substitute for rigid lines of management and hierarchical relations (Addicott, 2008). In essence, decentralization is deprived of a good infrastructure where the system is linked in terms of exchange of information, knowledge sharing, and mutual support among independent organizational units; decentralization is deprived of a quality control function too, which can be harmful rather than beneficial.

It should be emphasized that decentralization is conducted more easily in developed countries (Fenwick and Bailey, 1999; Guga, 2018), since simply having a good idea about a high-quality process is not enough. What it takes too is to properly communicate the strategy and have all stakeholders involved. Therefore, decentralization should be done in phases, in such a way as to allow the system to accommodate to functional changes and to the division of responsibilities; not to forget, the fundamental pillar of quality of every decentralization and *conditio sine qua non*, is the quality of legislation.

The purpose of decentralization that is achieved by relocating public functions to organizations beyond the public administration system is as follows:

- increased level of efficiency of the organizational system (increased system flexibility, and managerial independence in execution of such tasks);
- greater involvement of civil society in the decision-making process (e.g., through memberships in councils of public services, among others);
- higher level of transparency (Regmi, 2010) and by that, a higher level of trust in the system;
- higher level of professional integrity and of other forms of independence, and thereby a "distance from any political influence or pressure in doing important public affairs or providing public services" (Blažić, 2009: 138);
- higher likelihood that set goals would be closer to local citizens, as opposed in the case of centralized management (Goddard and Mannion, 2006); and
- strengthening of lower decision-making levels and participative decision-making allows for an organizational learning and knowledge sharing (Ford and Angermeier, 2008), and a "stronger motivation of public officials in democratic systems" (Prysmakova, 2016: 895).

For all the above reasons, decentralization guarantees a more efficient and rational execution of affairs through non-state administration than through state administration bodies. An important argument is the fact that no constant political oversight is required in the area of public services. On the contrary, to perform any public service, it is necessary to be distanced from any political or other influence.

However, potential risks that lure from the uncontrolled decentralization of the system call for caution:

- lower likelihood of control over public services (as opposed to executing the same affairs under the jurisdiction of a ministry or a body within the ministry);
- lower level of ministerial responsibility (reduction of responsibility is proportional to the degree of independence of public services in legal, professional, organizational, personal, and financial sense);
- increase of costs due to loss of the economy of scale (Athanasiadis, Ratsika, Trompoukis, and Philalithis, 2018);
- dysfunctionality in institutions, "various forms of risks on the central level and in organizational units of the decentralization" (Kennewell and Baker, 2016: 453), "having too many units" within a system results in lower capacities of such units and in lower possibility of a systemic control, which is the case in Scandinavian countries (Byrkjeflot and Neby, 2008);
- different levels of motivation and dedication of decentralized units to the joint vision (Kingsnorth, 2013);
- problems with the implementation and monitoring of policies in case of poorer managerial capacities on lower levels (Regmi, 2010); and
- if the system is decentralized in case of municipalities, it is natural that some municipalities will be able to allocate more funds for health care unlike others; hence, inequality is easy to arise, and "in case of any sort of intervention to overcome the inequality it would cause a lower motivation of a municipality that is willing to invest more" (Collins and Green, 1993: 61).

The risks are particularly pronounced in institutions that have no tradition or sufficient experience in operational activities either. For example, establishment of public services as regulatory bodies that may have certain quasi-judicial competences, but lack a direct democratic base (unlike, for example, democratic legitimacy of the parliament). To that sense, it is difficult to ensure independence of these bodies, that is, free them from any political influence of entities that appoint members to such bodies. Therefore, special attention has to be paid to the regulatory role in the administrative system (Blažić, 2009: 140).

There is a significant link between the decentralization and quality of health services (Meirovich, G., Brender-Ilan, and Meirovich, A., 2007). The empirical analysis of this author has shown that both the decentralization and formalization affects the quality of services in parallel, as two dimensions of organizational structures. That is the reason due to which the quality decentralization of the system cannot be implemented without proper legal regulations and procedures, that would guarantee the formalization of actions of the health system.

HEALTH SYSTEM IN MONTENEGRO—LEGAL AND ORGANIZATIONAL ASPECT

The trend of liberalization, deregulation, and privatization has become ever more present in modern forms of state administration, and in some segments, they are even "dictated" through requirements and regulations of supranational instructions that Montenegro is to fulfil in the process of accession to the European Union.[2] Slovenia had a similar experience with the decentralization of the administration system due to its membership in the European Union (McCluskey and Bevc, 2007).

Health system of Montenegro is regulated by a number of laws, with the Law on Health Care as an umbrella law. The activity of health care is recognized as an activity of public interest by this Law (Article 8 paragraph 2). Pursuant to the Law on State Administration (Article 21) "securing of the performance of affairs of public interest comprises the performance of such affairs through institutions, commercial entities, entrepreneurs, through direct enforcement, awarding concessions, capital investments and other measures which enable efficient and cost-effective performance of such activities." Public services are established in social and economic areas that are defined as areas of public interest, regardless of who performs those activities and who their founder may be; therefore, health institutions can be listed among public services that perform social activities.

Pursuant to the Law on Health Care (Article 2) "health care is an organized and comprehensive activity of the society with the aim to achieve the maximum possible level of preservation of health of its citizens." It is exercised through a set of measures and activities on preservation, protection, and improvement of health of citizens. In accordance with Article 6 "citizens are entitled to information that are required for preservation of health and for healthy lifestyles."

Basic principles of the Law on Health Care are comprehensiveness, continuity, accessibility, integrity, and expediency, a specialized approach to health care and constant improvement of the quality of health care. Decentralization of the system, that is, responsibility divided on all entities of the system with the purpose of having a quality health care is shown in Article 10, which insists on comprehensiveness of health care through inclusion of all citizens in implementation of appropriate measures and activities for preservation, protection, and improvement of health. These activities include promotion of health, prevention of illnesses, early detection of illnesses, treatment, and rehabilitation.

The Law on Health Care (Article 58) sets forth the possibility that founders of a health institution can be "the state, municipality, a national or foreign legal or natural person. As an exception to the above, the state founds health institutions on tertiary level of health care i.e. institutions that practice activities of blood transfusion, typification, body parts transplantation, tissue and cell transplantation, activities of preventive and epidemiological surveillance of contagious illnesses and urgent medical assistance." The decision on establishment is made by the government, or by a competent body within a municipality, depending on who the founder is—the government or municipality (Article 60). The ministry issues a formal decision on fulfilment of conditions for commencement of health care activities (Article 61).

Within the domain of rights and possibilities of municipalities to create conditions for primary health care on their own territory, the law defined that the municipality: (1) monitors the state of play, initiates, and proposes measures in the area of primary health care; (2) participates in the planning and implementation of primary health care, which is of direct interest for the local population; (3) participates in management of a health institution that was founded by the state, in accordance with the Law on Health Care; (4) undertakes other activities with the aim of improvement of primary health care (Article 18). In addition to the above, there is room for municipalities "to take part in financing of a share of costs of primary health care—during the tourist season, and in line with the agreement concluded with a health institution."

Article 31 defines that for the purpose of public interest and for the implementation of health care programs, a network of health institutions is to be formed "in accordance with the population size, number of insurers, state of health of the population, prevalent number of citizens, characteristics of specific territories, availability of health resources and their accessibility to citizens." The health network of municipalities, the capital city, and the Old Royal Capital consist of health institutions founded by the state, and certain other health institutions or parts of health institutions that are founded by another legal and/or natural person; furthermore, it covers some legal persons that perform activities that are linked with the right to health care (Decision on network of health institutions, Article 2).

The Health Insurance Fund of Montenegro is in charge to fund the health care and other rights arising from health insurance, and is in charge for the intended spending of funds. It is an independent financial institution whose task is to adopt annual program of health care and to adopt the draft financial plan in accordance with the Law.

In accordance with the Law on Territorial Organization of Montenegro (Articles 2, 5, 6, and 7), units of local self-government are Capital City of Podgorica, city municipality Golubovci—as a municipality within the capital city, Old Royal Capital of Cetinje, and municipalities: Andrijevica, Bar, Berane, Bijelo Polje, Budva, Gusinje, Danilovgrad, Žabljak, Kotor, Kolašin, Mojkovac, Nikšić, Petnjica, Plav, Plužine, Pljevlja, Rožaje, Tivat, Tuzi, Ulcinj, Herceg Novi, and Šavnik.

In accordance with the decision on network of health institutions, the network of health institutions founded by the state, on primary level, consists of eighteen health centers: Andrijevica, Bar, Berane, Bijelo Polje, Budva, Cetinje, Danilovgrad, Herceg Novi, Kolašin, Kotor, Mojkovac, Nikšić, Plav, Pljevlja, Podgorica, Rožaje, Tivat, and Ulcinj (Article 3). The Public Health Institute provides services of primary health protection (even though it is an institution for public health on tertiary level of health care with the associated activities, under Article 50). There are eight hospitals that are providers of health care (Bar, Berane, Bijelo Polje, Cetinje, Kotor, Meljine, Nikšić, Pljevlja) and three specialized hospitals (Brezovik, Dobrota, Risan). In addition to general and special hospitals, hospitals that provide health care on secondary and tertiary level are Codra Hospital, Tesla Medical polyclinic in Berane, and the Clinical Center of Montenegro (Article 10). Provider of the service of emergency medical care on the primary level is the Emergency Medical Service, while the blood transfusion is covered by the Office for Blood Transfusion (Articles 12–14). Exercise of the right to medicines is done through the institution Pharmacies of Montenegro “'Montefarm” (and other pharmacies that have signed an agreement with the Pension and Insurance Fund), while “Rudo Montenegro” supplies the medical and technical devices (Article 14).[3]

Under the law, bodies of health institutions in Montenegro are a board of directors (a governing body) and a director (a managing body). They are appointed and dismissed by the founder (i.e., government being the founder in case of state institutions). It is peculiar that board of directors is a mandatory body in health institutions such as the Clinical Center of Montenegro and the Public Health Institute, whereas in other health institutions (health clinics, general, and special hospitals, etc.) it cannot be formed (Article 70 of the Law on Health Care). In such institutions, governing body is the executive director at the same time. One representative of the municipality must be is appointed as a board member of institutions.

Following a proposal by the minister, Government of Montenegro appoints and dismisses directors of the Clinical Center of Montenegro and of the Public

Health Institute. Directors of other health institutions founded by the state are appointed and dismissed by the minister following a public call (Article 74).

In cases of emergency, the ministry is entitled to take measures and activities concerning the organization of activities in any entity that operate in health care-related activities. This is in line with Article 101 paragraph 1 of the Constitution that says that during the state of war or the state of emergency, the government may adopt decrees with legal power, if the Parliament is not able to meet.

An important thing for decentralization and a more efficient organization of the system is a possibility for institutions founded by the state or municipalities, to lease their premises and equipment under previously obtained approval from the ministry. Financing of health institutions is provided from the following sources: (1) founders, (2) budget of Montenegro (through the Health Insurance Fund), (3) budget of municipalities, (4) natural and legal persons under terms stipulated by the law, (5) voluntary insurance, and (6) other sources.

PROCESS OF DECENTRALIZATION OF HEALTH SYSTEM OF MONTENEGRO—KEY CHALLENGES

Health system in Montenegro is predominantly centralized, and the same applies to the entire administrative system. Through its regulations, and in accordance with recommendations dictated by the European Union, the state works on building a more efficient system of administration. Comparative analyses of a number of countries that have reformed their health care systems showed that their goal was the same (Burau and Vrangbæk, 2008). Decentralization of the system is mainly taken for the reform of health care system. Impediments for the decentralization of the system—which could result in an improved quality of services, can be found both in the legal regulations and in (non)enforcement of laws.

Features of quality of small successful systems are typically based on a good integration of elements of the system, their mutual support, and trust. Any integration of the system is based on a good systematic legal regulations and implementation of laws, on their mutual support in the process of decentralization, that is, on delegation and transfer of powers from the central level to lower level entities, and as a result of it all, trust of beneficiaries of services and their satisfaction improves, which, in essence, contributes to a more favorable social and economic environment.

This analysis has shown the following impediments for a quality decentralization of the health system of Montenegro and for achievement of a better and more efficient health care system:

1. *Lack of an appropriate legal framework.* Montenegro does not have a systemic law that would regulate the non-state administration properly, while the number of non-state administration entities is rather varied and as such makes the functioning of the system more difficult. What was lacking too was the Law on Public and Private Partnership, adopted in late 2019, but its implementation did not make any major effects due to the COVID-19 pandemic. Its adoption made the process of decentralization of health care system easier, and it increased the motivation of legal entities to take part in the system, especially in the field of outsourcing nonhealth care services (food catering, cleaning, maintenance, etc.). Public and private partnership is a form that links public and private organizations. Both sides assume different logic and objectives at the beginning, but with the purpose of recognizing the synergy of their association, increasing the efficiency and quality of management in fulfilling the needs of local population (Saviano, Parida, Caputo, and Kumar Datta, 2014). To that context, models of public and private partnerships are widely popular in health systems all over the world (Sciulli, 2008; Gerstlberger and Schneider, 2012) emphasize that a private partner is strongly interested in a long-term success (to be able to return the investment, mostly in infrastructure), which compels the government to adopt a more strategic way of thinking. The institutional prerequisites are good legislation, appropriate sector policies, and differentiation in provision of services from the system of regulation.

2. *Poor enforcement of the Law that causes a lack of democracy and autonomy.* Only in case the central authorities clearly demonstrate consistency, accuracy, and responsibility in enforcement of laws, one can expect a stronger inclusion and stronger motivation of lower levels in the organizational chain. Involvement of citizens in decision-making process is limited. An interesting research made by the IPSOS agency for the Institute Alternativa showed that as many as 58 percent of citizens were not informed about public discussions organized by public administration bodies, 38 percent were partly informed, whereas only 4 percent were well informed (Milošević, 2018: 27–28). Worth noting is the fact that not a single representative of the public (citizens) took part in discussions about local budget for year 2017 in as many as five units of local self-government, including the capital city of Podgorica and Old Royal Capital of Cetinje, according to the data of the Institut Alternativa that analyzed reports of local self-governments.[4] This is alarming, even though experience from regional countries show that civil organization in most cases lack best terms for an efficient participation in preparation of policy papers (Lajh and Krašovec, 2010; Kavčić, Pahor, and Domajnko,

2015). In addition, this is in conflict with Article 157 of the Law on Local Self-Government, according to which "a municipality creates conditions, stimulates and assists the participation of the local population in their exercise of local self-government." Still, it is in conflict with contemporary management practices that insist on inclusion of as many stakeholders as possible into the decision-making process and setting out priorities as that implies the stakeholders would act upon them, and for which a number of techniques and forms of communication have been developed (Garpenby and Bäckman, 2016: 893–894). The Law on Local Self-Government (2018, Article 29) sets forth the conditions and procedure for a territorial change, which is in accordance with Article 5 of the European Charter of Local Self-Government. Enforcement of this law means that local assembly would have to call for the (consultative) local referendum so the citizens could state their mind about territorial changes. This law was applicable for two out of three newest municipalities in Montenegro (Petnjica, Gusinje and Tuzi), whereas in the case of Tuzi, it was not implemented. And last but not the least, the citizens do not have an option to choose directly their local counsellors at elections; they have to vote for a list of a political party or civil initiative, contrary to Article 113 of the Constitution of Montenegro and to Article 6 of the Law on Local Self-Government and to the European Charter of Local Self-Government (Article 3 paragraph 2). In addition, during the height of COVID-19 pandemic, the National Coordination Body adopted a set of measures. However, there were multiple breaches of these measures (face masks, distance, no public gatherings) and of recommendations by other professionals, not just in individual cases, but rather mass violations at rallies, by members of the ruling majority and the opposition.

3. *Inability of municipalities to take part in the financing of health care system.* The fact that as many as two-thirds of Montenegrin municipalities (15) got their funding from the Equalization fund,[5] in 2018, speaks for itself about poor fiscal capacities of local self-governments in Montenegro.[6] These data are complimentary with the fact that the estimated population in 2017 was lower in two-thirds of Montenegrin municipalities than in 2016, which altogether speaks about problems of uneven development of the country, predominantly of insufficient development of the northern region.[7] However, one should not forget that health care performances are linked with economic performances, and that sound health is a source of economic and social stability, and "a key for poverty reduction and sustainable development too" (WHO—Health 2020: a European policy framework: 8). The Law on Local Self-Government in Article 21 says that the task of local self-government is to create

conditions and to care about development of tourism, and of other activities that improve tourism. In that context, it is clear that through a harder care about the health system, municipalities themselves could contribute to development of local and state tourist potentials, that is, to increase the number of tourists, revenues to both the municipality and state through the exploitation of comparative advantages of our health care system (competitive prices, nature, geographical position, climate, etc.). Sport tourism could be seen as a part of complementary activities, as well as the promotion of healthy lifestyle, spending time outdoors, among others.

4. *Insufficient motivation of persons in charge of health institutions.* Health institutions are dominantly founded by the state. Current state of play allows directors of health institutions to manage, but not to govern; therefore, there is no necessary flexibility in governing. Hence, it is impossible to establish an adequate motivational system. Contemporary initiatives of the reconfiguration of health system focus on employees who are allowed to develop new ways of thinking and acting (Rule, Dunston, and Solomon, 2016). Health institutions in Montenegro are by definition "money spending units," and their employees are not motivated to be innovative or cost-efficient, due to lack of any benefits. The Clinical Center of Montenegro and the Public Health Institute are only health institutions that have a board of directors (Article 70 of the Law on Health Care), which leads to conclusion that other health institutions have limited possibilities for development through advantages of collective decision-making and distribution of competences. A way to increase motivation and achieve stronger efficiency of the decentralized units of the system is to introduce stimuli for better efficiency and competitiveness in the hospital sector. To that effect, and based on the comparative experience of regional countries, there is a gradual introduction of the payment system that is based on DRG model (Diagnostic Related Group). It promotes control of consumption in the hospital sector and eliminates inefficient capacities. The objective is to improve the management and exploitation of resources, that is, to allocate costs to cost-effective services and to strengthen equality in financing of different units of the system. This system increases autonomy in terms of possibilities for reorganization of the model of services and input management.

5. *Insufficient cooperation between health institutions from different municipalities.* The centralization of health institutions and the reduction of a role of the director to a mere manager diminishes possibilities of health institutions to cooperate at municipal level. The cooperation and networking is a globally recognized trend that is important for the quality of

services. It leads to a higher efficiency, spurs the innovation, and results in a higher flexibility of the system (Sorrentino and Simonetta, 2011). Within the health field, it is proven that inter-professional teams can improve health outcomes (Katon, Lin, Von Korff, Ciechanowsk, Ludman, Young, Peterson, Rutter, McGregor, and McCulloch, 2011; Rayner, Muldoon, Bayoumi, McMurchy, Mulligan, and Tharao, 2018), and can offer better health protection than individual service providers (Dinh and Bounajm, 2013; Rayner, Muldoon, Bayoumi, McMurchy, Mulligan and Tharao, 2018). Inter-municipal cooperation is important (Bigdeli, Kamal, De Cesare, 2013) but so is the internationalization of the health system, as the strategy "Health 2020" of the World Health Organization suggests. The integrative role of that type could strengthen the increased participation of municipalities in health management, in parallel with other sectoral policies with shared interest for networking.

6. *Insufficient motivation of municipalities.* Municipalities do not want to allocate their scarce financial resources to the health system. There are no health institutions founded by a local municipality in Montenegro. Only a few municipalities finance some costs of primary health care during the tourist seasons (tourist ambulances), whereas some municipalities finance the construction, adaption, or reconstruction of health facilities on their own territory or offer housing for health care workers mostly by giving the land, or by releasing them from communal fees and granting them construction permits. In spite of high expectations of local self-governments about quality and accessibility of health system, their specific contribution to the implementation of activities and measures that could result in improved quality of the health system is somewhat modest, as seen above. Most of local self-governments lack funds for health care in their budgets, or in some cases, they allocate substantially less money for health care than for other areas, so general impression is that health care is not among priorities of local policies. One of the reasons is poor fiscal capacity and short-term strategic orientation of municipal bodies toward their term of office only, as opposed to the need for strategic thinking. The management style of public sector from the standpoint of an entrepreneur is often perceived as "putting out small fires" instead of searching for long-term sustainable solutions for improvement of health services (Sinisammal, Leviäkangas, Autio, and Hyrkäs, 2016). If we take into account that the quality of health care affects both the quality and quantity of foreign investments, and the quality of tourist season too, it seems that, by strategic approach, local self-governments should register stronger activities in providing services of health protection. It seems that with the current state of play the best form of organization of health

care is the public and private partnership in which all parts—the state, municipality, and investors—could recognize their interests and protect themselves through a strategic approach. In terms of a never-ending need to seek for more efficient solutions, Heilman (2008) recommends that central authorities should encourage local officials to try new methods for problem-solving, which he names as "experimentation under hierarchy." Regardless of the need for a proactive approach of local self-governments on the course toward the decentralization, textbooks say that the role of the government is a key to change the system and to spur changes (Millar, Jian, Mannion, and Miller, 2016: 328).

7. *Lack of teamwork and effects of synergy*. The centralization of the system can be seen in the structure of health organizations. There are only two private entities among health institutions. The state founded every other health institution. Municipalities in Montenegro are not among founders of health institutions, although the law provides for such a possibility. Public and private partnerships have not gained momentum yet, in spite of intensive analyses of an inclusion of the private sector, especially in the field of nonhealth care-related activities. Given the poor fiscal capacity of municipalities, the state could work on a gradual, multiphase decentralization of the system in parallel with strengthening of the local self-governments—to begin with, by conferring (by law) or by entrusting (by government regulations) certain affairs from health system to local self-governments. In this case, the government would reserve the right to control such affairs that are exercised by the local self-government (Article 39–40 of the Law on State Administration).

8. *Databases of insufficient quality*. Quality of information system is an underlying assumption of quality of decision-making, and the *conditio sine qua non* of the decentralization. This is due to the reason that the mission of information system is 'to allow for the central control and coordination of mutually separated parts (Walker, 1993: 11). The existing health information system has not gained its full momentum yet, it is not whole nor is connected entirely—in the functional sense it does not provide sufficient information for planning and monitoring of costs, services, or needs of the health system. To that sense, the Ministry of Health has worked continuously on improvements of the information system, and among current priorities of the ministry stands out the information system of the Clinical Center of Montenegro and the development of e-health card. Continuous investments into the information system and adjustments to new Internet-based business models are important not just for the possibility of networking of health institutions and greater

efficiency, but also for the rationalization of performance, improved cost-effectiveness, development of different analyses and assessments of economic and financial performances, and an improved use of available capacities (particularly in terms of lease of equipment).

RECOMMENDATIONS TO IMPROVE THE ORGANIZATIONAL-LEGAL DIMENSION OF HEALTH SYSTEM OF MONTENEGRO

Global competitive environment implies constant adjustments of organizations to changes or, if they want to survive, they have to initiate changes. If we understand the state as an organization, or as a network of public organizations, then constant reforms are necessary that need a systematic approach and full commitment of all social structures on the road to development of an efficient, professional, and service-oriented administration. Montenegrin administration is predominantly centralized. The state, in accordance with its own needs and with the principle of subsidiarity, is strongly committed to development of quality conditions for the system decentralization. Through creation of normative and institutional conditions for a quality functioning of local self-governments, public services, and public private partnerships allow for better organizational structuring of the public health system.

Local self-government in Montenegro functions according to the model of general jurisdiction. Consequently, all municipalities perform the same tasks, regardless of any differences among them. For the purpose of more rational operations, it is vital to have a good communication and intensified cooperation among municipalities from the same region, and thus rationalize the costs if possible.

The quality of services in public administration is of crucial importance for the creation of favorable economic and social environment, which defines the overall stage of development of a society. Organizational structure of the public state administration has to be flexible enough to use, depending on the state of play, the advantages and models of both the centralization and decentralization when necessary, that is, to react in accordance with the theory of contingence (Treiblmaier, 2018).

It is necessary to develop a higher level of motivation of all social structures to improve the health system. To begin with citizens, who could contribute by taking part in public discussions and at elections (Steiner, Kaiser, Tapscott, and Navarro, 2018). To continue with local self-governments that should define specific measures and activities to contribute to the improvement of the quality of health care on their own territories, and in accordance with their strategies and plans, government policy papers and guidelines in the health sector. Better management and monitoring of implementation of health-related policies could be achieved through establishment of special organizational units of local self-governments that would be competent for health care too. That would make for a possibility to entrust or confer powers from the state to local self-governments in the fields of health care. Inclusion of the units of local self-government and of private sector in terms of reconstruction and development of health infrastructure, clinical, and nonhealth-related services would contribute to improved accessibility of health services to the entire population, improve the quality of services, and rationalize the costs.

Reform of the public administration in Montenegro is on the way to create institutional and systemic conditions for a quality system decentralization. The assumption of quality of organization of the public administration system is a legal dimension. To that effect, a key problem in the public administration system of Montenegro is a wide range of divergences in entities that exercise public powers. Therefore, it is vital to establish a precise typology of organizations with public powers and unified rules for their establishment and functioning. It is necessary to adopt a Law on Public and Private Partnership too.

Hence, it is necessary to strengthen the local self-governments in Montenegro, which is in line with recommendations of the European Charter of Local Self-Government, where the strengthening of local self-government in different European countries is treated as "an important contribution to development of Europe that is based on principles of democracy and decentralization of power."

The health system of Montenegro has noted a growth of trust of its citizens, which is a result of intensive activities of the Government of Montenegro and competent ministries that work to improve the system. Yet, just as any other process of reformation, this one requires time and room for further adjustments too. Basic problems that Montenegrin health system faces in terms of the implementation of decentralization strategy are inconsistent legal framework and the lack of a number of systematic laws, poor law enforcement, insufficient transparency and level of democracy in public administration, poor financial capacities of local self-governments, insufficient flexibility of the system, lack of motivation for additional entrepreneurial initiative in most health institutions where the directors are not entitled by law to govern, and the lack of a good database as a support for analyses and decision-making.

The research showed that Montenegrin health system is dominantly centralized and units of local self-governments do not have any major involvement in provision of health services. At the same time, results point to the need of greater involvement of municipalities and private partners in development of health policy papers in order to have health services of higher level.

NOTES

1. Furthermore, Montenegro does not have subsystemic laws in the field of public services. In 2010, Montenegro abolished the Law on Social Affairs and the Law on Public Companies, as a step within the project Guillotine of Regulations in order to simplify the administrative procedures and to improve the business environment. Those two laws regulated the subsystems of public services in social and commercial affairs.

2. For example, Directive (EU) 2018/1972 of the European Parliament and of the Council from December 11, 2018, Available at: https://eur-lex.europa.eu/legal-content/EN/TXT/PDF/?uri=CELEX:32018L1972&from=DE, 30. 11. 2019.

3. More details on types of health services: Article 32–57 Law on Health Protection of Montenegro, 2019. Available at: https://www.paragraf.me/propisi-crnegore/zakon-o-zdravstvenoj-zastiti.html, 30. 11. 2019.

4. More details at: http://www.mojgrad.me/images/infografici/mojgrad-koliko-gradjani-cg-ucestvuju-u-javnim-raspravama-o-budzetu-opstina.png, 30. 11. 2019.

5. Equalization fund has funds that are intended for equalization of financing of municipalities. Money from this fund is available to municipalities whose fiscal capacities per capita is below an average fiscal capacity per capita for all municipalities.

6. For more details on financial indicators of Montenegrin municipalities go to: http://uom.me/baze-podataka/opstinske-finansije, 30. 11. 2019.

7. More details at: https://www.monstat.org/cg/page.php?id=47&pageid=47n, 2. 1. 2019.

Chapter 7

Organizational Determinants of Health System of Montenegro (Strategy, Structure, Culture, and Climate)

Based on a string of empirical data, this chapter will present the organization of health system through the lens of four important organizational determinants: organizational strategy, organizational structure, organizational culture, and organizational climate. The results stem from the research that was carried out in 2019 and included forty-five health institutions (thirty-two public and thirteen private institutions), and in line with the methodology briefly described in the introduction and in the sample in chapter 5.

ORGANIZATIONAL STRATEGY

The analysis of organizational strategy was conducted from the standpoint of organizational focus. In most cases, as explained in chapter two, most organizational strategies are differentiated in accordance with two dimensions—efficiency and effectiveness. For that reason, below is the analysis of strategies of health institutions of Montenegro by region and by type of ownership. In the central region, the focus of strategy on efficiency and effectiveness was rated at 4.41 and 4.37, respectively. In the northern region, efficiency was rated at 4.14, while effectiveness was somewhat lower and stood at 4.05. As for health institutions from the southern part of Montenegro, strategy is more focused on effectiveness (4.25) than on efficiency (4.09), unlike in institutions in the central and northern region of the country.

Specifically, innovation by comparison with competitors (private health institutions are considered competition by public health institutions and vice versa) received the highest rating in the southern region (76.2%), followed by the central (72.2%), and the northern region earned the lowest rating (61.5%). The largest focus on knowledge about the latest health-related work methods was registered in the central region (83.3%), followed by the northern region (82.1%), while the lowest was in the southern region (76.2%). Doctors from the central region are most confident in their good reputation among patients (98.2%), followed by their peers from the south (92.8%), and the northern region (84.6%). Moreover, 88.9 percent of respondents from the central region, 74.4 percent from the north and 71.5 percent from the south of Montenegro are sure that the price-quality ratio of services is appropriate, especially when compared to their competitors.

The analysis from the standpoint of ownership structure showed that private health institutions have strategies of better quality in terms of efficiency and effectiveness. Interestingly, both public and private health facilities have balanced efficiency and effectiveness. Efficiency of strategy in public health institutions received a rating of 4.20 and effectiveness received a score of 4.22. As for private health facilities, the efficiency of the strategy was rated at 4.33, while the effectiveness was rated at 4.32.

A more detailed analysis indicates differences between strategic values in public and private health institutions. Specifically, respondents from private health institutions are more confident in giving higher priority to innovation than their colleagues from public health institutions. As much as 79.5 percent of respondents from private health institutions believe they are more innovative than their competitors, while this percentage in public health institutions is 66.7 percent. There are tangible differences in terms of giving priority to command of the latest health-related work methods. In this respect, 89.8 percent of respondents from private health institutions believe that they have advantage, while the same indicator stands at 71.1 percent for public health institutions. Employees from private (94.8%) and employees from public health institutions (91.7%) consider that they have a good reputation among their patients too. The only aspect that gives advantage to the public sector, strategically speaking, is the price-quality ratio. As many as 80.3 percent of respondents from public health institutions believe that the services of public health institutions are more competitive in terms of price and quality, while 77.0 percent of doctors from private health institutions take a different view.

ORGANIZATIONAL STRUCTURE

The quality of organizational structure in figures (scale from 1 to 5) is 3.71 in Montenegrin health institutions. There are no statistically significant differences in ratings of the organizational structure among institutions from different regions. The organizational structure has approximately the same value in health institutions from the central (3.76) and northern region (3.74), while it is somewhat lower in institutions from the southern region (3.62).

When it comes to ownership of health institutions, our results suggest that the quality of organizational structure is higher (3.84) in public health institutions than in private health institutions (3.78). There are no statistically significant differences in ratings between private and public health institutions either.

From the standpoint of suitability for development of knowledge management, organizational structure was rated with an average score of 4.10 (on a scale from 1 to 5). The importance of authority and hierarchy in the health system received a score of 3.22 and the organizational focus had an average score of 3.80 and tells that work processes are concentrated around teams and not around individual employees.

This study ranked the characteristics of organizational structure of health institutions by region too. The highest degree of suitability of the organizational structure for the development of knowledge management is present in health institutions from the southern region, then the central, and finally from the northern region. On the other hand, the most pronounced hierarchy and importance of authority occur in the northern region, then the central, and finally in the south. Team orientation versus individual one is most present in health facilities in the central region, followed by the northern, while it is least prevalent in health facilities in the southern region. Still, differences in characteristics of the organizational structure are not statistically significant.

As for the differences in characteristics of the organizational structure between private and public health institutions, the conclusion is that all three dimensions were evaluated with a higher average grade in public health institutions than in private ones. However, this is not a statistically significant difference either.

ORGANIZATIONAL CULTURE

The organizational culture plays an important role in creating the appropriate quality of health care (Domnariu, Cernuşcă-Miţariu, and Boitan, 2013; Alsoulami, Banjar, and Mahran, 2018). Therefore, in what follows the author will present the organizational culture of health organizations in Montenegro based on the OCAI instrument.

According to the analysis, the family type of organizational culture is predominantly represented in Montenegro (38.66%). This type of culture is based on great commitment, a high degree of mutual trust and respect and focuses on cooperation, internal processes, system integration, and sufficient flexibility. Organizational climate is an important prerequisite for success according to this cultural pattern. Therefore, it is dominantly found in the health sector (Bremer, 2008). This is followed by the hierarchical type with 25.67 percent. Hierarchical culture implies a high level of bureaucracy and multiple rules and regulations. The goal is to ensure the smooth operation of the organization, standardize policies and procedures, define precise lines of authority, responsibilities, and control mechanisms. In this sense, the hierarchical type of culture is a common feature of health organizations too. Adhocracy culture is represented by 20.84 percent in Montenegrin health institutions. This culture is characterized by flexibility, open system, constant change, creativity, and innovation. Finally, the market culture is the least represented one, with 14.84 percent. This model is externally oriented and focuses on results and competitiveness.

There are no significant differences between the regions in terms of the above summary indicators. However, family and hierarchical cultures are most evident in the northern region, adhocracy in the southern, and market culture in the central region. On the other hand, comparatively speaking, family culture is least present in institutions of the central region, adhocracy and market cultures in the northern, and hierarchical culture in institutions of the southern part of Montenegro.

Therefore, two predominant types of organizational culture (family and hierarchical) are mostly internally oriented. If the ratio between internal and external focus was calculated, it would be approximately 2:1. In that sense, it can be stated that, in order to strive for balance and an ideal situation in terms of the organizational culture, there is room to strengthen the external (market) orientation of health institutions in Montenegro.

The family type of culture is dominant in health institutions in Montenegro, both in public (37.28%) and private health institutions (42.03%). In terms of representation in public health institutions, hierarchical culture is in second place (27.55%), adhocracy culture is in third place (20.36%), and market culture is in last place (14.81%). As for private health institutions, the strongest is adhocracy culture (22.01%), hierarchical ranks second (21.05%), while the market culture is the least strong (14.91%).

In private health institutions, the family type of culture is more noticeable, unlike in public health institutions that prefer the hierarchical organizational culture. There are no significant differences between private and public health institutions when it comes to adhocracy and market type of culture.

A more detailed analysis shows that employees in private health institutions (41.8%) recognize the organization as a personal place, like a larger family where colleagues share information with each other. The same indicator is 30.4 percent in public health institutions, which indicates a lack of freedom and trust in public health institutions compared to private ones.

ORGANIZATIONAL CLIMATE

Organizational climate is, as shown in the second chapter of the book, one of more important factors of organizational design. The following section focuses on the assessment of organizational climate aggregately, and on the analysis of organizational climate from the standpoint of its basic determinants—the level of tension within the organization and the readiness of its members for change.

When it comes to rating of organizational climate by region, the best organizational climate is in health institutions in the central region (3.97), then in the north (3.83), while the southern region notes the worst organizational climate in health institutions (3.79).

The research wanted to observe the matter of organizational climate through the standpoint of its basic dimensions, as shown in figure 7.1. Readiness for change is highest in institutions from the central part of Montenegro (3.19), followed by institutions from the southern region 2.74, while in institutions from the northern region it amounts to 2.72. The level of tensions is lowest in health institutions in the central region (1.90). A slightly higher degree of tension was recorded in institutions from the northern region (1.99), and the highest level of tension, according to this research, is present in health institutions from the southern region.

According to the respondents, fair remuneration of employees is most prevalent in the central region (75.9%), followed by the northern region (56.4%), and the lowest in the southern region (47.7%). Furthermore, the respondents feel

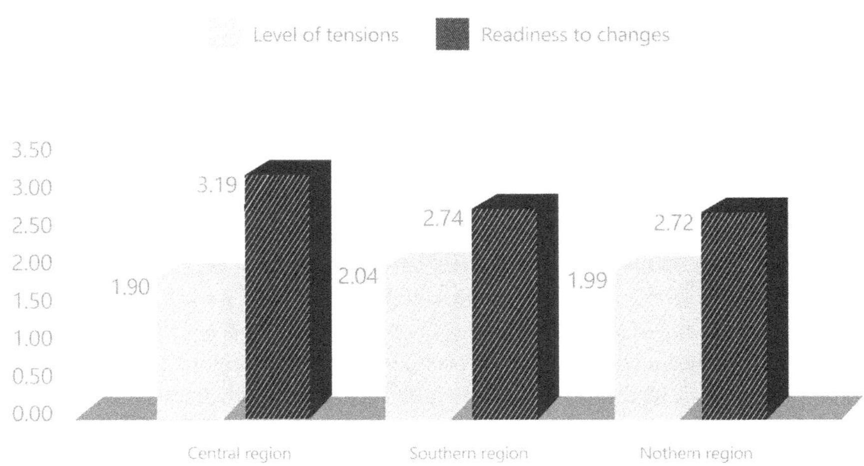

Figure 7.1 Analysis of Determinants of Organizational Climate in Health Institutions in Montenegro by Regions. *Source:* Data collected by author.

that the central region shows greatest organizational flexibility, when observed from the standpoint of possibility of introducing changes in the organization, while it is significantly poorer in the northern and southern region. A many as 38.9 percent of respondents from the central region believe that it is not difficult to implement changes in the organization, and that percentage in the northern and southern regions stands at 25.6 percent and 28.6 percent, respectively. Moreover, the responsibility of employees is mostly expected in institutions from the southern region (88.1%), followed by the northern (82.0%), while it is lowest in the central region (64.8%), according to the respondents.

The analysis by type of ownership shows that the organizational climate in private health institutions (4.10) is better than in public health institutions (3.78). The analysis of basic factors of the organizational climate indicates a lower level of tensions and a greater readiness for changes in private health institutions. The level of tension earned the score of 2.04 in public health institutions, while in private ones the same indicator stood at 1.80. Additionally, ratings for readiness for change in private and public facilities stand at 3.51 and 2.67, respectively.

Trust among employees is greater in private (82.1%) than in public health institutions (77.1%). According to respondents, the commitment to work (in terms of ethics, morality, and energy of employees) is higher in private health institutions. While as many as 85.4 percent of respondents recognize commitment in public health institutions and that percentage is even higher in private health institutions and stands at 92.3 percent. Also, there are big differences in the perception of fairness of the compensation system. While 51.1 percent of employees in public health institutions believe that employees are fairly rewarded for their efforts, this percentage is 87.2 percent in private health institutions. When it comes to organizational flexibility and the likelihood of implementing changes, private health institutions are in advantage over public ones. While 62.5 percent of employees in public health institutions find it difficult to implement changes, only 18.9 percent of their colleagues from private health institutions share that view.

According to the analysis, the management and respondents from health institutions that were delegated upon suggestion of the Ministry of Health largely (78.5%) believe that employees can trust each other. In addition, 69.6 percent of them emphasize that disagreements in decision-making are very rare or nonexistent. In addition, 87.4 percent point out that the level of commitment to work ethics and morality, energy, is at a high level. As many as 61.4 percent of respondents from the same sample highlight that the compensation system is fair, while 49.6 percent state that making changes within the organization is often difficult. As many as 83.7 percent of respondents believe that employees have confidence in their leaders. However, these indicators will be particularly interesting after we compare two independent samples, in chapter 9.

Chapter 8

Quality of Services of Health Organizations in Montenegro

The fact is that stakeholders continuously (re)evaluate all the entities they come in contact with. Therefore, it is very important for the organization to manage these perceptions as much as possible, in order to make its business performance stable and sustainable in the long run (Zavyalova, Pfarrer, Reger, and Shapiro, 2012; Bednar, Boivie, and Prince, 2013; Harrison, Thurgood, Boivie, and Pfarrer, 2018).

In the spirit of the marketing approach, it is advisable to create an organization strategy that will direct resources toward sustainable competitive advantage and customer/consumer satisfaction. In this sense, market signals are very important for the purpose of creating a strategy that will match supply with demand. Thus, service users are increasingly being used as active participants in creation of strategies, or as Prahalad and Ramaswamy (2004) put it, "consumers are increasingly transforming from a passive audience to active players" (Hsu, 2017: 3). For these reasons, the perception of health care users can be extremely important for creation of an adequate national strategy.

This chapter presents the analysis of quality of services of health organizations in Montenegro. It was carried out from the standpoint of citizens, as users of services of health system. In addition to specific evaluations of the quality of health services, this chapter presents determinants of the environment that are important for an adequate configuration of the health system's organization.

SAMPLE STRUCTURE

This section provides a more detailed insight into the structure of the sample of 1.769 persons from Montenegro, who were included in the survey in order to evaluate their perceptions about the quality of health services of Montenegrin health institutions, as well as the health system in general. Sex structure of persons included in the research is uniform. Of the total number of respondents (1.769), the majority of the sample is female (51%), while 49 percent of respondents are male.

The sample consisted of persons aged eighteen and over. When it comes to age structure, people aged sixty and over were in majority percentagewise or 23.90 percent, while the representation of people aged eighteen to twenty-nine was 22.41 percent. The population aged thirty to fifty-nine was evenly represented: persons aged thirty to thirty-nine—18.20 percent; persons aged forty to forty-nine—17.61 percent; and persons aged fifty to fifty-nine—17.88 percent, of the total number of respondents.

From the aspect of the level of education, almost two-thirds of respondents have secondary education (62.95%). They are, according to the representation in the sample, followed by persons with primary education (12.95%), and those with higher education (12.57%). Persons with higher education make 9.97 percent, while there are only few of respondents without any formal education that make 1.56 percent.

When it comes to the territorial affiliation of the respondents, the largest part of the sample consists of persons from the central region of Montenegro (Podgorica, Danilovgrad, Nikšić and Cetinje)—45 percent. The share of respondents from the northern region (Berane, Bijelo Polje, Gusinje, Kolašin, Mojkovac, Petnjica, Plav, Pljevlja, Plužine, Rožaje, and Žabljak) is 31 percent, while the lowest percentage of respondents in the total sample is from the southern region (Bar, Budva, Herceg Novi, Kotor, Tivat, and Ulcinj)—24 percent.

When observed locally, that is, from the standpoint of municipalities, majority of respondents come from the capital city (Podgorica): 28.46 percent. It is followed by the municipalities of Nikšić (10.80%), Bijelo Polje (8.21%), Bar (6.75%), Berane (5.54%), Herceg Novi and Ulcinj (4.68% each) and Rožaje (4.02%). Respondents from Pljevlja made 3.95 percent, Danilovgrad 3.88 percent, Kotor 3.49 percent and Budva 3.22 percent. The sample also included 2.02 percent of respondents from Cetinje, 1.76 percent from Plav, 1.72 percent from Mojkovac, 1.59 percent from Plužine, while there were 1.25 percent and 1.15 percent from Petnjica and Tivat, respectively. There were fewest respondents from municipalities of Žabljak and Kolašin, that is, 0.89 percent and 0.86 percent, respectively. For the sake of rationality, it is worth mentioning that three smaller municipalities were not covered by the sample: Andrijevica, Šavnik, and Tuzi. However, that did not affect the representativeness of the sample.

COMPARATIVE ANALYSIS OF THE QUALITY OF HEALTH SERVICES BY REGIONS

An important aspect of the quality of health care is the waiting time for an examination. Therefore, this chapter will present an overview of the waiting time for an examination in different regions. As many as 81.8 percent citizens of Montenegro wait less than a week to be examined by their chosen doctor, while 13.0 percent of the population state that their waiting time is from one week to one month. The analysis of the quality of health services by regions, from the aspect of efficiency, that is, waiting time for an examination by a chosen doctor, showed that majority of examinations are done in less than a week in health institutions in the northern (91.4%) and southern regions (89.8%). A slightly smaller number of examinations are performed within the same timeframe in health institutions located in the central part of Montenegro: 71.0 percent.

When it comes to specialist examinations, the research showed a lower efficiency of the system. Specifically, 51.6 percent of the population stated that their waiting time for a specialist examination was less than a week, 27.9 percent from one week to a month, while 9.4 percent of persons stated that they had to wait between 30 and 90 days for such an examination. By region, majority of examinations are performed in less than a week in the north (53.3%), followed by the central region (51.1%), while in the southern region that percentage stands at 50.2 percent. The highest percentage of respondents who stated that their waiting time was from one to three months for an examination is in the northern region (23.6%), followed by the central region (9.4%), and the southern region (5.5%).

Table 8.1 shows results of the analysis of perception of determinants of the quality of health services: commitment of doctors, knowledge of doctors, waiting time for an examination, modern technology, kindness of nurses, price of service, and quality of service. When it comes to public health institutions, citizens of the northern region showed the greatest satisfaction with the quality of health services, while citizens in the southern part cited a lower level of satisfaction, and the lowest quality ratings are given in the central part of Montenegro. This distribution of scores was established for almost all observed determinants of the quality of services of public health institutions (highest scores in the northern region, followed by the southern, and lowest scores in the central region), with the exception of modern technology and knowledge of doctors that scored approximately the same in southern and northern region.

In the case of public health facilities, the lowest average score (on a scale of 1 to 5—the lowest score means the longest wait) regarding the waiting time for an examination was recorded in the central region (3.21). On the

Table 8.1 Comparative Analysis of the Perception of Determinants of the Quality of Health Services by Region

		Central Region		*Southern Region*		*Northern Region*	
Institution type	*Determinants of quality of health services/region*	*Average rating (AR)*	*Standard deviation (SD)*	*AR*	*SD*	*AR*	*SD*
Public health institutions	Dedication of doctors	3.74	1.180	4.01	1,149	4.20	1,054
	Doctors' knowledge	3.92	1.040	4.27	0.965	4.28	1.041
	Waiting time for an examination	3.21	1.297	3.57	1.388	3.85	1.245
	Modern technology equipment (machines, devices)	3.36	1.135	3.55	1.212	3.55	1.228
	Kindness of nurses	3.72	1.234	3.86	1.207	4.13	1.154
	Price of service	3.85	1.154	4.29	1.132	4.48	.955
	Quality of services	3.74	1.072	3.97	1.122	4.23	1.051
Private health institutions	Dedication of doctors	4.29	0.893	4.45	0.844	4.73	0.617
	Doctors' knowledge	4.27	0.885	4.41	0.849	4.66	0.706
	Waiting time for an examination	4.38	0.897	4.43	0.921	4.69	0.676
	Modern technology equipment (machines, devices)	4.33	0.902	4.50	0.851	4.72	0.634
	Kindness of nurses	4.34	0.883	4.41	0.868	4.68	0.693
	Price of service	3.76	1.200	3.23	1.446	3.60	1.365
	Quality of services	4.30	0.884	4.43	0.874	4.69	0.659

Source: Author's empirical research.

other hand, the waiting time for an examination was rated at 3.57 in the southern region, and the highest score is in the northern region, that is, 3.85. The largest dispersion of scores is evident in relation to the waiting time for an examination (standard deviation is 1.39 in the southern region), and the biggest difference in average scores by regions (0.64). When it comes to quality of determinants, the highest average score in public health institutions was recorded in the price of services. Satisfaction with the price of services of public health institutions in the northern region earned an average score of 4.48. A slightly lower score was recorded in the southern region, 4.29, while the lowest one was in the central part of Montenegro, that is, 3.85.

When asked to give an open statement about the quality of services of public health institutions, the population stated that the highest quality of services was in the north of Montenegro (4.23), followed by the southern region (3.97), and the lowest score was assigned to the central part (3.74).

When it comes to private health institutions, by region, the distribution of scores is such that except for the price of services, all other determinants record the highest scores in the northern region, medium scores in the southern, and lowest scores in the central region (table 8.1). The price of services of private health institutions was rated with the highest score in the central part of Montenegro (3.76), followed by the northern part (3.60), and the lowest score was assigned to the southern region (3.23). When it comes to the observed determinants in the quality of private health institutions, the highest rating was given to the dedication of doctors (4.73) in the northern region. The lowest score referred to the abovementioned price of services (southern region), and this variable recorded the largest dispersion in scores (standard deviation was 1.45), as well as the largest difference in average scores by region (0.54).

When asked openly to rate the quality of services of private health institutions from 1 to 5, measured by the average score, the respondents rated as following: northern region (4.69), southern region (4.43), and central region (4.30).

A comparative overview of public and private institutions by region, based on the average score as a derived size that is based on seven determinants of the quality of health services, is such that private health institutions are listed above public health institutions in all regions, from the standpoint of respondents' perception of quality of health services.

An additional set of questions about the quality of health institutions was dimensioned through the rating of four features of health care quality (adequacy of process of treatment, care of medical staff, care of doctors, and material things). A scale of 1 to 7 was used in this set of questions. The results are largely consistent with those regarding the determinants of quality.

Table 8.2 Evaluation of Characteristics of the Quality of Health Services in Montenegro by Region

Characteristic of Health Service Quality	*Type of Health Care Institution*	*Region*			
		Central region	*Southern region*	*Northern region*	*Total*
Adequacy of the process of treatment	Public health institutions	4.88	5.41	5.53	5.21
	Private health institutions	5.68	5.91	6.19	5.89
Care of medical staff	Public health institutions	5.05	5.23	5.52	5.24
	Private health institutions	5.97	6.06	6.37	6.11
Care of doctors	Public health institutions	5.29	5.59	5.69	5.48
	Private health institutions	5.95	6.10	6.44	6.13
Material things	Public health institutions	4.11	4.81	4.60	4.43
	Private health institutions	5.59	6.01	6.32	5.91
Total		5.31	5.63	5.81	5.59

Source: Author's empirical research.

As table 8.2 shows users of health services from the northern region are happiest with the quality (5.81), followed by users in the southern region (5.63), while the central region received the lowest rating (5.31).

On the other hand, the lowest score was given to material items in public health institutions in the central region (4.11), and the highest went to the care of medical doctors in private health institutions in the northern region (6.44).

To summarize, perception of quality is highest in the northern region and lowest in the central part, in almost all characteristics. Material resources are the only exception to this, as they are rated better in the southern than in the northern region.

COMPARATIVE ANALYSIS OF THE QUALITY OF SERVICES OF STATE AND PRIVATE HEALTH INSTITUTIONS

The evaluation of the share of private and public health institutions that is based on the respondents' answers to the question in which institution they were last treated by their chosen doctor shows the dominant position of the public health system in Montenegro. Specifically, at the level of primary health care, when it comes to the chosen doctor, public health institutions have a dominant market share, that is, 92.9 percent, while the share of private health institutions stands at 7.1 percent.

When it comes to the analysis of quality of health services from the standpoint of waiting time for an examination by a chosen doctor, the results show that majority of examinations are done in less than a week—in public health institutions (82.5%), while in private health institutions, there are 72.6 percent of those who wait for an examination by the chosen doctor less than seven days. As many as 12.7 percent respondents wait for an examination in public health institutions from one week to one month, while this percentage stands at 17.6 percent for private institutions. In this sense (speed), the public health system is more efficient than the private health system.

The market share of private and public health institutions in terms of treatment by specialist doctors was assessed on the basis of respondents' answers about the institution where they last had that type of treatment. It is evident that public health institutions are dominant in this domain too, with a share of 71.6 percent, while private health institutions cover 28.4 percent of the market of Montenegro.

On average, however, the waiting time for a specialist examination is shorter in private health institutions. More than two-thirds of respondents (69.7%) stated that their waiting time for a specialist examination in private health institutions is under a week, while the percentage of persons who are examined in public health institutions within that period is 44.4 percent. As many as 32.7 percent of respondents wait for a specialist examination in public health institutions from one week to one month, while 16.1 percent of them wait for a specialist examination between one and three months. On the other hand, 19.6 percent of respondents have a specialist examination within one week to one month in private health institutions, while 5.9 percent have it within one to three months. This analysis indicates that the waiting time for a specialist examination is significantly shorter in private health institutions.

What follows is an evaluation of determinants of the quality of services of public and private health institutions. The population agrees that dedication and knowledge of doctors, equipment, scheduling and waiting time for examinations, kindness of nurses and quality of service are at a higher level than in public health institutions, except for the price of the service. In this regard, according to comparison of average grades, respondents agree that the price of services is more affordable in public health institutions.

Table 8.3 shows in more details ratings of determinants of quality in public and private health institutions. Evidently, waiting time for an examination and equipment in private health institutions received the highest score of 4.49, while the dedication of doctors and the kindness of nurses in private health institutions were evaluated with approximately same high score (4.47).

Table 8.3 Analysis of Differences in the Perception of Determinants of Quality of Services in Public and Private Health Institutions in Montenegro

Determinants of quality of health services	*Type of Ownership*	*Average Rating*	*Standard Error*	*Standard Deviation*
Dedication of doctors	Public health institutions	3.95	0.002	1.151
	Private health institutions	4.47	0.001	0.827
Doctors' knowledge	Public health institutions	4.12	0.002	1.035
	Private health institutions	4.43	0.001	.840
Waiting time for an examination	Public health institutions	3.51	0.002	1.334
	Private health institutions	4.49	0.001	0.854
Modern technology equipment (machines, devices)	Public health institutions	3.47	0.002	1.188
	Private health institutions	4.49	0.001	0.832
Kindness of nurses	Public health institutions	3.88	.002	1.216
	Private health institutions	4.47	0.001	0.839
Price of service	Public health institutions	4.17	0.002	1.123
	Private health institutions	3.57	0.002	1.339
Quality of services	Public health institutions	3.95	0.002	1.099
	Private health institutions	4.46	0.001	0.836

Source: Author's empirical research.

On the other hand, the lowest scores were given to equipment and waiting time for examination in public health institutions (3.47 and 3.51, respectively), while the approximate score (3.57) was given to the price of services in private health institutions. The largest dispersion of scores is in the price of services in private health institutions (standard deviation is 1.34) and waiting time for examination in public health institutions (the value of the standard deviation is 1.33). The largest difference in the average scores of determinants of the quality of private and public health institutions was identified in the equipment in the northern region (4.72 private institutions, 3.55 public) and waiting time for examination in the central region (3.21 is the average score in public health institutions and 4.38 in private ones). An open question about the quality of services in public and private health institutions (scale from 1 to 5) resulted in an average score of 3.95 for the quality of services in public health institutions and 4.46 for the quality of services in private health institutions.

In addition to the above determinants, a special questionnaire with four sets of questions was designed to analyze the following variables (features of the quality of services of health organizations): adequacy of the process of treatment, care of medical staff, care of doctors, and material things. In this case, the rating scale was from 1 to 7.

Results of this part of the research are complementary with the set of questions about determinants of the quality of health services that were elaborated above. Specifically, the quality of services of private health institutions was rated higher than that of public health institutions in this domain too (table 8.2). The adequacy of the process of treatment scored 5.21 in public health institutions, while this variable received an average score of 5.89 in private health institutions. The care of medical staff and doctors in public health institutions was rated at 5.24 and 5.48 (respectively), while these indicators in private health institutions were rated at 6.11 and 6.13, respectively. The biggest difference was in material things (equipment, technology, premises, etc.). In public health institutions, this indicator was rated at 4.43, while in private institutions it was significantly higher and amounted to 5.91.

AMBIENT DETERMINANTS OF THE HEALTH SYSTEM OF MONTENEGRO

Ambient determinants of the health system are crucial to formulating a strategy for development of health system. Health care is an area with constantly growing, extremely high expectations of system users, which is confirmed by this research. In it, respondents rated from 1 to 7 the importance of individual characteristics in health services: (1) reliability, (2) professionalism/skills, (3) empathy, (4) security and trust, (5) key medical services, (6) responsibility, and (7) tangible things.

Average scores for all seven characteristics are extremely high. Security and trust were rated as most important (6.19), followed by professionalism and skills (6.16). An average score of 6.09 was assigned to reliability and accountability, while empathy received a score of 6.02. Key medical services and material items were rated lower than others, but still received high average scores of 5.99 and 5.72, respectively.

Interestingly, statistically significant differences in scores for all seven categories were found for all three regions. According to this research, the most demanding are patients from the northern region (6.53), followed by the southern region (6.09), while the lowest overall average score was noted in the central region (5.67).

Growing expectations of clients include staff that is motivated and ready to respond to growing expectations with their dedication, attention, and professional attitude. Even though financial motivation is not the only type of motivation, it is still very important. Given the overall dissatisfaction of Montenegrin doctors with their earning, and the readiness of the Government of Montenegro to find a model to increase health workers' salaries in the future, this research conducted an analysis of public perceptions of doctors' salaries in Montenegro.

Specifically, as many as 62.9 percent of Montenegrin citizens think that doctors' salaries are lower than what they deserve, 31.1 percent think that the salaries are appropriate, and 6.0 percent feel that salaries are higher than what doctors deserve. The highest percentage of those who think that salaries of doctors in Montenegro are lower than they deserve is in the southern part of the country (74.1%), while that percentage in the northern and central part of Montenegro is 62.5 percent and 57.2 percent, respectively. Respondents from the central region agreed with view that salaries are adequate (35.8%), followed by the northern 31.1 percent, and the southern region 21.9 percent.

The Matter of Corruption

In this research, citizens commented on the level of corruption in Montenegrin health system too. Only 5 percent believe that there is no corruption in the health system at all, while a high percentage of respondents were confident it existed. Of the total number of respondents, 14.9 percent believe that corruption is widely present, while 26.9 percent believe that it is certainly present. Apart from 5 percent of those who believe that there is no corruption at all, there are 16.7 percent of those who claim that it is present to a small extent. Among those who were not confident that corruption existed in the system, there are 19.5 percent respondents who claim that "there is maybe some," while 17.1 percent answered with "I don't know."

By region, corruption is least present in the northern region, while the problem is more pronounced in the central and southern part of the country. Specifically, 17.2 percent of respondents from the central region, 15.1 percent from the southern region, and 11.3 percent from the northern region claim that corruption is largely present. As many as 8.1 percent of respondents from the north of Montenegro, 4.0 percent from the central region, and 2.9 percent of respondents from the southern region claim that there is no corruption at all. Similar answers were given to the question about the view that corruption is present to a small extent, which is considered by 21.9 percent of respondents from the northern region, 16.2 percent from the central, and 10.7 percent from the southern region. The highest number of "I don't know" answers was in the northern region (24.6%), followed by the southern region (18.7%), and the central region (11.2%).

Analysis of the presence of corruption in the health system of Montenegro showed that there have been no major positive changes in that area since 2012, when the Center for Monitoring and Research researched that topic, under the support of the German Embassy in Podgorica.

Interestingly, only 5.0 percent of respondents point out that "there is no corruption at all" in 2019, while that number was 11.5 percent in 2012. On the other hand, the "high presence of corruption" in 2019 is highlighted by 14.9 percent of respondents, while the percentage was 17.1 percent in 2012. However, the difference between the two observed periods is seven years, so one may conclude that management of health institutions should address this matter in a better way. If we take into account that the number of those who agreed the corruption existed was 26.9 percent in 2019 (together with those respondents who claim the corruption is present at large extent, the percentage is 41.8%), as opposed to 26.0 percent in 2012 (together with those respondents who claim the corruption is present at large extent, the percentage is 43.1%). A comparative analysis of results from 2012 and 2019 showed that no major progress was made in that area.

There are a few facts that support the statement on presence of corruption. As many as 11.5 percent of respondents confirmed they had paid extra to a health worker in a health institution over the past year, to perform some procedure that is otherwise covered by health insurance. While 5.3 percent of respondents claim to have given money unofficially to a health worker on several occasion over the past year, 6.2 percent point out that they have done so once in the previous year. On the other hand, 81.7 percent of respondents claim that they did not pay extra for health services, while 6.8 percent say that they are "not sure" or "do not remember." Among those who unofficially paid extra money to medical doctors, 70.4 percent say that the payment was monetary, while 13.4 percent say it was in the form of coffee, chocolates, or drinks. As many as 4.3 percent gave an expensive gift (a watch, jewelry, and home appliance), and 0.9 percent did some favor in return. The rest of respondents (11.0%) did not want to specify how they made the payment. According to respondents, unofficial additional payments to health workers, as a kind of corruptive activity, are prevalent in the southern region (17.1%), followed by the central region (10.8%) while that percentage stands at 8.1 percent for the northern region.

When it comes to perception of citizens about the most important roots of corruption, the reasons ranked as follows: (1) poor financial motivation of doctors, that is, low salaries, (2) moral crisis, underpinned by poor economic situation and mentality of the people, (3) legal problems predominantly addressed to bad legislation, that is, poor law enforcement.

Citizens feel that low salaries of medical staff are the main cause of corruption, according to 51.1 percent of respondents. Moreover, almost one-third of respondents cite the moral crisis (31.0%) and Montenegrin mentality in terms of special features of national culture (29.9%). Furthermore, 23.7 percent of the population believes that bad legislation is the culprit, while 19.3 percent finds nonsanctioning of corruption as the problem, followed by the lack of strict internal control in health institutions (19.1%) and disrespect of professional and moral duties (19.0%). Also, as many as 16.1 percent of respondents mention inefficiency of the health system as a fertile ground for corruption.

In addition to the research on causes of corruption on providers side, this analysis included the causes of corrupt practices on the side of health service users, that is, their reasons for additional—unofficial payments for health services in Montenegro.

Desire to get the best possible service or to avoid a bad service and long waiting time are most often reasons why people opt for additional payments to doctors, the analysis showed. In particular, most citizens opt for corruption to get better health care, more kindness and attention from doctors (44.2%). As many as 41 percent of respondents feel that waiting time is a cause of corruption, while 30.4 percent point out that they are afraid of poor treatment. In addition, 22.9 percent of respondents cite corruption as a reason to reach a certain doctor/nurse, and 9.9 percent to get some kind of comfort (special room, visits by family and friends) that they would not receive otherwise. Not a small percentage of population speaks about corruption as of a step toward receiving medical findings that would qualify them for the disability pension commission (7.2%) or sick leave (7%). The findings on the perception of corruption in the health system of Montenegro underpin the conclusion that this problem should be worked on continuously and systemically.

When it comes to preferences of the population of Montenegro regarding the choice of public or private health institution, 67.1 percent would rather opt for treatment in a private than in a state health institution. Regardless of different demographic criteria (sex, education, monthly income, and region), majority of population of Montenegro would choose a private health institution, if asked to do so.

Autonomy of Health System

This research analyzed the perception of the autonomy of health system in terms of the absence of political factors in decision-making. Statement that Montenegrin health system is not susceptible to influence of political factors was supported by 19.6 percent of the population, while 38.3 percent do not know the answer, or—they are not sure. As many as 42.1 percent of respondents opposed this statement.

Since health care is vital for any society (public good), and the fact that public health system covers 92.9 percent of the Montenegrin market when it comes to treatments by chosen doctor and 71.6 percent market share when it comes to treatments by specialists, the presence of political factors is inevitable. However, knowledge management implies monitoring and managing of perception of users (explained in more detail in third chapter). In this sense, it is necessary to work on changing the perception of the population, in terms of recognizing knowledge as a fundamental factor of every system and every institution, and in terms of recognizing politics as a way to achieve that goal through an adequate configuration of the organizational design of macrosystem.

Analysis of Preventive Activities in the Function of Protection of Health

Any health strategy must include preventive activities, which is in line with the famous saying attributed to Hippocrates: "The most important branch of medicine is the one that teaches people how to live without needing medicines." In that sense, it is necessary to pay special attention to matters, such as diet, use of nicotine and alcohol, sports and recreational activities, and lifestyle in general. Therefore, the following lines will present some basic research results that partly determine the lifestyle of the population of Montenegro.

On average, according to the research, citizens of Montenegro spend five hours and fifty-seven minutes sitting. Furthermore, they consume an average of 1.8 meals prepared in fast food stores, with the number being positively correlated with the income (the higher the income of respondents, the higher the number of meals consumed that are prepared in fast food stores). As many as 78.9 percent of men and 42.8 percent of women consume alcohol. Furthermore, 37.1 percent of men and 29.8 percent of women smoke. As many as 96.0 percent of respondents have a chosen doctor, unlike 3.3 percent who do not (0.7% do not know). Women in Montenegro visit doctors more often, and men are more involved in sports and recreational activities. Majority of intense sport, fitness, and recreational activities are practiced in the central region, followed by the southern and the northern region. Moderate-intensity activities, such as walking and static exercise, are prevalent in the northern region, followed by the central, and the southern. Almost one-fifth of men (18.5%) are not at all aware of their rights as patients, and 14.9 percent of women say that too.

Detailed analysis of these and other indicators should be included in systemic activities in the field of health (and related) activities in Montenegro. The basis for action lies in analysis, knowledge and teamwork for the purpose of continuous improvement of conditions related to being healthy.

THE COMPLEXITY OF BEING HEALTHY IN MODERN TIME

Complexity of the matter of being healthy and managing the health system often leads to the dilemma concerning the qualifications required from a top person in a health organization (Scholten and Van Der Grinten, 1998). In this sense, the author made a survey of citizens' perceptions about that problem. Results of that study show that 85.8 percent of respondents believe that a doctor should be in the position of the head of a health institution, and 11.7 percent believe that an expert in management should take that position, and 2.5 percent believe that it should be "someone else." It is interesting that mostly citizens from the central region (16.9%) favor the option of an expert in the field of management, unlike their fellow countrymen from the northern (8.6%) and southern (5.9%) region. Also, respondents with high and higher education opted for an expert in the field of management in 15.6 percent of cases, while respondents with secondary education did so in 12.1 percent of cases, and respondents with primary education in 4.6 percent. Respondents with no formal education in zero cases opted for an expert in the field of management, but rather for a medical doctor (92.8%).

In any case, the head of a health institution should be familiar with many things, mostly from the field of medicine and management. In that sense, if a candidate lacks knowledge in both areas, then the team leadership is the only option, where team members are complementary and create a balance of their weaknesses and strengths.

Over the past two years, the level of quality of health services has polarized the population of Montenegro. The majority believe that the quality of services in Montenegro is unchanged (40.7%), while 27.3 percent believe that it has improved, compared to 16.6 percent of those who feel that it deteriorated. Citizens of the northern region are satisfied with health services (29.4% notice a trend of improvement), and the citizens of the southern region are least satisfied (21.1%).

Respondents were asked to name the country they considered to have the most developed health system, and according to their answers, their preference is with the health system of Serbia (44.3%), followed by Croatia (14.9%), Slovenia (9.7%), while slightly fewer respondents chose Albania (1.8%), Bosnia and Herzegovina (1.5%) and Macedonia (1.4%). Although not in the immediate vicinity, Turkey's health system was cited as the most reliable one by 3.5 percent respondents. It is interesting that respondents from the northern region prefer the health system of Serbia that is 63.1 percent, unlike the central and southern region, where only 34.5 percent and 38.5 percent of respondents (respectively) chose the health system of that country.

When it comes to the analysis of the matter of being healthy in modern times, more than two-thirds of respondents (68.4%) believe that it is more difficult to be healthy now than two decades ago, while 20.2 percent claim the opposite. In addition, 11.4 percent of respondents believe that it is just as easy (difficult) to be healthy today as it was two decades ago. Respondents from the northern region are most confident that health is harder to keep today than two decades ago (75.5%), while respondents from the central region claim the opposite (24.9%).

This research attempted to identify factors that affect the complexity of being healthy in modern times. According to this research, the most important factors are poor nutrition (14.1%), followed by pollution (11.8%) and stress (10.3%). Poor quality of life was rated as an important factor by 6.2 percent of population, and a hasty life with too much work by 6.1 percent. Poverty is seen as a problem by 2.7 percent of the population, while 2.2 percent perceive the emergence of many new and unknown diseases as a problem. Some of the positive factors that respondents single out are the progress of medicine and technology (8.2% of respondents), better living conditions (3.6%), and greater availability of medicines (1.7%).

Chapter 9

The Influence of Knowledge Management and Organizational Design on the Quality of Health Services

This chapter will present a cross-analysis of the basic constructs of research—knowledge management and organizational design, in the function of the quality of health services. Since previous chapters discussed important factors of knowledge management and organizational determinants, this chapter will present combined results. A special part of this chapter will be dedicated to the comparison of views of members of administration of health institutions and medical doctors—respondents delegated by the administration, with the views of medical doctors who are members of the Union (independent sample).

KNOWLEDGE MANAGEMENT AND ORGANIZATIONAL DESIGN IN THE FUNCTION OF QUALITY OF HEALTH SERVICES

Organization of the health system and the level of application of knowledge management significantly determine the quality of health services. The level of application of knowledge management will depend on whether the organizational strategy supports the concept of knowledge management or not, and the quality of health services will ultimately depend on the level of knowledge management. Similarly, organizational structure, organizational culture, and organizational climate are vital to the quality of knowledge flow within an organization, but they also affect circumstances in which knowledge is created, stored, and applied. Consequently, all of that affects the quality of health system and its sustainability.

In particular, the level of application of knowledge management affects the quality of health services—through improved cooperation, a higher level of flexibility and willingness to learn, improved communication, and organizational performance of the health institution. Basic variables of the organizational design, such as formalization, centralization, and complexity, show a lower level of interrelationship with knowledge management, which is consistent with the contingency theory. While every organization prefers knowledge management, regardless of its size and contextual factors, the preferred dimensions of organizational design depend on many contextual factors. This means that there are no predefined solutions for every situation in terms of dimensions of the ideal organization. On the contrary, one must take into account the internal and external harmonization of elements of organizational design, as will be discussed later in this chapter. Nevertheless, formalization, when understood as adherence to rules, procedures, and standardization of behavior, contributes to the application of knowledge management. In addition, complexity does not have a significant effect on the level of knowledge management, while centralization has a negative impact on the quality of knowledge management application. This is in line with theoretical principles that a higher level of knowledge within the organization allows for greater decentralization.

Given all of that, one may conclude that greater representation and application of knowledge management in the organization affects the increase in the quality of services of health organizations and significantly determines it.

ANALYSIS OF THE QUALITY OF INTERNAL HARMONIZATION OF ELEMENTS OF HEALTH SYSTEM'S ORGANIZATIONAL DESIGN

Homogeneity within health care organizations is a prerequisite for the quality of system functioning. Since people make the basis of any system, their homogeneity and compatibility are vital. This does not mean that employees have to be homogeneous in terms of their knowledge levels and ways of thinking. On the contrary, a team should be heterogeneous in terms of knowledge, skills, interests, and many other characteristics (sex, age, etc.). Differences in above aspects are wanted because by building a team and having members integrate internally mean that differences are transformed into advantages, which is reflected through a harmonious and complementary team. However, there is one thing that all team members should share and those are the values. In that sense, it is crucial to build an organizational culture that will be shared by all. As explained in chapter 3, internal team integration is an underlying assumption of effectiveness of the management of health institutions and the quality of health services. The emergence of collective emotions, shared values, and their convergence, initiate and facilitate interactions between members of the organization, and have a positive effect on the organizational performance (Wang and Zeng, 2017). Collective emotions and shared values are significantly determined by organizational culture, manner of communication, leadership style, and organizational structure. Therefore, it is highly important to pay attention to all the above factors in the process of designing the organization.

Having obtained results of the initial sample of 135 surveyed members of health institutions from Montenegro (ninety-six respondents from public and thirty-nine respondents from private health institutions) who were delegated by the administration of health institutions and the Ministry of Health, the author randomly selected sixteen doctors—all members of the Union of Medical Doctors from (sixteen) different public health institutions. This was done in order to compare the ratings of members of the Union on key variables of knowledge management and organizational design with the opinion (ratings) of sixteen doctors, members of the same (sixteen) institutions who were interviewed together with management of the health institutions delegated at a proposal of the Ministry of Health (they made up the basic sample of a total of 135 respondents). Therefore, on the following pages, we will see a comparison of ratings of (sixteen) Union members with the ratings of (sixteen) doctors from the same (sixteen) institutions, as well as with the ratings on the scale of public health institutions as a whole.

Major Differences in the Opinions of Representatives of the Management of Health Institutions and Members of the Union of Medical Doctors

Results of the abovementioned research showed no major differences in ratings on public health institutions given by one member of the administration, one medical doctor, and one medical technician (delegated by the Ministry of Health). However, if these ratings are compared to the perception of members of the Union, we will see extremely significant differences, which speaks about a high degree of organizational bifurcation.

Union members rate the level of application of knowledge management with a score of 2.03, which differs significantly (more than twice and statistically significantly) from the average score given by doctors from the same institutions who were delegated by the administration of health institution (4.17), and from the summary score obtained at the level of the public health system in the initial sample (4.06).

There are statistically significant differences in the perception of the effectiveness of knowledge management, which is mirrored in the quality of provided services. Union members gave the score of 2.07 to the effectiveness of knowledge management, while their colleagues from the same institutions scored that same variable with a grade of 4.10 (average of individual grades of sixteen doctors from the basic sample), and 4.12—average at the level of public health institutions (based on the basic sample).

Slightly smaller but equally significant (and statistically relevant) differences are evident in the perception of the quality of organizational infrastructure. On average, Union members rate the organizational infrastructure at 2.27, while their peers from the same institutions rate it at 3.76 (average of individual ratings of sixteen doctors from the basic sample), and 3.84 (at the level of public health institutions from the basic sample). When it comes to the organizational culture, Union members rate it with 2.57, doctors from the same institutions rate it at 4.02 (individually on average, based on the basic sample), while the average rating at the level of the public health system in the basic sample is 4.10. Finally, there are significant differences in terms of leadership too. While the average score of leadership based on the scores from the sample of Union members was 2.46, the average score given by doctors from the same institutions from the basic sample was 3.55, and the average score at the level of institutions from the basic sample 3.58.

Figure 9.1 shows the size of differences in perception. On the one hand, these differences suggest that employees in public health institutions may have given the so-called socially acceptable responses, or, in other words, their ratings may have been biased. Also, the presented indicators suggest that the quality of alignment of elements of organizational design is not at the best

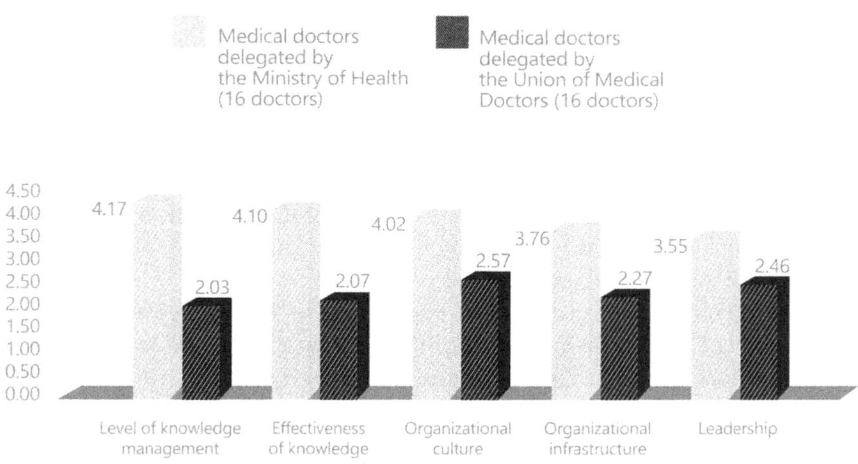

Figure 9.1 Analysis of the Internal Integration of Public Health Institutions Based on Two Samples. *Source:* Data collected by author.

level, especially from the point of view of shared values as a key dimension of the organizational model, which is elaborated in more detail in chapter 3.

However, both samples showed the link between the basic variables that are the subject of research. Specifically, a high degree of (statistically significant) correlation between the application of knowledge management, effectiveness of knowledge management, and the quality of health services was found in a sample of members of the Union (regardless of the fact that scores are quantitatively lower).

Differences in the Perception of Organizational Culture Within the Public Health System of Montenegro

Organizational culture also shows the difference between the perception of doctors from the basic sample and doctors who are members of the Union, as shown in figure 9.2. However, the internal focus reached consensus. Based on the answers of both groups of respondents, the ratio between the internal and external orientation of health institutions is approximately 2:1. In that sense, it is vital to strengthen the external focus, as will be discussed in the next section.

Comparison of differences in the perception of organizational culture based on two samples showed a high inconsistency in the perception of organizational culture between members of the administration and employees. The differences are evident from the example of the dominant type of organizational

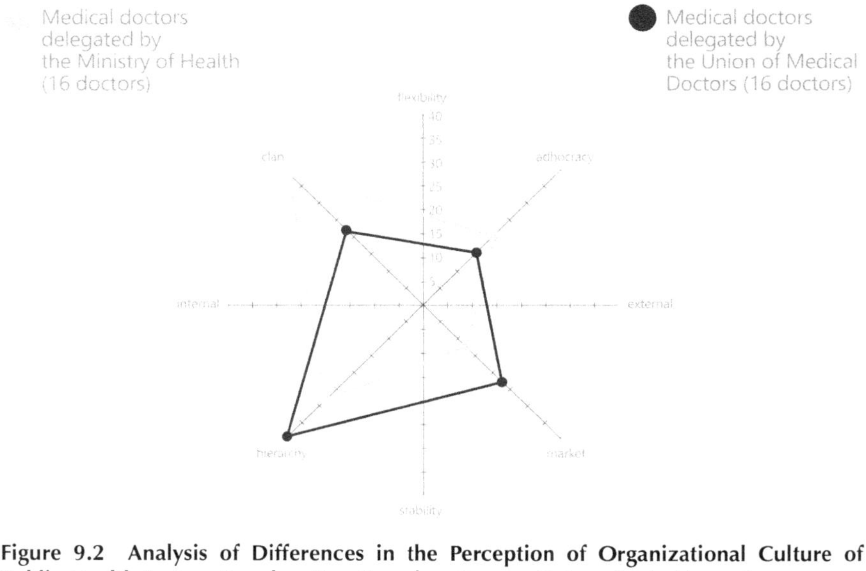

Figure 9.2 Analysis of Differences in the Perception of Organizational Culture of Public Health System Based on Two Samples. *Source:* Data collected by author.

culture. While one group of doctors (members of the administration) believes that family organizational culture (38.54%) is a dominant pattern of public health institutions, the other group (members of the Union) feels that dominant cultural pattern of public health institutions is hierarchical (39.22%). Although both these types have an internal focus, the difference is that the family type implies freedom and flexibility of members, and the hierarchical one implies stability and control. This speaks in favor of significantly opposing views and different perceptions of respondents from the same institutions.

Differences in the perception of family as a type of organizational culture are significant (in absolute terms, the value of the difference is 16.52). Members of the administration value familiarity with 38.54 percent, while Union members value that type in 22.02 percent of cases. The next big difference in perception of types concerns the hierarchical dimension of organizational culture (10.73). Medical doctors, representatives of the administration, recognize the hierarchical culture through 28.49 percent of the total organizational culture, while Union members see the representation of this type of culture in 39.22 percent of cases. A double-digit difference is evident in the perception of market culture (10.55). Members of the administration recognize this type of culture in 12.50 percent of cases, and Union members see the same pattern of culture in 232.05 percent of situations. The smallest differences are present in the adhocracy type of culture (4.76). Members of the administration see the representation of this type of culture in 20.47 percent cases, while members of the Union see this cultural pattern in 15.71 percent of situations.

While members of public health institutions, delegated at the proposal of the Ministry of Health, believe that the organization of the system is largely entrepreneurial and that people are willing to take risks (which they recognize in the organizational culture with 22.2%), their colleagues from the same institutions, but delegated by the Union, believe that risk-taking and entrepreneurship are present in only 7.7 percent of cases. While the doctors delegated by the management accentuate that the organization is focused on achieving its goal, has strong competitive spirit and strong orientation toward results (percentagewise, that number stands at 24.1%), their colleagues from the same institutions and members of the Union believe that to be true in 9.9 percent of cases. A large, more than double difference is also noticeable in terms of the perception of the structure of the organization. While members of the management believe that formal procedures dictate people what to do and consider the organization to be a controlled and structured place (25.9%), members of the Union share that view in 52.7 percent of cases, which is more than double.

Their perceptions of organizational leadership are different too. While members of the management of health institutions view leadership as mentoring behavior (29.1%), medical doctors from the Union share that view in 13.1 percent cases. Members of the management occasionally recognize leadership as aggressively oriented toward results (11.9%), and 44.7 percent of respondents from the Union share that view. In terms of management style, members of the management highly value teamwork, participation, and consensus in decision-making (54.1%), while members of the Union do not value this aspect as much (18.8%). While on the one hand doctors delegated by the management claim that loyalty and mutual trust, as well as commitment to the organization are high (42.5%), and commitment to innovation and application of latest technology are evident (24.1%), employee trainings and open communication are important (34.4%), as well as caring for people and teamwork (43.4%), Union members have a very different opinion. Thus, they value loyalty, mutual trust, and commitment to the organization with 27.1 percent, commitment to innovation and the application of latest technology with 11.7 percent, employee training and encouraging open communication with 18.8 percent, and caring for people and encouraging teamwork are rated with 24.7 percent.

The analysis shows a significant ambivalence in the domain of shared values within the organizational culture at the level of the public health institutions. Therefore, specific measures should be taken to prevent the emergence of a kind of organizational bifurcation.

Comparative Analysis of Different Attitudes of Two Groups of Respondents About the Organizational Climate in Public Health Institutions

Conclusions from the previous part regarding the organizational culture are confirmed through the results on the quality of the organizational climate at the level of the public health system, which showed differences in perception between the two groups of doctors. While one group of doctors rates the organizational climate with an average score of 3.85, the other group thinks that the quality of the organizational climate is weaker and evaluates it with a score of 2.52.

When it comes to the basic determinants of the organizational climate (figure 9.3), there are significant differences in perception too. Doctors (selected at the suggestion of the administration) rate it at 1.96, while the same indicator based on responses of members of the Union is significantly higher and amounts to 3.45. On the other hand, the readiness for change evaluated by the members of the Union is lower than by the doctors from the basic sample (2.31 and 2.69, respectively).

A more detailed analysis indicates a strong organizational bifurcation. As many as 56.3 percent of interviewed doctors from the Union absolutely

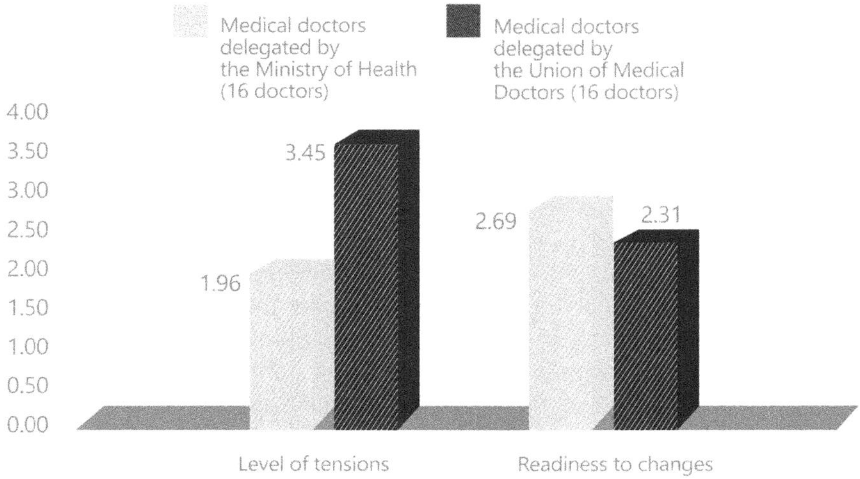

Figure 9.3 Comparative Analysis of the Perception of Organizational Climate Determinants Based on Two Samples. *Source:* Data collected by author.

disagree with the statement that employees in the public health system can trust each other. On the other hand, 85.1 percent of doctors delegated by the management of a public health institution point out that employees within the organization can trust each other, while only 37.5 percent of respondents share this view and only partially agree with it. As members of the Union—43.8 percent of them—state that there is often or almost always a strong disagreement in decision-making between employees involved in the process, representatives of the administration, and doctors delegated at the Ministry's suggestion in 62.6 percent of cases believe it happens rarely or never. The high level of commitment to work is witnessed by 87.6 percent of respondents from the management of health institutions, while the number of members of the Union is lower and amounts to 50.0 percent. As many as 43.8 percent of respondents delegated by the management chose the remuneration to be fair, only 6.3 percent of the members of the Union shared that view. Furthermore, as many as 62.5 percent absolutely disagree with the claim of fair remuneration, and 25.0 percent members of the Union partially disagreed with it. When it comes to the perception of system flexibility, the differences are somewhat smaller. In general, both sides find it difficult to make changes in the organization. Specifically, 43.8 percent of the management partially and 12.5 percent absolutely agree that it is difficult to make changes, while 56.3 percent of members of the Union absolutely agreed with it. When asked about taking responsibility, even in situations when mistakes are made, members of the management say that it is a common case in 93.8 percent of cases, while Union members claim that it happens in 68.8 percent of situations. In the end, the biggest discrepancy probably relates to the perception of trust in one's leaders. Doctors delegated by the management say the level of trust in the leaders is 87.6 percent, while their colleagues from the Union feel that to be true in 6.3 percent cases.

All of the above suggest that organization model of health systems needs reconfiguration through internal harmonization of elements of organizational design, which would result in increased quality of health services, be based on greater motivation, higher spirits, greater flexibility, higher level of kindness, and professionalism of health workers. Therefore, reconfiguration of organizational model based on internal harmonization of organizational design elements leads to an increased quality of services of health organizations.

ANALYSIS OF QUALITY OF EXTERNAL HARMONIZATION OF ELEMENTS OF ORGANIZATIONAL DESIGN OF HEALTH SYSTEM

The analysis of perception of strategic orientation of public health institutions in Montenegro, based on two samples, shows that the tendency toward efficiency is more pronounced than toward effectiveness in both cases. This indicates the need to improve external orientation, in order to increase the research component, monitor market signals, and increase the flexibility of the public health system (which is explained in more detail in the second chapter).

So members of the Union rate the efficiency of the public health system at 2.82, while their peers (basic sample—members delegated by the administration) rate focus to efficiency at 4.35. On the other hand, members of the Union rate effectiveness with 2.19, while doctors from the basic sample assigned it a significantly higher value (4.07).

From the standpoint of the focus on innovation in services, 56.2 percent of respondents from the basic sample believe that public health institutions have an advantage over private ones, while 31.3 percent of respondents are not sure about it, and 12.6 percent believe that private health institutions are more innovative. On the other hand, only 6.3 percent of respondents from the Union believe that public health institutions are more innovative than private ones, 12.5 percent are not sure, while as many as 81.3 percent of respondents from the Union share the opinion that private health institutions are more innovative. When it comes to knowing about latest methods of work, 81.3 percent of respondents from the basic sample believe that public health institutions give priority to improving the latest methods of work, while only 18.8 percent of respondents from the Union agree with this view. In addition, as many as 81.3 percent of respondents from the basic sample believe that the public health system has a good reputation among patients. Only 37.5 percent of doctors—members of the Union share that opinion. According to the criterion of the ratio between the price and quality of services, public health institutions have an advantage over private ones, all respondents from the basic sample agree (100.0%), while 68.8 percent of the members of the Union share that point of view.

The following is a comparison of the assessment of the quality of services of public and private health institutions measured by the perception of employees (internal perception) and the perception of the population (external perception)—figure 9.4.

As already shown, private health institutions have a stronger strategic focus on effectiveness, which corresponds to the perception of the population, who assign greater value to the quality of services of private institutions (4.46) than public health institutions (3.95). Interestingly, the analysis found that employees in private health institutions value the quality of services of their institutions (measured by the effectiveness of knowledge management) with 4.01, while employees in public health institutions value the quality of services of institutions with 4.12. Therefore, high scores of knowledge management and effectiveness of knowledge management, based on internal perception, do not have to coincide with scores measured by external

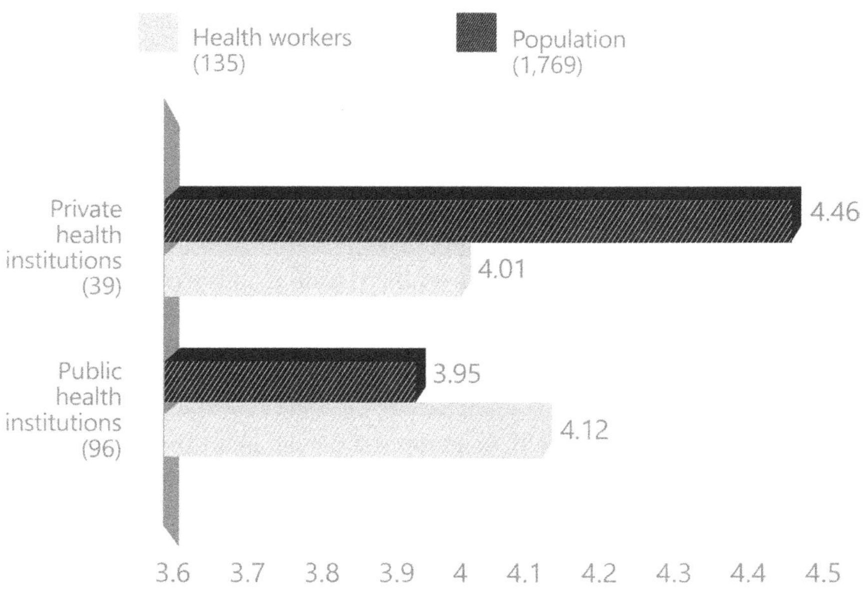

Figure 9.4 Comparative Analysis of Internal and External Perception of the Quality of Health Services in Public and Private Health Institutions. *Source:* Data collected by author.

perception. On the contrary in this particular case, based on internal perception, private health institutions earned a lower rating of the quality of services than public health institutions. That is, employees in public health institutions rated the quality of provided services with a higher score than employees in private health institutions. However, the external perception—the perception of the public, showed the opposite results. All of the above is in line with well-known saying attributed to Socrates: "the more we know, the more we are aware of what we don't really know and how much more room there is for further progress." For this reason, there is an external mismatch of elements of the organizational design of health system of Montenegro, so the organizational focus must be directed more toward effectiveness (as stated in chapter 6). Such a change of strategic focus in accordance with the multi-contingency approach implies changes in the organizational structure and other elements of organizational design, and requires a permanent process of harmonization of elements in order to ensure optimal business performance of the organizational system.

In addition to the above, previous chapters confirmed the discrepancy between public and private health institutions in terms of their organizational components, as well as between health institutions from different regions. Also, the organizational and legal context of the analysis (chapter 6) showed an insufficient integration of the health system due to inadequate information system. Furthermore, it showed that the existing legal framework is not supportive of modern design requirements (in particular those related to flexibility, teamwork, etc.).

In this sense, the reconfiguration of organizational model based on the external harmonization of elements of organizational design leads to an increased quality of services of health organizations.

Chapter 10

Montenegrin Health System at the Times of COVID-19 Pandemic

This chapter will include an analysis of the functioning of Montenegrin health system during the COVID-19 pandemic. One segment of this chapter is based on the data of a survey conducted in Montenegro during the pandemic. Hence, at the very beginning, this chapter will present profile of respondents. Having described the structure of the sample, this chapter will continue with the quality of the response of health system of Montenegro to the constraints of COVID-19, from the point of view of knowledge management and organizational design.

SAMPLE STRUCTURE

This section provides a more detailed insight into the structure of the sample of 12,359 persons from Montenegro, who took part in online research about the perception of quality of health services and the quality of organization of health system in general. The research was conducted from April 30 to May 4, 2020, during the COVID-19 pandemic.

The gender structure of respondents is such that females make majority of the sample (66%), while 34 percent of respondents are males.

The sample included persons aged eighteen and over. The age structure is such that the largest percentage in relation to the total number of respondents were young people aged eighteen to twenty-nine, that is, 64.40 percent, while the representation of people aged thirty to thirty-nine was 15.60 percent. The population aged forty to forty-nine years made up 11 percent of the sample, and persons aged fifty to fifty-nine years made 7 percent of the sample. Finally, persons aged sixty and over accounted for 2.00 percent of the total number of respondents.

From the aspect of the level of education, the dominant group were persons with secondary education (48.60%). They were followed by respondents with high education (30.00%), and those with higher education (19.20%). Respondents with primary education accounted for 1.90 percent, while those without any education made by far the lowest share: 0.30 percent.

When it comes to the geographical location of respondents, the sample involved persons from all municipalities of Montenegro.

Although the structure of the sample does not ideally reflect the structure of entire population of Montenegro, the sample size is such that it covers about 2 percent of the total population (according to Monstat estimates on January 1, 2020, Montenegro's population is 621,873), therefore, the validity of the results of this research is undisputable.

THE COUNTRY OF EXTREMES

Sociopolitical, economic, and health environment in Montenegro in the wake of the health crisis caused by COVID-19, speaks in favor of the thesis that Montenegrin and Yugoslav revolutionary and politician, Veljko Vlahović (1914–1975) gave the best description of Montenegro in his speech "Montenegro." Among other things, Vlahović points out that Montenegro is "a country of greatest extremes" that is "drunk with its own history" (Radonjić, 2013b: 586–587). The same author gaudily explains that Montenegro is "a land of deep darkness and lavish light, a free prisoner and enslaved freedom" (Radonjić, 2013b: 586–587).

Although small in territory, Montenegro is extremely proud of its history, which has often been permeated with the struggle for freedom and the pursuit of the ideal "he who stands up is not small." William Ewart Gladstone (1809–1898), British politician and statesman, supports this by stating "the magnitude of human action and human character does not depend mainly on the size of the stage on which it occurs" (Radonjić, 2011: 242). Regarding the troubles that Montenegrins struggled with, Gladstone points out that "the most romantic and shocking images of other histories fade before the ordinary life of Montenegro" (Radonjić, 2011: 616). Vlahović synthesizes Montenegrin history by stating that Montenegro is "an eternally open window of freedom that constantly carries broken chains of slavery, always in the wounds that it washes away with drops of dew" (Radonjić, 2013b: 586–587).

Historical events and the turbulent past of the Balkans, permeated by wars and great sufferings, have left traces in Montenegro as well. During wartimes, people typically grouped in two opposing sides, and those memories are still fresh and reflected in deep polarizations within the population. In this context, although a small, rather heterogeneous environment, Montenegro reacts very emotionally to topics such as their language, nation, religion, and even the anthem and the state flag. All these reactions are permeated and further complicated by the economic situation, which is highly complex during the times of pandemic. In practice, public debt has almost reached the glass ceiling, citizens are deeply dissatisfied with the economic situation and quality of life, sociopolitical instability, and law violations are getting stronger. This is reinforced by the latest analysis of the International Monetary Fund on inequality of income, according to which Montenegro ranks second among sixteen countries in the region, right after Bulgaria. Such a social environment, as well as the historical context, makes it even more difficult to fight constraints of the COVID-19 pandemic.

COVID-19 PANDEMIC AND THE HEALTH SYSTEM OF ULTIMATE EXTREMES

On the last day of 2019, the World Health Organization received an information about a cluster of atypical pneumonia in China (Wuhan, Hubei Province). After detailed analyzes, it was found that a large number of cases of infection in Wuhan were caused by a new type of corona virus, which on January 7, 2020, was identified as the new corona virus (2019-nCoV). The new virus is classified in the family of viruses just like severe acute respiratory syndrome (SARS). On February 11, 2020, the World Health Organization announced the official name of the disease—COVID-19, which is caused by the corona virus—SARS-CoV-2, (CoronaInfoCG, 2020). The corona virus (CoV) causes various types of diseases, and its clinical picture can be anything between milder diseases to severe respiratory infections, with a fatal outcome in most difficult situations.

After the first case of CoV infection was recorded, the virus spread to all continents except Antarctica. The number of patients increases every day, while all countries are trying to reduce the spread of the disease. According to the dashboard of the global COVID-19 statistics Worldometers (2021), a total of 98,670,343 cases of CoV have been reported worldwide, from the day of onset of the corona virus, more than a year ago (data as of January 22, 2021). There are 2,113,765 fatalities, while the reported number of recoveries was 70,859,648. The number of active cases (as of January 22, 2021) is 25,696,930.

While activities on finding a vaccine were rather intensive, countries across the globe made recommendations to prevent and combat the spread of the virus, in order to reduce its consequences until the vaccine is found. The basic measures for prevention of CoV are social distancing, face masks, and hand hygiene, and reduced contact, that is, avoiding all mass gatherings. In addition to the devastating effects of the virus on the health system (health systems in most countries are facing exhaustion) and the health of the population, measures that are necessarily implemented to preserve health in many countries cause and deepen social, economic, and political crisis. The biggest problems of that kind occur in small countries that are predominantly dependent on tourism as an industry, which is currently the case with Montenegro as well.

The First Wave of the Pandemic and the Successful Response of the Health System

The first two cases of CoV in Montenegro were confirmed on March 17, 2020. Thus, Montenegro was the last country in Europe to register the corona virus, that is, about three months after it first appeared in Europe. Therefore, first measures in terms of combating the spread of CoV were taken in a timely manner. The Government of Montenegro resolutely started the fight against the corona virus, and received an unbroken support of the people and the media at the very beginning. Through the formation of the National Coordination Body for Infectious Diseases, citizens received relevant information on daily basis through the national television and the social media. The measures were quite restrictive (restriction of movement, ban on some economic activities, and transition to the online mode of operation), and that citizens were scared, considering the disturbing news and images from, for example, neighboring Italy (large number of infected people, collapse of the health system) and Spain. Therefore, the level of compliance with the measures was at an extremely high level, and any violation, no matter how small, was sanctioned by competent authorities. The solidarity of citizens was also at a high level. A large number of individuals and companies responded to the call for fundraising to mitigate the effects of the pandemic. In the first five days alone, over 2 million euros were donated to the account of the National Coordination Body for Infectious Diseases of Montenegro, while a significant part was in the form of medical and other equipment (a significant part came from Montenegrin citizens living abroad). Due to the closure of borders and restrictions on movement in many countries, a number of Montenegrin citizens had troubles returning to Montenegro. The government responded by sending planes to evacuate them. The centralization of the health system in this case, the unity of the system and solidarity, had a positive impact on the health situation, because in emergencies, centralization is both theoretically and practically recommended as desirable.

Three regional COVID centers were established according to the model—center, north, and south. There was some proactive thinking and the system was ready for a much more difficult scenario than the one that happened. Healthcare professionals were respected in various ways, and it seemed that finally profession and knowledge were more important than the politics. All that gave the result. The prime minister of Montenegro stated that sixty-eight days after the first recorded case of coronavirus (March 17–May 24, 2020), there are no cases in Montenegro. Thus, according to him, Montenegro became the first corona free destination in Europe, with the score of 324 sick citizens, of which 315 recovered and 9 died in the first wave of the pandemic. Based on all the above, it can be said that the response of the Montenegrin health system in the first wave was satisfactory, although there were mistakes (contradictions in prescribing measures, problems with protection of personal data of the infected, legal justification of the prescribed measures, etc.). Nevertheless, enthusiasm, solidarity, and motivation of all the subjects to enter together in the fight "against the unknown" led to a positive outcome.

The Second Wave of the Pandemic—Politics Before the Profession and the Loss of Trust in the Health System

Officially, the first case of the CoV after the proclamation of Montenegro as the corona free destination was registered on June 14, 2020. Thus, twenty days after the end of the first wave, the so-called second wave of the pandemic officially started. Although this time more prepared than in the first wave, it turned out that the response of the health care system, but also of the wider state system, was worse. In order to maintain enthusiasm, solidarity, unity of doctors, media, decision-makers and citizens, appropriate organizational support is vital. However, the accumulated problems that were present in the first wave but were neglected in the short term, were further intensified as the crisis caused by the CoV continued. A large part of the economy was blocked, especially tourism, on which the Montenegrin economy relies to the greatest extent due to weak diversification of its economic activity. That caused a high rate of economic decline, the highest in the region. On top of all that, for Montenegro, the second wave of the pandemic came in a bad time, mostly because the parliamentary and local elections in Montenegro were approaching, and they were held on August 30, 2020. The stability (and continuity) of government on the one hand (for three decades the government in Montenegro has not been changed) and instability in many spheres of life were contrasts in their own right. Problems in many spheres of life of the citizens, a large number of examples of imperfections of the social organization and unprincipledness, a significant number of unemployed and people on the edge of existence, escalated with a decline in confidence in the governing structure and the desire of the population for change. Thus, a large number of political entities (and this time in two columns) began fighting for the trust of the citizens before the elections. The organization of elections posed a health risk in the conditions affected by corona (that the government has decided to take).

Taught by experience from the first wave of the pandemic, everyone was aware that adherence to measures to combat the spread of the pandemic was crucial. However, as the time went on, not only the population slowly lost patience, but also the initially present fear of the virus. People adhered less and less to the measures which used to be quite contradictory and illogical, as a result of insufficiently good analysis in their introduction. Initial trust in health workers and the profession began to decline, so people began to question those measures that are meaningful. However, the key problem in the second wave was that politics took a key role in the run-up to the elections, while the pandemic was put in the background, knowledge and the profession alike, and often even the common sense. In addition, the government faced the protests and mass gatherings because of the Law on Freedom of Religion, which was adopted at the end of 2019 in a formal and regular procedure. This law was adopted due to the votes and the will of the representatives of the ruling majority, but with great opposition from the Serbian Orthodox Church in Montenegro, which regarded this law as discriminatory. The protests that were announced on that occasion (and which presented a health risk), were supposed to be replaced by a dialogue at the proposal of the prime minister hoping to find a compromise. However, no agreement was reached. Therefore, the representatives of the Serbian Orthodox Church called for protests on the occasion of the adoption of this (for them disputable) Law, to which a large number of members of the opposition, as well as the people, responded. In the run-up to the elections, the number of protests has grown, and over time, the goal of the protests shifted and became directed toward the ongoing election campaign. Although Montenegro is a secular state, and according to the Constitution of Montenegro (Article 14) "religious communities are separated from the state," the Serbian Orthodox Church found itself at the head of the opposition block before the elections. Even though the representatives of the Serbian Orthodox Church stated that they did not interfere in the election process, it was clear from their actions that the situation was not like that. On the other hand, the authorities were unable or unwilling: first, to implement the Law on Freedom of Religion; and second, to ensure compliance with the measures of the National Coordination Body for Infectious Diseases that exclude the possibility of mass gatherings during a pandemic. Thus, during the so-called "litija"—protest walks, in a situation when the second wave of the pandemic in Montenegro began, thousands of Montenegrin citizens, who took to the streets not only because of the Law, but also because of the generally bad economic situation, could be seen (which worked for the organizers of "litija"). Despite the obvious violation of measures, and except from the occasional hearing of the organizers of mass gatherings, there were no sanctions. The unprincipledness of the authorities in this situation was more than visible. While during the first wave thousands of people were prosecuted for noncompliance with measures (in some cases due to very mild violations of measures by individuals), during the second wave mass violations of measures through rallies did not result in sanctions. Not only were there mass gatherings, but often representatives of the Serbian Orthodox Church often declared that the virus was powerless in relation to the believing people, and thus "assumed the role of a profession." After several gatherings with more than ten thousand people, the campaign of the opposition before the elections was completed. The parliamentary elections held on August 30, 2020, ended in such a way that the opposition parties had the opportunity to form the government, and after three decades, they sent the representatives of the authorities to the opposition benches. After acknowledging the election results, supporters of the "outgoing government" organized their mass gathering in the form of a "counter-meeting"—which was attended by thousands of citizens. This time it was about pro-Montenegrin citizens who felt threatened by messages from mass gatherings led by the Serbian Orthodox Church (within which there were often highlighted the features of neighboring Serbia).

What does this have to do with management, organizational design and the quality of health services? The health care system was not supported by the authorities in the direction of implementing prevention measures. The organizational design at the macrolevel did not work. On the other hand, the knowledge of health workers and their recommendations were put aside, in order to meet political goals. At the beginning, the measures were violated by the representatives of the opposition, who were joined in the protest walks even by a certain number of medical doctors, which confirmed that there is great dissatisfaction within the health system and the presence of a kind of organizational bifurcation. Then, the representatives of the government, with their supporters, supported "their own" mass gathering, and thus violated the measures they adopted, it was the same violation for which they criticized their colleagues from the opposition in the previous days. And to make matters worse, in this case as well, a number of doctors took part, again, forgetting the profession, as well as their colleagues who participated in the *litije*. Such unprincipledness is inadmissible from the point of view of management, trust, and leadership. After all that, there was a third situation of gross violation of measures through mass gatherings. Namely, due to the consequences of the corona virus, the leader of the Serbian Orthodox Church in Montenegro passed away. Although there were measures in place to organize funerals of this kind in the closest circle of the family, due to the risk of spreading the virus, the Serbian Orthodox Church in Montenegro organized another mass gathering to see off the metropolitan. The event was attended by thousands of people at the Church of Christ's Resurrection in Podgorica, including representatives of the new parliamentary majority, including the (current) prime minister-designate for the composition of the new government, with gross violations of measures, which were reported by many world media. All these events caused a significant number of infected citizens with the CoV and a much more difficult situation compared to the first wave.

These circumstances are another confirmation of the thesis that Montenegro is a "country of the greatest extremes." In the context of the pandemic, in the first wave, the system reacted in an excellent way (the last country to register the corona virus, and the first country to get rid of the corona virus). In the second wave, there is a second extreme, and Montenegro is among the record holders, but this time in a negative way. The total number of registered cases of CoV in Montenegro is 57,482, of which 765 with fatal outcome. These are the results on January 22, 2021. According to global statistics Worldometers, on this same date, Montenegro, according to the total number of registered cases of CoV per million inhabitants is in third place (with 91,516 cases per million inhabitants), behind Andorra (121,758) which is in first place, and Gibraltar (115,927) which is in the second place. However, it is important to point out that Andorra performed 180,088 tests, which when compared to the population of this small country (77,334) means that on average each inhabitant of Andorra was tested 2.33 times. On the other hand, in Gibraltar, each inhabitant was tested as many as 4.40 times for the presence of CoV (148,195 tests per 33,685 inhabitants). As for Montenegro, it conducted 215,765 tests. Therefore, in Montenegro, on average, every third citizen was tested. For this reason, it seems that if the number of tests in Montenegro were close to that of Andorra (6.78 times more tests per capita in Andorra than in Montenegro), or Gibraltar (12.81 times more tests per capita than in Montenegro) that Montenegro would rank as first on the list of recorded cases of CoV per million inhabitants in the world. In addition, it is interesting to compare Montenegro and Luxembourg, whose population is approximately the same as Montenegro's. The number of infections in Luxembourg is by 8,044 lower (78,270 cases per million inhabitants). However, Luxembourg conducted 8.43 times more tests per capita than Montenegro, which means that every citizen of Luxembourg was tested 2.89 times on average (Worldometers, 2021). This is an indicator of Montenegro's failure to respond to the second wave of the pandemic in the right way. Despite the funds raised, the country did not procure additional testing equipment in due time, so people had to wait for their results for days. Even more, a part of tests was sent out to Germany for analysis, within the outsourcing model. Moreover, Montenegro did not react in time in terms of the procurement of vaccines, so the vaccination, which has largely started in many countries around the world and in the region (Slovenia, Croatia, and Serbia), did not begin in Montenegro until February 20, 2021.

Inconsistencies in the actions of the health and state authorities during the second wave of the COVID-19 pandemic caused the number of infections to increase, while the citizens' trust in health workers decreased. While two political opponents violated the measures, involving medical doctors in their mass gatherings and compromising them, a number of medical doctors left the public health system during the pandemic.

The election of a new government took place on December 4, 2020, and the citizens have high hopes for changes. However, it is worth noting that a significant number of candidates themselves violated the measures during the ban on mass gatherings, probably not thinking that, when coming to power, they would have to appeal to citizens to adhere to measures against the spread of corona virus. In this context, the continuity of unprincipledness in action continues in the field of health, like and in many other fields too, despite the fact that the government changed after three decades, and so did the key political actors on which the system depends.

From all the above, it seems that politicians in Montenegro, regardless of whether they are in the position or in the opposition, forget three important facts: first, that trust is gained through action and personal example, and second, that trust is hard to come by, and easy to lose, and third, that in the times we live in, knowledge has no alternative and should not be, by any means, substituted by political references.

A HEALTH CARE SYSTEM DRUNK FROM ITS OWN HISTORY

Just like Montenegro is described as "drunk from its own history," this could be stated for its health system as well. It is important to point out that health and knowledge cannot be built quickly, but require patience, long-term investment, commitment, and building of trust. A situation where doctors and scientists are practically lower-class citizens than politicians does not guarantee the sustainability of the system. It is not enough to give recognition to doctors and scientists only when problems that no one can solve but them arise, while in the normal circumstances they are forgotten. It is forgotten that the doctors and scientists are a source of progress even when there is no state of emergency.

Sources of Problems in the Organization of Health System

The COVID-19 pandemic in Montenegro has shown that the history of the development of the health system in terms of knowledge management and organizational design in Montenegro provides much room for improvement:

First, it is a devastating fact that as many as 52.0 percent of Montenegrin citizens do not agree with the thesis that in Montenegro knowledge is a key condition for individual career advancement. As many as 75.4 percent of respondents believe that the salaries of doctors in Montenegro are lower than they deserve. As many as 46.7 percent of Montenegrin citizens believe that the Montenegrin health care system is not autonomous in relation to political influences, while 63 percent of respondents believe that corruption in the health care system of Montenegro is more or less present.

Second, according to the latest survey from 2020, as many as 75.6 percent of respondents, if they could choose, would rather be treated in a private than in a state health institution. Waiting time for an examination in private health institutions is shorter, commitment of the doctors is higher. A large number of doctors from the health system are forced to work additionally in private health care institutions in order to provide for themselves. Because of this fact and the small system with a limited number of staff, the same doctors often work in both private and public health institutions. As the doctor is the basis for the quality of health services, it seems that the advantage of private health care institutions is crucial in terms of motivation and quality of the organization (and not because of specific, professional medical knowledge). However, it should be noted that citizens, just as they pay for an examination in a private health institution, also finance the public health system through allocations of money for health insurance. According to the Law on Contributions for Compulsory Social Insurance (Article 17), 8.5 percent of the gross amount is allocated to health insurance at the expense of the employee and 2.3 percent at the expense of the employer. If we put this percentage of health care expenditures in relation to the average salary in Montenegro, we come to the conclusion that over three decades, a citizen of Montenegro spends on average about 30,000 euros for health care. In that sense, they naturally expect to have quality treatment by the public health system. In addition, the form of ownership does not determine the level of efficiency of the system, but the quality of its organization and management (knowledge).

Third, according to Monstat (2020), the average gross monthly salary is 783 euros which makes an average net monthly salary of 524 euros. This is very similar to the basic salary of, for example, a university teaching assistant who holds a PhD degree, but whose full-time engagement may be possible after ten years of work. When we compare an average salary in Montenegro to salaries of employees in education (regardless of their level) and health, it comes to light that salaries of health and education workers in Montenegro are in the range of average salaries or slightly above. Correspondingly, Montenegro does not give due importance to areas of knowledge and health. Likewise, that is the root of the problem of international migration of top talents from the country and their lack of motivation of young people to work in the fields of science and health. It is also the reason why many medical doctors leave the public health system and choose to either go abroad or start working in private practices.

Fourth, there is an omnipresent organizational bifurcation in the health system. Feuds, mistrust, and frequent provocations through the media. Doctors sacrifice their credibility and their profession at the expense of political goals, they violate measures they have brought, and lose trust. On the other hand, many doctors do whatever they can to ensure the functioning of the system even in the times of pandemic. They are guided solely by enthusiasm and love for the job, albeit not being properly valued.

Organizational and Systemic Morals

COVID-19 pandemic was an opportunity for everyone to understand the importance of science, education, and organization.

First, faith in science is the source of progress. But one must be aware that the task of science is not ultimate pursuit of truth and absolute objectivity does not exist (Hoover & Donovan, 2011). In that sense, science is not claimed to be true, but rather striving to truth (Ilić, 1996; Radonjić, 2013a). It actually aspires to come up with the best ideas and explanations that help in better understanding of phenomena in the world (Powell, 1962). A typical feature of scientific observation and reasoning is that it is not based on beliefs, religious doctrines, intuition, imagination, or assumptions (Leary, 2001). Scientific research is based on research questions and answers to them. It implies systematic observation and analysis of observations that are structured according to an appropriate logical framework in order to obtain valid conclusions. In this sense, epistemological principles imply a combination of knowledge about (Porter, 1913; Bengson & Moffett, 2011): (1) concept ("know that"), (2) operations ("know how"), and (3) experience ("know from experience").

Second, education implies both knowledge and behavior (in terms of upbringing). Knowledge can be acquired at any time, but typically, acquisition of specialist knowledge starts at the age of eighteen at university. Behavior (upbringing) starts at the earliest age and is difficult to change later. In this context, acting by example is important. Therefore, to build a quality organization and correspondingly quality system, knowledge and behavior have to be in harmony.

Third, organization and management are critical success factors. Importance of the organization that implies transparency of the process, reliance on knowledge and science, work, order, and discipline (enforcement of laws), appropriate valuing of results and merits, is immeasurable. The importance of organization and management are best understood through problems, when there are none (organization and management). In that context, back in 1774, Katerina Radonjić, sister of a Montenegrin governor, stated that "anarchy is worse than slavery." Referring to the times she lived in, Radonjić adds that "injustice is seen at every turn, because there is no one with enough power to stop it or punish" (Radonjić, 2013b: 239–241).

The organization and management in Montenegro, as well as the health system as a whole, are as full of contrasts as the country itself and its people. As the mountains of Montenegro are "angry and cheerful," "calm and singing," Montenegro is "both sea foam and snow dust" (Radonjić, 2013b: 586–587). However, just as such a combination of natural contradictions makes a beautiful harmony of nature and makes Montenegro one of the most beautiful countries in the world, organization of health care in Montenegro should be approached with more knowledge and knowledge-based aspirations in order to reach harmony and quality.

Conclusion

KNOWLEDGE MANAGEMENT AND ORGANIZATIONAL DESIGN IN THE FUNCTION OF HEALTH QUALITY

Through each of its phases (creation, storage, sharing, and application), knowledge management significantly determines the quality of health services. A higher level of knowledge creation, storage, sharing, and application raises the level of knowledge management application in the organization. Consequently, a higher level of application of knowledge management has a positive effect on its effectiveness. From the standpoint of quality of service in the health sector, this means:

1. improving cooperation between employees in the health sector (more teamwork and better decision-making);
2. improved communication (better relations among employees, higher spirits, better cooperation, and kindness of staff);
3. higher level of flexibility and willingness to learn (greater efficiency and effectiveness of the organization through the constant acquisition of new knowledge);
4. improved organizational performance (reduction of waiting time for examinations, cost optimization, and increased competitiveness in terms of quality of health services).

Organizational design as a multidimensional construct affects the quality of health services in many ways.

First, mutual harmonization of elements of organizational design (according to the theory of multi-contingency) significantly determines the organizational performance, efficiency and effectiveness of the organization, and the quality of health services.

Second, system centralization affects organizational flexibility (higher degree of centralization—lower degree of flexibility, and vice versa) and the ability to react quickly to changes in the environment, hence, the level of centralization can largely determine the quality of health services.

Third, the organizational climate has a major effect on the characteristics of health services such as kindness, commitment, friendliness, and motivation of health workers in providing health services, while the organizational culture considerably dictates the level of professionalism in work in health institutions.

Fourth, the choice that is made between efficiency and effectiveness through the organization's goals and its strategy, affects the characteristics of quality of health services (higher efficiency will provide lower cost of health services, while higher effectiveness will result in greater customer satisfaction through tailoring the organization to customers' needs).

Fifth, the organizational structure affects the flow of information between different factors of the organizational system and their alignment, as well as the motivation of members of the organization. Therefore, the quality of health services consequently depends on the organizational structure.

Sixth, constant changes in health care require permanent vigilance of the organization and entail reactions to changes by reconfiguring the organizational system. That is done with the purpose of maintaining focus of the organization on patients and continuously improving the quality of health services.

These conclusions are in line with the findings of a number of studies in this field. Within knowledge management, there is a special emerging component that relates to knowledge about clients, as an important factor of organizational competitiveness. From the standpoint of strategic effectiveness, it aims to better understand market needs and provide better services (Gustavsson, Gremyr, and Kenne Sarenmalm, 2016; Mehdibeigi, Dehghani, and Yaghoubi, 2016). In this sense, the application of knowledge management is becoming a key factor of organizational effectiveness (Wickramasinghe, 2010; Cepeda-Carrion, Martelo-Landroguez, Leal-Rodríguez, and Leal-Millán, 2017). Exceptional progress of technology has made people accustomed to business innovation. For that reason, innovation strategies of health institutions have a positive effect on patient's satisfaction (Dobrzykowski, Callaway, and Vonderembse, 2015; Sahoo and Ghosh, 2016), and their application is significantly determined by the quality of leadership (Abdallah, 2014). Even though some consider that health care does not accept or respond to new management methods as quickly as other activities (Jorma, Tiirinki, Bloigu, and Turkki, 2016), the application of new knowledge-based management approaches can contribute to improving organizational performance and better quality of health services through appropriate organization design (Bouncken, 2002; El Morr and Subercaze, 2010). Organizational design affects the quality of health services in many ways (Coleman, Austin, Brac h and Wagner, 2009; Labonte, Benzer, Burgess, Cramer, Meterko, Pogoda, and Charns, 2016; Swensen, Gorringe, Caviness and Peters, 2016). Moreover, there is vast evidence that confirms how organizational culture is vitally important to the quality of health care (Davies and Mannion, 2013; Beardsmore and McSherry, 2017).

INTERDEPENDENCE OF KNOWLEDGE MANAGEMENT AND ORGANIZATIONAL DESIGN

According to this research, knowledge management affects the organizational design, and vice versa, organizational design affects knowledge management, which collectively determines the quality of services.

First, certain relationships between organizational design and knowledge management already exist in literature, including determinants of the two basic constructs and their relationships. The fact that the health sector is one of the biggest consumers of state budget results in the continuous aspiration of health institutions to develop more efficient and effective systems of delivery of services (Miller, 2015). In an economy, that increasingly becomes based on knowledge and the intangible assets (Barão, de Vasconcelos, Rocha, and Pereira, 2017; Hussinki, Kianto, Vanhala, and Ritala, 2017), organizations face persistent changes in many areas of social action. Under such conditions, the scientific field of knowledge management is becoming an increasingly relevant concept, as one of the most important sources of growth of efficiency and effectiveness of modern organizations (Assem and Pabbi, 2016). Knowledge management is especially important in developing countries that face limited resources (Asrar-ul-Haq and Anwar, 2016). From the standpoint of organizational perspective, knowledge sharing is the most important aspect of knowledge management. Knowledge sharing implies its circulation between individuals in the organization, between organizational departments, as well as between the organization itself and its environment (Bremer and Cohintz, 2004; Da Silva and Agusti-Cullell, 2008; Chidambaranathan and Swarooprani, 2017). Consequently, the management must establish an organizational structure that will allow for the creation and sharing of a large amount of knowledge (Koohborfardhaghighi and Altmann, 2017). The task of knowledge management in organizations is to design organizational structures of such a kind that will enable experts from different fields of expertise to connect into one whole, whose function is to meet the needs of its clients (Boder, 2006). As a rule, the knowledge management system gives better results with decentralized organizational structure (Mahmoudsalehi, Moradkhannejad, and Safari, 2012; Koohborfardhaghighi and Altmann, 2017). Therefore, knowledge management depends heavily on the organizational design, which significantly determines efficiency and effectiveness of the organization. Organizational culture is more important for the application of knowledge management than information systems as a form of support to knowledge sharing (Ghosh and Scott, 2007). Also, knowledge management has a positive impact on the level of organizational performances (Heisig, Suraj, Kianto, Kemboi, Perez Arrau, and Fathi Easa, 2016; Shahzad, Bajwa, Siddiqi, Ahmid, and Raza Sultani, 2016).

Organizational culture (as a common determinant of knowledge management and organizational design) is vital to health organizations because the quality of communication between employees and their teamwork largely affects the level of service they provide to patients (Drotz and Poksinska, 2014; Johnson, Nguyen, Groth, Wang, and Ng, 2016; Rydenfält, Odenrick and Larsson, 2017). Furthermore, continuous communication between the management and employees in health institutions plays a key role in establishing an appropriate leadership system in the health sector (Wikström and Dellve, 2009). The complexity of the leadership process and building an appropriate organizational culture in large health systems requires achieving an appropriate balance between needs and resources of medical doctors (as direct health care providers), professional managers, and policymakers in these institutions (Antwi and Kale, 2014).

Formalization (as a structural component of organizational design) in terms of adherence to rules, procedures, and standardization of behavior in the provision of health services, has a positive effect on the level of application of knowledge management. What is more, a negative correlation was found between centralization and the application of knowledge management. To illustrate this, a high degree of centralization has an inevitably negative effect on the level of application of knowledge management, as the research suggest. Furthermore, connection between formalization and the application of knowledge management was confirmed, because as much as flexibility can be accepted and required in other areas, the health sector must have at least some level of formalization, that is, adherence to standards, rules, and procedures.

Likewise, factors of organizational design greatly determine the level of application of knowledge management.

First, the very choice of goals and strategy of the organization crucially affects the degree of application of knowledge management. As a strategic direction in the health sector, effectiveness, rather than efficiency, requires from the organization a higher level of application of knowledge management. This is due to the fact that effectiveness implies the external orientation of the organization and the focus on innovation. Therefore, the complexity of changes in the environment and the need to be competitive implies a permanent focus on improving knowledge and skills in the process of providing health services.

Second, the size of the organization reflects on the knowledge management too. Large organizations require a higher level of knowledge quality, both in terms of opportunities for various specializations and in-depth studies of a particular area and in terms of the necessary knowledge in the field of management and work in large teams (communication, etc.).

Third, organizational culture, which does not have the prominent importance of knowledge as the most important resource of the organization, affects its lower level. Likewise, the organizational climate that encounters problems regarding mutual trust and respect makes the knowledge sharing between members of the organization more difficult and negatively affects the application of knowledge management.

Fourth, the leadership style is vital to the level of application of knowledge management in the organization. Primarily, leaders are required to lead by example. Only a leader who clearly demonstrates his focus on knowledge as a strategically important resource of the organization can count that knowledge management, as a concept, will be accepted by employees as a basic paradigm of development.

Fifth, depending on characteristics, the organizational structure can facilitate or hinder the dissemination of knowledge within the organization. As mentioned before, centralization disrupts the motivation to increase the level of application of knowledge management. Hierarchical organizational structures slow down the flow of information, which also complicates the knowledge sharing and has a negative effect on the level of application of knowledge management.

On the other hand, knowledge management determines the choice of organizational design. First, a higher level of application of knowledge management assumes that the organizational structure is as flexible and "flat" as possible. It is necessary to ensure the best possible communication between members of the organization. The organizational system should be decentralized, but networked and integrated too. Also, knowledge management implies a high level of mutual trust and respect within the organization, that is, an appropriate system of values determined by organizational culture and organizational climate.

Health, as well as education, is an area in which people and their knowledge cannot be replaced by capital or technology. From all the above, it is clear that knowledge management and organizational design are processes with a strong mutual dependence. In addition, the complementarity of knowledge management and organizational design enables better organizational performance, and accordingly, higher quality of health services.

KNOWLEDGE MANAGEMENT IN HEALTH SYSTEM OF MONTENEGRO

The level of application of knowledge management in health institutions in Montenegro was measured in two ways. First, members of health institutions delegated at the proposal of administration of health institutions filled in the questionnaire, and then their peers from public health institutions delegated by the Union did the same. Finally, a qualitative research based on focus groups and interviews followed to deepen the analysis and reach better conclusions.

Results of the basic sample gave an average score of 4.02 to the application of knowledge management. The central region earned the average score of 4.17, followed by the northern with 4.11, and the southern region that scored 3.76. The level of application of knowledge management was 4.06 in public health institutions, while the same indicator was 3.94 in private institutions.

Expected but remarkably large differences in scores turned out in the sample of members of the Union. Based on this independent sample, the level of application of knowledge management earned the score of 2.03. This is twice as low as the summary indicator at the level of public health institutions.

Differences in these scores and reasons behind them were analyzed in focus groups and interviews. Assuming that knowledge management is based on knowledge as the basic resource of an organization, and considering that the more you know, the more you become aware of how much more you need to learn, it is evident that the highest score of knowledge management—5, is an ideal to strive to. On the other hand, an average grade of 4, under assumption of self-criticism, could be almost a perfect system. In other words, there is a high level of knowledge application in the organization, awareness that knowledge management is a process, and that there is always room for improvement. However, the average score of the level of application of knowledge management of 4.02 can be argued to be too high (under assumption that respondents who are also managers gave socially desirable answers), which is supported by the following reasons:

First, the average score of the application of knowledge management based on questionnaires that respondents, members of the Union, filled in is 2.03. Therefore, such discrepancy in scores indicates that the level of application of knowledge management is overestimated.

Second, information infrastructure and technology networking are a prerequisite for the application of knowledge management (especially through the phases of storage and knowledge sharing). It is a fact that Montenegrin health system is not networked appropriately which means that institutions cannot communicate, share data, compare results, and the like. In particular, the Clinical Center of Montenegro and special hospitals are still outside the existing information system. Therefore, since prerequisites for knowledge management system are not fulfilled, it is evident that the level of application of the concept of knowledge management is not at a satisfactory level.

Third, speaking from the organizational and legal perspective, Montenegro's health system is centralized. Board of directors can be established in the Clinical Center and the Institute of Public Health only. Furthermore, quantitative analysis showed that most health care managers do not have information about their institutions' assets based on balance sheets or they may not want to share that information (75.08% of respondents). As already proven, centralization has a negative effect on the application of knowledge management, and that is another reason to conclude that the level of application of knowledge management is not at the appropriate level.

Fourth, one of the prerequisites for knowledge management is a positive organizational climate, readiness for change, and low level of tension. However, this research has shown that there is significant room for improvement. To begin with the financial motivation of employees, quality of communication, mutual trust and respect, and the last, but not the least, shared values.

Fifth, high scores of the management regarding the level of application of knowledge management indicate a lack of understanding of the concept by health institutions' leaders. Moreover, all the above data indicate it is necessary to strengthen managerial and leadership skills of leaders in health institutions.

Finally, the concept of knowledge management in health institutions in Montenegro is present, yet, at an early stage, and it is predominantly based on programs of continuing medical education. Continuing medical education is most prominent in the Clinical Center of Montenegro (Center of Science) and the Institute of Public Health, which established a special organizational unit to address that matter. Mathematically speaking, this is "a necessary but not sufficient condition" for the application of knowledge management to give expected results. Therefore, in order to improve the health system of Montenegro, knowledge management should be at the top of the agenda of policymakers in the field of health.

SOURCE OF OPPORTUNITIES TO IMPROVE THE ORGANIZATION AND QUALITY OF THE HEALTH SYSTEM'S SERVICES

Internal harmonization of elements of organizational design implies the application of a multi-contingency approach to organizational design within health institutions, that is, harmonization of elements such as size of the organization, technology, goals and strategy, organizational culture, leadership style, and organizational climate. In this case, external harmonization implies a balance in the level of quality of health services in different regions, and a balance between the quality of public and private health institutions. In addition, taking into account the fact that health is vital to general social interest, external harmonization implies an appropriate interaction of the health system with the environment.

The analysis showed that health organizations in Montenegro need to pay more attention to the permanent internal and external harmonization of elements of organizational design. The following facts speak in favor of that.

First, the way to achieve success is the reduction of internal disintegration (which is achieved through mutual trust and respect, positive organizational climate, and shared values of members of the organization). As shown in chapter 9, there are statistically significant differences among members of health institutions about the perception of organizational climate, culture, shared values, and leadership style. Taking into account insufficient financial motivation of employees, too much work, and, in some cases, conflicts between doctors, it is evident that the problem of internal integration of staff should be in greater focus of management of health institutions in Montenegro.

Second, lack of internal harmonization implies imminently external lack of harmonization too. External harmonization means external integration (harmonization with the market needs). Yet, there are important discrepancies between managers of health institutions and patients (e.g., members of public health institutions consider that the quality of their services is higher than the quality of services of private health institutions, while citizens oppose that view). In addition, continuous dissatisfaction of doctors, which drew media attention too, is just another reason for patients to worry if doctors would be committed enough to their medical state. Similarly, there is a problem of corruption too. Only 5 percent of citizens believe that there is no corruption in the health system of Montenegro, while as many as 41.8 percent of the population are sure it existed. In addition, representatives of the Union mention ninety assaults on medical doctors over the past four years, with an upward trend over the past two years, which is a signal of an inadequate external harmonization of elements of organizational design.

Third, it is important to emphasize that there are differences in the perception of quality of health services in different regions, as well as differences in the level of application of knowledge management and its effectiveness. Similarly, there are differences between public and private health institutions in terms of perception of quality by patients and managers alike.

Fourth, high system centralization leads to reduced system flexibility and weaker resistance to changes. On the other hand, the modern business necessitates quick reactions to events in the environment and continuous adjustments. Local self-government units are not sufficiently involved in the management of health institutions, even though health care, as an activity of general interest, requires greater involvement of the entire social community in order to increase the quality of health services.

Fifth, the research also showed an insufficient degree of cooperation between different health institutions. Therefore, the Strategy for improving the quality of health care and patient safety 2019–2023 of the Ministry of Health of Montenegro sheds more light on the matter of improving the integrated quality management system, based on continuous improvement of the system, and system integration. The strategy includes key quality indicators, that is, "effectiveness—in terms of improving health outcomes, security, appropriateness, orientation to patients, efficiency and equality" (Strategy for improving the quality of health care, 2019). The strategy recognizes that "coordination, cooperation and continuity at all levels of health care are a prerequisite for raising the quality of health services."

Sixth, the premise of harmonization of elements of organizational design implies their continuous follow-up, in order to create a quality information basis for decision-making. Due to the already stated shortcomings of both the information system and the rulebook for assessment of the quality of health services, it is crucial to make further efforts on building a quality management system. The Strategy for improving the quality of health care (2019) recognizes that too. Therefore, it envisages the establishment of a national body for quality in health care and other formal structures for quality management in health institutions.

These reasons lead to the conclusion that permanent internal and external harmonization of elements of organizational design has to be in the focus in order to increase the quality of health services.

RECONFIGURATION OF THE ORGANIZATIONAL MODEL AS A CONDITION FOR IMPROVING THE QUALITY OF HEALTH SERVICES

An organization that is strategically dominantly oriented to effectiveness is most often one of the initiators of changes in the market. On the other hand, a dominant focus on efficiency usually means adapting to changes in the environment. Still, modern business environment, regardless of the organization's strategic direction, requires continuity of changes. Just as knowledge multiplies rapidly, the application of new knowledge causes constant changes too. These changes require internal and external harmonization of elements of organizational design. Organizations that do not change, do not grow, and do not develop. Nowadays, that usually means that survival of the organization is endangered.

According to results of combined quantitative and qualitative methods from this research, the reconfiguration of the organizational model that is based on internal and external harmonization of elements of organizational design leads to increased quality of services of health organizations.

This section will present concrete indicators in support of evidence that reconfiguration of organizational model, along with the harmonization of elements of organizational design, results in increased quality of services of health organizations.

First, *kaizen* methodology, that many companies around the world owe their success to, requires constant work on incremental improvements within the organization, that is, reconfiguration of the organizational model. This methodology starts from the assumption "unless we progress, we regress." It is a philosophy that implies a critical approach to one's own activities, in order to re-examine their quality and constantly look for ways to improve them. Just as a person can improve oneself and become better, so can an organization. Members of the organization should increase their awareness that "one can always do better," and that this is constantly being strived for. Nevertheless, this does not mean that members of the organization should be unhappy with the present state of affairs even if they are aware that things can be better. On the contrary, they need to be motivated to do their best under the given circumstances and to strive for higher goals and improvements based on satisfaction with their present achievement. Thus, it will create a positive environment and organizational climate that will at the same time contribute to a reduction of internal disintegration of team members and increase external integration, which is in line with Adizes' philosophy and the formula for success of any organization.

Second, there are many ways to internally harmonize elements of organizational design to improve the quality of health services in health institutions in Montenegro. As already mentioned, change is inevitable, and with the change of goals, it is necessary to change strategies as well. The change in strategy causes a change in the organizational structure, which consequently, based on the theory of multi-contingency, indicates the need for permanent internal harmonization of elements of organizational design in order to increase the quality of health services. First, the internal integration of the system, positive organizational climate, and the leadership style in the function of shared values of team members has a positive effect on the organizational performance. Then, major differences in the perception of the quality of management between managers and employees negatively affect the motivation of employees and their communication with the management. For this reason, should these differences be overcome, based on constructive dialogue, transparency, and building trust, that will have a positive impact on the quality of health services. Greater strategic focus on effectiveness, along with the pursuit of decentralization of the system, will result in increased flexibility of the organization, greater motivation of employees, and greater opportunities for the application of knowledge management, which together lead to improved quality of health services.

Third, in addition to the internal harmonization of elements of organizational design, there is plenty of room to contribute to the quality of health services in Montenegro through external harmonization of elements of organizational design. Greater strategic focus on effectiveness and the market can contribute to a better understanding of patients' needs, and thus to creating better responses to meet them. The development of an integrated health information system and the networking of key stakeholders is a prerequisite for the development of adequate quality management of health services. The key stakeholders in this domain are "Ministry of Health, Committee for the Quality and Safety of Health Care, Institute of Public Health, Commissions for Quality Control in All Health Institutions, Managers of Health Institutions and the World Health Organization" (Strategy for Quality Improvement of health care, 2019), the Government of Montenegro, local self-governments, citizens, and the media. Improving the quality of health services requires a holistic approach and trust-based management (Weilandt, 2018), which necessitates the active participation of the wider community. Alignment of systems of employee motivation, organizational structure, and organizational culture will reduce corruption in the health system, which also affects the better quality of health services, based on the standardization of operational procedures, and the formalization of processes of delivery of services. The importance of health reflects in its impact on other economic activities too. For example, the quality of health care has a major effect on the quality of tourism. Therefore, given that tourism is one of Montenegro's strategic directions of development, it is necessary to take into account harmonization of the quality of health services with the expectations of tourists and their preferences. In this context, health tourism could be considered as an important segment of harmonization with the environment. Statistically significant differences in perception of the quality of health services by region and between public and private health institutions indicate the need for external harmonization of elements of organizational design. Continuous quality monitoring enables the application of benchmarking methods, or the use of best practices to improve and standardize quality of the system. External harmonization of elements of organizational design includes additional consideration of the environment. In particular, Montenegro is in the process of joining the European Union (EU). As a result, EU membership might have an increased migration of health workers to EU member states. Therefore, it is necessary to create an appropriate organizational design that will be proactive and prevent negative consequences. Finally, organizational design should be aligned with the legal framework of the country. In this context, the adoption of the Law on Public and Private Partnership contributes to greater possibilities for configuring organizational design by connecting the private and public sectors based on shared interests. Synergy effects based on the investment role of the private sector and its business efficiency on the one hand and the control role of the public sector on the other hand, can contribute to the increased quality of health services.

From all the above, it is certain that the health system of Montenegro needs a reconfiguration of the organizational model based on internal and external harmonization of elements of organizational design and greater application of knowledge management that will lead to increased quality of health care services.

Bibliography

Abdallah, Abdallah. 2014. "Implementing Quality Initiatives in Healthcare Organizations: Drivers and Challenges." *International Journal of Health Care Quality Assurance* 27 (3): 166–81. https://doi.org/10.1108/IJHCQA-05-2012-0047.

Addicott, Rachael. 2008. "Models of Governance and the Changing Role of the Board in the 'Modernised' UK Health Sector." *Journal of Health, Organisation and Management* 22 (2): 147–63. https://doi.org/10.1108/14777260810876312.

Adižes, Isak Kalderon. 2015. *Upravljanje organizacijama: Menadžment saradnjom i zajedništvom u preduzećima, ustanovama i institucijama.* Beograd: HESPERIA edu.

Adizes, Ichak Kalderon. 2018. *Insights on Management.* Santa Barbara: Adizes Institute Publications.

Akgül, Yakup, and Mustafa Zihni Tunca. 2016. "Knowledge Management and Strategic Orientation: Leveraging Innovativeness and Organizational Performance: The Case of Turkey." *International Conference on Intellectual Capital and Knowledge Management and Organisational Learning*, 1–8. Kidmore End: ACIL.

Allen, Davina. 2018. "Analysing Healthcare Coordination Using Translational Mobilization." *Journal of Health Organization and Management* 32 (3): 358–73. https://doi.org/10.1108/JHOM-05-2017-0116.

Almalki, Mohammed, Gerard Fitzgerald, and Michele Clark. 2011. "Health care system in Saudi Arabia: An overview." *Eastern Mediterranean Health Journal* 17 (10): 784–93.

Al-Otaibi, Abdulah Saleh. 2014. "Assessment of Dominant Organizational Cultures Role in Health Care Provision in Riyadh—Saudi Arabia." *Middle-East Journal of Scientific Research* 21 (10): 1898–907.

Alsoulami, Safe Mohammed, Hasnah Erfan Banjar, and Sabah Mahmoud Mahran. 2018. "Assessment of Organizational Culture at Two Governmental Hospitals in Jeddah City." *Journal of Nursing and Health Science (IOSR-JNHS)* 7 (3): 42–51. https://doi.org/10.9790/1959-0703044251.

Amayah, Angela Titi. 2013. "Determinants of Knowledge Sharing in a Public Sector Organization." *Journal of Knowledge Management* 17 (3): 454–71. https://doi.org/10.1108/JKM-11-2012-0369.

Anand, Bharat N., and Richard L. Daft. 2007. "What Is the Right Organization Design?" *Organizational Dynamics* 36 (4): 329–44. https://doi.org/10.1016/j.orgdyn.2007.06.001.

Andish, HamidAzad, Mojtaba Yousefipour, Hamidreza Shahsavaripour, and Abdolreza Ghorbanipour. 2013. "Organizational Culture and Its Impact in Organizations." *Interdisciplinary Journal of Contemporary Research in Business* 5 (1): 1126–30.

Anning-Dorson, Thomas. 2017. "Moderation-Mediation Effect of Market Demand and Organization Culture on Innovation and Performance Relationship." *Marketing Intelligence & Planning* 35 (2): 222–42.

Antwi, Michael, and Mruganka Kale. 2014. *Change management in healthcare.* Ottawa: The Monieson Centre for Business Research in Healthcare.

Arevuo, Mikko. 2002. *Book review: Knowledge Management: Best Practices in Europe.* http://www.providersedge.com/docs/book_reviews/km_-_best_practices_in_euorpe.pdf

Arrow, Kenneth. 1962. "The Economic Implications of Learning by Doing." *Review of Economic Studies* 29: 155–73.

Asrar-ul-Haq, Muhammad, and Sadia Anwar. 2016. "A Systematic Review of Knowledge Management and Knowledge Sharing: Trends, Issues, and Challenges." *Cogent Business and Management* 3 (1): 1–17. https://doi.org/10.1080/23311975.2015.1127744.

Assem, Patrick Boateng, and Kwaku Agyepong Pabbi. 2016. "Knowledge sharing among healthcare professionals in Ghana." *VINE Journal of Information and Knowledge Management Systems* 46 (4): 479–91. https://doi.org/10.1108/VJIKMS-08-2015-0048.

Athanasiadis, Athanasios, Nikoleta Ratsika, Constantinos Trompoukis, and Anastas Philalithis. 2018. "The Health Decentralization Process in Greece: The Insiders' Perspective." *International Journal of Health Governance* 23 (4): 316–29. https://doi.org/10.1108/IJHG-06-2018-0025.

Azim, Syed, Andy Gale, Therese Lawlor-Wright, Richard Kirkham, Ali Khan, and Mehmood Alam. 2010. "The Importance of Soft Skills in Complex Projects." *International Journal of Managing Projects in Business* 3 (3): 387–401. https://doi.org/10.1108/17538371011056048.

Bajza, Jozef. 2006. *Crnogorsko pitanje*. Podgorica: Vijesti.

Baloh, Peter, Kevin C. Desouza, and Scott Paquette. 2011. "The concept of knowledge." In *Knowledge Management: An Introduction*, edited by Desouza, Kevin C., and Scott Paquette, 35–71. New York: Neal-Schuman Publishers, Inc.

Barão, Alexandre, José Braga de Vasconcelos, Álvaro Rocha, and Ruben Pereira. 2017. "A Knowledge Management Approach to Capture Organizational Learning Networks." *International Journal of Information Management* 37 (6): 735–40. https://doi.org/10.1016/j.ijinfomgt.2017.07.013.

Baumol, William. 1993. "Health Care, Education and the Cost Disease: A Looming Crisis for Public Choice." *Public Choice* 77 (1): 17–28. http://www.jstor.org/stable/30027203

Beardsmore, Elizabeth, and Robert McSherry. 2017. "Healthcare Workers' Perceptions of Organisational Culture and the Impact on the Delivery of Compassionate Quality Care." *Journal of Research in Nursing* 22 (1–2): 42–56. https://doi.org/10.1177/1744987116685594.

Bednar, Michael K., Steven Boivie, and Nicholas R. Prince. 2013. "Burr under the saddle: How media coverage influences strategic change." *Organization Science* 24 (3): 910–25.

Benavides Espinosa, María del Mar, and José María Merigó Lindahl. 2016. "Organizational Design as a Learning Enabler: A Fuzzy-Set Approach." *Journal of Business Research* 69 (4): 1340–44. https://doi.org/10.1016/j.jbusres.2015.10.104.

Bengson, John, and Marc A. Moffett. 2011. *Essays on Knowledge, Mind, and Action.* New York: Oxford University Press.

Bensaou, M., and N. Venkatraman. 1995. "Configurations of interorganizational relationships: A comparison of U.S. and Japanese automakers." *Management Science* 41: 1471–92.

Berthier, Déborah. 2018. *Europe has a shortage of doctors.* Italia: Europe Explained Through Data. European Data Journalism Network.

Bierbooms, Joyce, Hans Van Oers, Jeroen Rijkers, and Inge Bongers. 2016. "Development of a Comprehensive Model for Stakeholder Management in Mental Healthcare." *Journal of Health, Organisation and Management* 30 (4): 630–47. https://doi.org/10.1108/JHOM-01-2016-0004.

Bill of the law on budget of Montenegro for year 2019. http://www.gov.me/ResourceManager/FileDownload.aspx?rId=341877&rType=2.

Bill of the law on budget of Montenegro for year 2020, as defined at 143rd session of the Government of Montenegro on November 14, 2019.

Björnberg, Arne, and Ann Yung Phang. 2019. *Euro Health Consumer Index—2018 Report.* France: Health Consumer Powerhouse.

Blackler, Frank. 1995. "Knowledge, Knowledge Work, and Organisations: An Overview and Interpretation." *Organisation Studies* 16 (6): 1021–46.

Blažić, Đorđije. 2009. *Sistem javne uprave u Crnoj Gori.* Podgorica: Fakultet za državne i evropske studije.

Blažić, Đorđije. 2011. *Sistem lokalne samouprave.* Podgorica: Fakultet za državne i evropske studije.

Bloch, Carter, Mads P. Sørensen, Ebbe K. Graversen, Jesper W. Schneider, Evanthia K. Schmidt, Kaare Aagaard, and Niels Mejlgaard. 2014. "Developing a Methodology to Assess the Impact of Research Grant Funding: A Mixed Methods Approach." *Evaluation and Program Planning* 43: 105–17.

Boder, André. 2006. "Collective Intelligence: A Keystone in Knowledge Management." *Journal of Knowledge Management* 10 (1): 81–93. https://doi.org/10.1108/13673270610650120.

Bosua, Rachelle, and Krishna Venkitachalam. 2013. "Aligning Strategies and Processes in Knowledge Management: A Framework." *Journal of Knowledge Management* 17 (3): 331–46. https://doi.org/10.1108/JKM-10-2012-0323.

Bouncken, Ricarda B. 2002. "Journal of Quality Assurance in Hospitality & Tourism Knowledge Management for Quality Improvements in Hotels." *Journal of Quality Assurance in Hospitality & Tourism* 3 (3–4): 25–59. https://doi.org/10.1300/J162v03n03.

Bremer, Manuel, and Daniel Cohnitz. 2004. *Information and information flow: an introduction.* München. Germany: Walter de Gruyter.

Bremer, Marcella M. W. 2008. *Health care sector examined with the OCAI. Diagnosis: dissatisfied… A National Survey in the Netherlands.* Zwolle, Netherlands: OCAI online.

Brezovšek, Marjan, and Simona Kukovič. 2015. *Evropska javna uprava.* Ljubljana: Fakulteta za družbene vede.

Brezovšek, Marjan, Miro Haček, and Simona Kukovič. 2015. *Javna uprava.* Ljubljana: Faculty of Social Sciences.

Burau, Viola, and Karsten Vrangbæk. 2008. "Institutions and Non-Linear Change in Governance: Reforming the Governance of Medical Performance in Europe." *Journal of Health, Organisation and Management* 22 (4): 350–67. https://doi.org/10.1108/14777260810893953.

Burton, Richard M. 2013. "The Future of Organization Design: An Interpretative Synthesis in Three Themes." *Journal of Organization Design* 2 (1): 42. https://doi.org/10.7146/jod.7363.

Burton, Richard M., and Børge Obel. 1998. *Strategic Organizational Diagnosis and Design: Developing Theory for Application.* Boston, Massachusetts: Kluwer Publishers.

Burton, Richard M., Jørgen Lauridsen, and Børge Obel. 2003. "Erratum: Return on Assets Loss from Situational and Contingency Misfits (Management Science (2002) 48: 1461–585)." *Management Science* 49 (8): 1119. https://doi.org/10.1287/mnsc.49.8.1119.16404.

Burton, Richard. M., Børge Obel, and Dorthe Døjbak Håkonsson. 2015. *Organizational Design: A Step-By-Step Approach.* Cambridge: Cambridge University Press.

Cabrera, Elizabeth, and Angel Cabrera. 2005. "Fostering knowledge sharing through people management practices." *International Journal of Human Resource Management* 16 (5), 720–35.

Cameron, Kim S., and Robert E. Quinn. 2011. *Diagnosing and Changing Organizational Cutlure: Based on the Competing Values Framework.* San Francisco, California: John Wiley & Sons.

Carmeli, Abraham, Roy Gelbard, and David Gefen. 2010. "The Importance of Innovation Leadership in Cultivating Strategic Fit and Enhancing Firm Performance." *Leadership Quarterly* 21 (3): 339–49. https://doi.org/10.1016/j.leaqua.2010.03.001.

Carvalho, Marly Monteiro De, and Roque Rabechini Junior. 2015. "Impact of Risk Management on Project Performance: The Importance of Soft Skills." *International*

Journal of Production Research 53 (2): 321–40. https://doi.org/10.1080/00207543.2014.919423.

Cavicchi, Caterina. 2017. "Healthcare Sustainability and the Role of Intellectual Capital: Evidence from an Italian Regional Health Service." *Journal of Intellectual Capital* 18 (3): 544–63. https://doi.org/10.1108/JIC-12-2016-0128.

Cegarra-Navarro, Juan Gabriel, and Gabriel Cepeda-Carrión. 2010. "How to Implement a Knowledge Management Program in Hospital-in-the-Home Units." *Leadership in Health Services* 23 (1): 46–56. https://doi.org/10.1108/17511871011013760.

Cegarra-Navarro, Juan-Gabriel, Pedro Soto-Acosta, and Anthony K. P. Wensley. 2016. "Structured knowledge processes and firm performance: the role of organizational agility." *Journal of Business Research* 69 (5): 1544–49.

CEMI—Center for Monitoring and Research. 2012. "What is the price of health care? Public opinion survey on corruption in health care and patients' rights in the Public Health System of Montenegro—Analytical report." http://cemi.org.me/wp-content/uploads/2017/01/Rezultati-istrazivanja-KORUPCIJI-U-ZDRAVSTVU.pdf

Cepeda-Carrion, Ignacio, Silvia Martelo-Landroguez, Antonio L. Leal-Rodríguez, and Antonio Leal-Millán. 2017. "Critical Processes of Knowledge Management: An Approach toward the Creation of Customer Value." *European Research on Management and Business Economics* 23 (1): 1–7. https://doi.org/10.1016/j.iedeen.2016.03.001.

Certo, Samuel C., and Travis S. Certo. 2011. *Modern Management: Concepts and Skills*. Upper Saddle River, NJ: Prentice Hall.

Chambers, Naomi. 2012. Healthcare board governance. *Journal of Health Organization and Management* 26(1): 6–14. https://doi.org/10.1108/14777261211211133.

Chandler, Alfred Dupont. 1962. *Strategy and Structure: Chapters in the History of American Enterprise*. Boston: MIT Press.

Chidambaranathan, Kumaresan, and B. S. Swarooprani. 2017. "Analyzing the Relationship between Organizational Culture and Knowledge Management Dimensions in Higher Education Libraries." *Journal of Librarianship and Information Science* 49 (1): 57–68. https://doi.org/10.1177/0961000615622678.

Choi, Kui Son, Woo Hyun Cho, Sunhee Lee, Hanjoon Lee, and Chankon Kim. 2004. "The Relationships among Quality, Value, Satisfaction and Behavioral Intention in Health Care Provider Choice: A South Korean Study." *Journal of Business Research* 57 (8): 913–21. https://doi.org/10.1016/S0148-2963(02)00293-X.

Clark, Peter. 1975. "Organizational Design: A Review of Key Problems." *Administration & Society* 7(2), 213–56. London: Sage Publications.

Claver-Cortés, Enrique, Patrocinio Zaragoza-Sáez, and Eva Pertusa-Ortega. 2007. "Organizational Structure Features Supporting Knowledge Management Processes." *Journal of Knowledge Management* 11 (4): 45–57. https://doi.org/10.1108/13673270710762701.

Coaffee, Jon, and Lorraine Johnston. 2005. "The Management of Local Government Modernisation: Area Decentralisation and Pragmatic Localism." *International Journal of Public Sector Management* 18 (2): 164–77. https://doi.org/10.1108/09513550510584982.

Coleman, Katie, Brian T. Austin, Cindy Brach, and Edward H. Wagner. 2009. Evidence on the Chronic Care Model in the New Millennium. *Health Affairs* 28: 75–85. https://doi.org/10.1377/hlthaff.28.1.7528/1/75.

Collins, C., and A. Green. 1994. "Decentralization and Primary Health Care: Some Negative Implications in Developing Countries." *International Journal of Health Services* 24 (3): 459–75. https://doi.org/10.2190/G1XJ-PX06-1LVD-2FXQ.

CoronaInfoCG—Web-site of the Government of Montenegro and the National Coordination Body for Contagious Diseases of Montenegro. www.coronainfocg.me.

Da Silva, Flavio Soares Correa, and Jaume Agusti-Cullell. 2008. *Information Flow and Knowledge Sharing*. Amsterdam, Netherlands: Elsevier Science.

Daft, Richard L. 2013. *Understanding the Theory & Design of Organizations (11th edition—international edition)*. Canada: Cengage Learning.

Dalkir, Kimiz. 2005. *Knowledge Management in Theory and Practice*. Oxford: Elsevier.

Damanpour, Fariborz, and Marguerite Schneider. 2006. "Phases of the Adoption of Innovation in Organizations: Effects of Environment, Organization and Top Managers." *British Journal of Management* 17 (3): 215–36. https://doi.org/10.1111/j.1467-8551.2006.00498.x.

Davenport, Thomas H., David W. De Long, and Michael C. Beers. 1998. "Successful knowledge management projects." *Sloan Management Review* 39 (2): 43–57.

Davenport, Thomas H., and Laurence Prusak. 1998. *Working knowledge: How organisations manage what they know?* Boston: Harvard Business School Press.

Davies, Huw Talfryn Oakley, and Russell Mannion. 2013. "Will Prescriptions for Cultural Change Improve the NHS?" *BMJ (Online)* 346 (7900): 1–4. https://doi.org/10.1136/bmj.f1305.

Deakins, David, and Mark Freel. 2012. *Entrepreneurship and Small Firms.*McGraw-Hill Europe.

Decision on network of health institutions (Official Gazette of Montenegro 37/16, 48/17 and 12/18).

Decree on organization and manner of work of state administration of Montenegro. 2018. (Official Gazette of Montenegro 87/18, 02/19 and 38/19).

Denscombe, Martyn. 2008. "Communities of practice: A research paradigm for the mixed methods approach." *Journal of Mixed Methods Research* 2 (3): 270–83.

Denzin, Norman. K. 2017. *The Research Act: A Theoretical Introduction to Sociological Methods*. United Kingdom: Routledge.

Desouza, Kevin C. 2011. "An Introduction to Knowledge Management." In *Knowledge Management: An Introduction* 3–34, edited by Kevin C. Desouza. New York: Neal-Schuman Publishers, Inc.

Dickinson, Helen, and Jon Pierre. 2016. "Between Substance and Governance: Healthcare Governance and the Limits to Reform." *Journal of Health Organization and Management* 30 (1), 109–16. https://doi.org/10.1108/JHOM-09-2015-0144.

Dierickx, Ingemar, and Karel Cool. 1989. "Asset Stock Accumulation and Sustainability of Competitive Advantage." *Management Science* 35: 1504–11.

Dimovski, Vlado, Sandra Penger, and Miha Škerlavaj. 2007. *Organising and Decision-Making, Selected Chapters for Post-Graduate Studies.* Ljubljana: Ekonomski fakultet.

Dimovski, Vlado, Sandra Penger, Judita Peterlin, Barbara Grah, Matej Černe, and Maja Klepec. 2017. *Advanced Management and Leadership Practice.* Harlow, England: Pearson.

Dimovski, Vlado, Sandra Penger, Miha Škerlavaj, and Jana Žnidaršić. 2005. *Učeća se Organizacija: Ustvarite Podjetje Znanja [Learning Organization: Creathe the Company of Knowledge].* Ljubljana: GV založba.

Dinh, Thy, and Fares Bounajm. 2013. *Improving Primary Health Care Through Collaboration: Briefing 3—Measuring the Missed Opportunity.* The Conference Board of Canada. www.conferenceboard.ca/e-library/abstract.aspx?did=5479.

Dobrzykowski, David D., Stephen K. Callaway, and Mark A. Vonderembse. 2015. "Examining Pathways from Innovation Orientation to Patient Satisfaction: A Relational View of Healthcare Delivery." *Decision Sciences* 46 (5): 863–99. https://doi.org/10.1111/deci.12161.

Domnariu, Carmen, Mihaela Cernuşcă-Miţariu, and Minerva Boitan. 2013. "Organizational Culture—Important Factor in Delivering High Quality Health Care." *Metalurgia International* 18 (8): 5–7.

Đorđević-Boljanović, Jelena. 2009. *Menadžment znanja.* Beograd: Data Status.

Dotty, Harold D., William H. Glick, and George P. Huber. 1993. "Fit, Equifinality and Organizational Effectiveness: A Test of Two Configurational Theories." *Academy of Management Journal* 38 (6): 1196–250.

Downes, Trevor Vernon. 2014. *An Evaluation of Knowledge Management Practices in Nonprofit Community Services Organisations in Australia (DBA thesis).* Lismore: Southern Cross University.

Drotz, Erik, and Bozena Poksinska. 2014. "Lean in Healthcare from Employees' Perspectives." *Journal of Health, Organisation and Management* 28 (2): 177–95. https://doi.org/10.1108/JHOM-03-2013-0066.

Drucker, Peter F. 1999. "Knowledge—Worker Productivity: The Biggest Challenge." *California Management Review* 41 (2): 79–94.

Drucker, Peter F. 1999. *Management Challenges for the 21th Century.* New York: Harper Collins.

Drucker, Peter. F. 2007. *The Effective Executive.* London: Routledge. https://doi.org/10.4324/9780080549354.

Dumitriu, Petru. 2016. *Knowledge Management in the United Nations System.* Geneva: United Nations.

Dunić, Mirjana. 2017. "Metodičko uputstvo za primenu mape znanja u nastavi informatike i računarstva." *Informacione tehnologije, obrazovanje i preduzetništvo* 17: 209–16.

Đurović, Gordana. 2017. *Evropska unija i Crna Gora: Proces pristupanja.* Podgorica: EU Info centar.

Eisenmann, Charles. 1988. *Cours de droit administratif, Tome I, X edition* 221–250. Paris; LGDJ editions.

Eklof, Mats, and Gunnar Ahlborg. 2016. "Improving Communication Among Healthcare Workers: A Controlled Study." *Journal of Workplace Learning* 28 (2): 81–96. https://doi.org/10.1108/JWL-06-2015-0050.

El Morr, Christo, and Julien Subercaze. 2010. "Knowledge Management in Healthcare." In *Handbook of Research on Developments in E-health and Telemedicine: Technological and Social Perspectives*, edited by Cruz-Cunha, Maria Manuela, Antonio J. Tavares, and Ricardo Simoes, 490–510. Hershey: IGI Global.

Elona, Guga. 2018. "Local Government Modernization in Albania: Historical Background and the Territorial Reform 2015–2020." *International Journal of Public Sector Management* 31 (4): 466–506.

Epetimehin, Festus M., and Oluwayomi Ekundayo. 2011. "Organisational Knowledge Management: Survival strategy for Nigeria Insurance Industry." *Interdisciplinary Review of Economics and Management* 1 (2): 9–15.

Epstein, Joshua. 2013. *Agent_Zero: Toward Neurocognitive Foundations of Generative Social Science.* Princeton: Princeton University Press.

Erzberger, Christian, and Udo Kelle. 2003. "Making inferences in mixed methods: the rules of integration." In *Handbook of Mixed Methods in Social and Behavioural Research*, edited by Tashakkori, Abbas, and Charles Teddlie. London: Sage.

European Union. 2018. "Directive (EU) 2018/1972 of the European Parliament and of the Council of 11 December 2018." https://eur-lex.europa.eu/legal-content/EN/TXT/PDF/?uri=CELEX:32018L1972&from=DE.

Eurostat. 2020. "Database." https://ec.europa.eu/eurostat/data/database

Farjoun, Moshe. 1994. "Beyond Industry Boundaries: Human Expertise, Diversification and Resource-Related Industry Groups." *Organization Science* 5: 185–199.

Farnham, Daniel, and Sylvia Horton. 1996. *Managing the New Public Services.* London: Macmillan.

Fenwick, John, and Mark Bailey. 1999. "Local Government Reorganisation in the UK: Decentralisation or Corporatism?" *International Journal of Public Sector Management* 12 (3): 249–261. https://doi.org/10.1108/09513559910267404.

Fields, Dail L. 2007. "Determinants of Follower Perceptions of a Leader's Authenticity and Integrity." *European Management Journal* 25 (3): 195–206.

Forcadell, Francisco J., and Fátima Guadamillas. 2002. "A Case Study on the Implementation of a Knowledge Management Strategy Oriented to Innovation." *Knowledge and Process Management* 9 (3): 162–171.

Ford, Randal, and Ingo Angermeier. 2008. "Creating a Learning Health Care Organization for Participatory Management: A Case Analysis." *Journal of Health, Organisation and Management* 22 (3): 269–93. https://doi.org/10.1108/14777260810883549.

Galbraith, Jay R. 1974. "Organization design: An information processing view." In *Organizational Sociology*, edited by Scott, W. Richard. Brookfield: Dartmouth Publishing Company.

Galbraith, Jay R. 1995. *Designing Organizations. An Executive Briefing on Strategy, Structure + Process.* San Francisco, CA: Jossey-Bass.

Gao, Fei, M. Meng, and Steve Clarke. 2008. "Knowledge, Management, and Knowledge Management in Business Operations." *Journal of Knowledge Management* 12 (2): 3–17. https://doi.org/10.1108/13673270810859479.

Garpenby, Peter, and Karin Bäckman. 2016. "Formal Priority Setting in Health Care: The Swedish Experience." *Journal of Health, Organisation and Management* 30 (6): 891–907. https://doi.org/10.1108/JHOM-09-2014-0150.

Gerstlberger, Wolfgang Dieter, and Karsten Schneider. 2013. "Outsourcing and Concession Models as Door Opener for Public-Private Partnerships in the European Health Sector?" *International Journal of Public Sector Management* 26 (7): 554–75. https://doi.org/10.1108/IJPSM-12-2011-0143.

Ghosh, Biswadip, and Judy E. Scott. 2007. "Effective Knowledge Management Systems for a Clinical Nursing Setting." *Information Systems Management* 24 (1): 73–84. https://doi.org/10.1080/10580530601038188.

Goddard, Maria, and Russell Mannion. 2006. "Decentralising the NHS: Rhetoric, Reality and Paradox." *Journal of Health, Organisation and Management* 20 (1): 67–73. https://doi.org/10.1108/14777260610656561.

Gohary, Ali, and Bahman Hamzelu. 2016. "Modeling Customer Knowledge Management to Make Value Co-Creation." *Business Information Review* 33 (1): 19–27. https://doi.org/10.1177/0266382116631850.

Government of Montenegro—Press release from 143rd session of the Government. Available at: http://www.gsv.gov.me/vijesti/214755/Saopstenje-sa-143-sjednice-Vlade-Crne-Gore.html, 26. 11. 2019

Grafenauer, Božo, and Boštjan Brezovnik. 2006. *Javna uprava.* Maribor: Faculty of Law.

Grah, Barbara. 2016. *Mind-Based Learning Organization Model Building—Unpublished Doctoral Dissertation.* Ljubljana: University of Ljubljana, Faculty of Economics.

Greer, Patrick, Anne Murphy, and Morten Ogard. 2005. *Guide to participatory democracy in Bosnia and Herzegovina and Serbia and Montenegro.* Strasbourg: Council of Europe Publishing.

Greiner, Martina E., Tilo Bohmann, and Helmut Krcmar. 2007. "A Strategy for Knowledge Management." *Journal of Knowledge Management* 11 (6): 3–15. https://doi.org/10.1108/13673270710832127.

Grønhaug, Kjell, and Odd Nordhaug. 1992. "Strategy and Competence in Firms." *European Management Journal* 10 (4): 438–44.

Gururajan, Vijaya, and Dieter Fink. 2010. "Attitudes towards knowledge transfer in an environment to perform." *Journal of Knowledge Management* 14 (6): 828–40. https://doi.org/10.1108/13673211011084880.

Gustavsson, Susanne, Ida Gremyr, and Elisabeth Kenne Sarenmalm. 2016. "Using an Adapted Approach to the Kano Model to Identify Patient Needs from Various Patient Roles." *TQM Journal* 28 (1): 151–62. https://doi.org/10.1108/TQM-04-2013-0050.

Haček, Miro, Simona Kukovič, and Marjan Brezovšek. 2017. *Slovenian Politics and the State.* Lanham, Boulder, New York and London: Lexington Books.

Hammad, Salah A., Ruzita Jusoh, and Imam Ghozali. 2013. "Decentralization, Perceived Environmental Uncertainty, Managerial Performance and Management

Accounting System Information in Egyptian hospitals." *International Journal of Accounting and Information Management* 21 (4): 314–30. http://dx.doi.org/10.1108/IJAIM-02-2012-0005.

Hansen, Morten T., Nitin Nohria, and Thomas J. Tierney. 1999. "What's your strategy for managing knowledge?" *Harvard Business Review* 77 (2): 106.

Harding, Kelli. 2019a. *The Rabbit Effect: Live Longer, Happier, and Healthier with the Groundbreaking Science of Kindness.* Columbia University Medical Center, Atria Books—Simon & Schuster.

Harding, Kelli. 2019b. *Why Kindness Is the Key to Improved Well-being. Knowledge & Wharton. Online Research and Business Analysis Journal.* Wharton School of the University of Pennsylvania. https://knowledge.wharton.upenn.edu/article/science-kindness-harding-book

Harrington, H. James, and Frank Voehl. 2010. "Innovation in Health Care." *International Journal of Innovation Science* 2 (1): 13–27. https://doi.org/10.1260/1757-2223.2.1.13(2010).

Harrison, Joseph S., Gary R. Thurgood, Steven Boivie and Michael D. Pfarrer. 2018. "Perception Is Reality: How CEOs' Observed Personality Influences Market Perceptions of Firm Risk and Shareholder Returns." *Academy of Management Journal, In Press.* https://journals.aom.org/doi/abs/10.5465/amj.2018.0626.

Hedman, Jonas, and Thomas Kalling. 2002. *IT and Business Models: Concepts and Theories.* Copenhagen: Copenhagen Business School Press.

Heilmann, Sebastian. 2008. "From Local Experiments to National Policy: The Origins of China's Distinctive Policy Process." *The China Journal* 59: 1–30.

Heiser, Stuart. 2019. *New Findings Confirm Predictions on Physician Shortage.* Washington: Association of American Medical Colleges. https://www.aamc.org/news-insights/press-releases/new-findings-confirm-predictions-physician-shortage

Heisig, Peter, Suraj Olunifesi, Adekunle Aino, Kianto Cosmas Kemboi, Gregorio Perez-Arrau, Nasser Easa, and Gregorio Perez. 2016. "Journal of Knowledge Management For Authors Knowledge Management and Business Performance: Global Ex- Perts' Views on Future Research Needs." *Journal of Knowledge Management* 20 (6). http://dx.doi.org/10.1108/JKM-12-2015-0521.

Hinrichs, Gina. 2009. "Organic Organizational Design." *OD Practitioner* 41 (4): 4–12.

Hislop, Donald. 2010. "Knowledge Management As An Ephemeral Management Fashion?" *Journal of Knowledge Management* 14 (6): 779–90.

Hislop, Donald. 2013. *Knowledge Management in Organisations: A Critical Introduction (3rd Ed.).* Oxford University Press.

Hodge, Billy J., William P. Anthony, and Lawrence M. Gales. 2003. *Teoría de la organización: Un enfoque estratégico.* Madrid: Prentice Hall.

Hooper, Daire, Joseph Coughlan, and Michael R. Mullen. 2008. "Structural Equation Modeling: Guidelines for Determining Model Fit." *Electronic Journal of Business Research Methods* 6: 53–60.

Hoover, Kenneth, and Todd Donovan. 2011. *The Elements of Social Scientific Thinking.* Spain: Wadsworth Cengage Learning.

Hoss, Robert, and Art Schlussel. 2009. *Metrics that assess an organization's KM state*. Pennsylvania: United States Army War College. www.digitalgovernment.com/media/Downloads/asset_upload_file66_2654.pdf

HR Magazine. 2009. "Leveraging HR and Knowledge Management in a Challenging Economy." *SHRM Research Quarterly* 54 (6): 1–10.

Hsu, Yen. 2017. "Organizational Innovation, Design and Npd Performance: The Role of Co-Creation Strategy." *International Journal of Innovation Management* 21 (4): 1–19. https://doi.org/10.1142/S1363919617500335.

Hussinki, Henri, Aino Kianto, Mika Vanhala, and Paavo Ritala. 2017. "Assessing the Universality of Knowledge Management Practices." *Journal of Knowledge Management* 21 (6). https://doi.org/10.1108/JKM-09-2016-0394.

Idris, Ahmad. 2017. "Penggunaan Organizational Culture Assesment Instrument Pada Organisasi Non Formal." *Jurnal Ekonomi Modernisasi* 13 (2): 53. https://doi.org/10.21067/jem.v13i2.1767.

Ilić, Mirjana. 1996. *Naučno istraživanje—opšta metodologija*. Beograd: Filološki fakultet.

Institut Alternativa (2016). *Koliko građana u Crnoj Gori učestvuje u javnim raspravama o budžetima svojih opština?* http://www.mojgrad.me/images/infografici/mojgrad-koliko-gradjani-cg-ucestvuju-u-javnim-raspravama-o-budzetu-opstina.png

International Monetary Fund 2020. https://www.imf.org/en/Countries/MNE.

Ivanović, Predrag. 2007. *Strategijski menadžment*. Podgorica: Ekonomski fakultet Univerziteta Crne Gore.

Jacobs, Jane. 1969. *The Economy of Cities*. New York: Vintage.

Jandavath, Rama Krishna Naik, and Anand Byram. 2016. "Healthcare Service Quality Effect on Patient Satisfaction and Behavioural Intentions in Corporate Hospitals in India." *International Journal of Pharmaceutical and Healthcare Marketing* 10 (1): 48–74. https://doi.org/10.1108/IJPHM-07-2014-0043.

Jasimuddin, Sajjad M. 2008. "A Holistic View of Knowledge Management Strategy." *Journal of Knowledge Management* 12 (2): 57–66. https://doi.org/10.1108/13673270810859514.

Johnson, Anya, Helena Nguyen, Markus Groth, Karyn Wang, and Ju Li Ng. 2016. "Time to change: a review of organisational culture change in health care organisations." *Journal of Organizational Effectiveness: People and Performance* 3 (3): 265–88. https://doi.org/10.1108/joepp-06-2016-0040.

Jorma, Tapani, Hanna Tiirinki, Risto Bloigu, and Leena Turkki. 2016. "Leadership in Health Services LEAN Thinking in Finnish Healthcare LEAN Thinking in Finnish Healthcare." *Leadership in Health Services International Journal of Health Care Quality Assurance Iss Leadership in Health Services* 29 (2): 9–36.

Kamhawi, Emad M. 2012. "Knowledge Management Fishbone: A Standard Framework of Organizational Enablers." *Journal of Knowledge Management* 16 (5): 808–28. https://doi.org/10.1108/13673271211262826.

Kassak, Kassem M., A. Mohammad Ali, Mitra Tauk, and A. M. Abdallah. 2007. "The Quest for Health Care Decentralization: Revisiting decree 159." *Journal of Public Budgeting, Accounting & Financial Management* 19 (4): 447–61. https://doi.org/10.1108/JPBAFM-19-04-2007-B002.

Katon, Wayne, Elizabeth Lin, Michael Von Korff, Paul Ciechanowski, Evette Ludman, Bessie Young, Do Peterson, Carolyn M. Rutter, Mary McGregor, and David McCulloch. 2011. "Collaborative Care for Depression and Chronic Illnesses." *New England Journal of Medicine* 364 (13): 1278–79.

Kavčić, Matic, Majda Pahor, and Barbara Domajnko. 2015. "User involvement in Slovenian healthcare." *Journal of Health Organization and Management* 29 (5): 595–610. https://doi.org/10.1108/JHOM-06-2014-0095.

Kennewell, Suzanne, and Laura Baker. 2016. "Benefits and Risks of Shared Services in Healthcare." *Journal of Health, Organisation and Management* 30 (3): 441–56. https://doi.org/10.1108/JHOM-03-2014-0044.

Kern, Anja. 2006. "Exploring the Relation Between Creativity and Rules: The Case of the Performing Arts." *International Studies of Management & Organization* 36 (1): 63–80. https://doi.org/10.2753/imo0020-8825360104.

Ketchen, David. J., and Donald D. Bergh. 2004. *Research Methodology in Strategy and Management.* Germany: Heidelberg.

Kim, Daniel H. 1993. "The link between individual and organizational learning." *Sloan Management Review* 35 (1): 37–50.

Kingsnorth, Rebecca. 2013. "Partnerships for Health and Wellbeing: Transferring Public Health Responsibilities to Local Authorities." *Journal of Integrated Care* 21 (2): 64–76. https://doi.org/10.1108/14769011311316006.

Kojo Sakyi, Emmanuel, John Koku Awoonor-Williams, and Francis Anderson Adzei. 2011. "Barriers to implementing health sector administrative decentralisation in Ghana: a study of the Nkwanta district health management team." *Journal of Health Organization and Management* 25 (4): 400–19. http://dx.doi.org/10.1108/14777261111155038.

Koohborfardhaghighi, S., and J. Altmann. 2017. "How Organizational Structure Affects Organizational Learning." *Journal of Integrated Design and Process Science* 21 (1): 43–60. https://doi.org/10.3233/jid-2017-0006.

Košutić, Budimir. 2002. *Uvod u velike pravne sisteme današnjice.* Beograd: Službeni list SRJ.

Kotler, Philip. 2000. *Marketing management.* Upper Saddle River: Prentice Hall.

Koufteros, Xenophon A., Abraham Y. Nahm, T. C. Edwin Cheng, and Kee-hung Lai. 2007. "An Empirical Assessment of a Nomological Network of Organizational Design Constructs: From Culture to Structure to Pull Production to Performance." *International Journal of Production Economics* 106 (2): 468–92.

Kukovič, Simona. 2018. "Coping with Demographic Challenges: Case of Slovenian Local Communities." *Journal of Comparative Politics* 11 (2): 83–100.

Labonte, Alan J., Justin K. Benzer, James F. Burgess, Irene E. Cramer, Mark Meterko, Terri K. Pogoda, and Martin P. Charns. 2016. "The Effects of Organization Design and Patient Perceptions of Care on Switching Behavior and Reliance on a Health Care System Across Time." *Medical Care Research and Review* 73 (2): 182–204. https://doi.org/10.1177/1077558715601543.

Lajh, Damjan, and Alenka Krašovec. 2010. "Slovenia." In *Nations in Transit 2010: Democratization from Central Europe to Eurasia*, edited by Lisa Mootz, 495–510. New York: Freedom House. www.refworld.org/pdfid/4d53f0261a.pdf

Larson, Anne M., and Jesse Ribot. 2004. "Natural resources lens: an introduction." *European Journal of Development Research* 16 (1): 1–25.
Law on Accounting of Montenegro—2016. (Official Gazzette of Montenegro 52/16).
Law on Administrative Procedure of Montenegro—2017 (Official Gazzette of Montenegro 56/14, 20/15, 40/16 and 37/17).
Law on Contributions for Mandatory Social Insurance Official Gazzette of Montenegro 13/2007, 79/2008, 86/2009, 78/2010, 40/2011—second law 14/2012, 62/2013, 8/2015, 22/2017 and 42/2019).
Law on Health Care—2018. (Official Gazzette of Montenegro 03/16, 39/16, 02/17, 44/18 and 24/19).
Law on Self-Government of Montenegro—2018. (Official Gazzette of Montenegro 02/18 and 34/19).
Law on State Administration of Montenegro—2018. (Official Gazzette of Montenegro 78/18).
Law on Territorial Organization of Montenegro (Official Gazzette of Montenegro 54/11, 26/12, 27/13, 62/13, 12/14, 03/16, 31/17 and 86/18).
Lawrence, Paul R., and Jay W. Lorsch. 1967. "Differentiation and Integration in Complex Organizations." *Administrative Science Quarterly* 12 (1): 1–47.
Lazović, Vujica, and Tamara Đuričković. 2018. *Digitalna ekonomija: Nešto već znamo, nešto naslućujemo, a nečega još uvijek nijesmo svjesni!* Autorsko izdanje. Cetinje: Štamparija Obod.
Leary, R. Mark. 2001. *Introduction to Behavioral Research Methods.* Boston: Allyn and Bacon.
Leavitt, Harold J. 1964. "Applied Organization Change in Industry: Structural, Technical and Human Approaches." In *New Perspectives in Organization Research*, edited by William W. Cooper, Harold J. Leavitt, and Maynard Wolfe Shelly. New York: John Wiley & Sons.
Lee, Hanjoon, Linda M. Delene, Anne Mary Bunda, and Kim Chankon. 2000. "Methods of Measuring Health-Care Service Quality." *Journal of Business Research* 48 (3): 233–46. https://doi.org/10.1016/s0148-2963(98)00089-7.
Lee, Heeseok, and Byounggu Choi. 2003. "Knowledge Management Enablers, Processes, and Organizational Performance: An Integrative View and Empirical Examination." *Journal of Management Information Systems* 20 (1): 179–228. https://doi.org/10.1080/07421222.2003.11045756.
Lojpur, Anđelko and Mirjana Kuljak. 2005. *Menadžment.* Podgorica: Ekonomski fakultet.
López, Susana Pérez, José Manuel Montes Peón, and Camilo José Vázquez Ordás. 2006. "The Organisational Context of Learning: An Empirical Analysis." *International Journal of Technology Management* 35 (1–4): 196–223. https://doi.org/10.1504/ijtm.2006.009235.
Mahmoudsalehi, Mehdi, Roya Moradkhannejad, and Khalil Safari. 2012. "How Knowledge Management Is Affected by Organizational Structure." *Learning Organization* 19 (6): 518–28. https://doi.org/10.1108/09696471211266974.
Mandal, Santanu. 2017. "The Influence of Organizational Culture on Healthcare Supply Chain Resilience: Moderating Role of Technology Orientation." *Journal of*

Business and Industrial Marketing 32 (8): 1021–37. https://doi.org/10.1108/JBIM-08-2016-0187.

Marshall, Alfred. 1890. *Principles of Economics*. London: Macmillan.

Mårtensson, Maria. 2000. "A Critical Review of Knowledge Management as a Management Tool." *Journal of Knowledge Management* 4 (3): 204–16. https://doi.org/10.1108/13673270010350002.

Mašić, Branislav, Lepa Babić, Jelena Đorđević-Boljanović, Gordana Dobrijević, and Sveto Veselinović. 2010. *Menadžment*. Beograd: Univerzitet Singidunum.

Maslow, Abraham Harold. 1943. "A Theory of Human Motivation." *Psychological Review* 50 (4): 370–96.

McCluskey, William J., and Igor Bevc. 2007. "Fiscal Decentralization in the Republic of Slovenia: An Opportunity for the Property Tax." *Property Management* 25 (4): 400–19. https://doi.org/10.1108/02637470710775220.

McColl-Kennedy, Janet, Lillemay Cheung, Elizabeth Ferrier. 2015. "Co-creating service experience practices." *Journal of Service Management* 26: 249–75. doi: 10.1108/JOSM-08-2014-0204.

Mehdibeigi, Najme, Masoud Dehghani, and Mohammad Nour Yaghoubi. 2016. "Customer Knowledge Management and Organization's Effectiveness: Explaining the Mediator Role of Organizational Agility." *Procedia - Social and Behavioral Sciences* 230 (May): 94–103. https://doi.org/10.1016/j.sbspro.2016.09.012.

Meirovich, Gavriel, Yael Brender-Ilan, and Alexander Meirovich. 2013. "Quality of Hospital Service: The Impact of Formalization and Decentralization." *International Journal of Health Care Quality Assurance* 20: 572–84. http://dx.doi.org/10.1108/09526860710822716.

Miles, Raymond E., and Charles Curtis Snow. 1978. *Organizational Strategy, Structure and Process*. New York: McGraw-Hill.

Miles, Raymond E., Grant Miles, and Charles Curtis Snow. 2005. *Collaborative Entrepreneurship: How Communities of Networked Firms Use Continuous Innovation to create Economic Wealth*. Palo Alto: Stanford University Press.

Millar, Ross, Weiyan Jian, Russel Mannion, and Robin Miller. 2016. "Healthcare Reform in China: Making Sense of a Policy Experiment?" *Journal of Health Organization and Management* 30 (3): 324–30. https://doi.org/10.1108/JHOM-12-2014-0200(2016).

Miller, Leon Monroe. 2015. "E-health: Knowledge Generation, Value Intangibles, and Intellectual Capital." *International Journal of Healthcare Management* 8 (2): 100–11.

Milošević, Milena. 2018. *Reforma javne uprave: Koliko daleko je 2020?* Podgorica: Institut Alternativa. http://media.mojauprava.me/2017/09/Reforma-javne-uprave_web.pdf.

Ministry of Finance of Montenegro—Explanation of the Current Budget, Reserves and Budget by Functional Classification (2009–2019).

Ministry of Public Administration. 2019. "European Charter of Local Self-Governments." http://www.mju.gov.me/ResourceManager/FileDownload.aspx?rId=268782&rType=2

Mintzberg, Henry. 1980. "Structure in 5's: A Synthesis of the Research on Organization Design." *Management Science* 26 (3): 322–41. https://doi.org/10.1287/mnsc.26.3.322.

Mohrman, Susan Albers, and Abraham B. Rami Shani. 2014. *Healthcare: An Ecosystem in Transition. Organizing for Sustainable Effectiveness,* Vol. 4. Emerald Group Publishing Limited. https://doi.org/10.1108/S2045-060520140000004005.

Monenegrin Employers Federation. 2020. https://www.poslodavci.org/biblioteka/publikacije/ko-vid-je-zaustavio-biznis.

Montenegro Travel—The Official website of Montenegro Tourism. 2021. www.montenegro.travel.

Monteverde, Kirk, and David J. Teece. 1982. "Supplier Switching Costs and Vertical Integration in the Automobile Industry." *The Bell Journal of Economics* 13 (1): 206. https://doi.org/10.2307/3003441.

Muriana, Cinzia, and Giovanni Vizzini. 2017. "Project Risk Management: A Deterministic Quantitative Technique for Assessment and Mitigation." *International Journal of Project Management* 35 (3): 320–40. https://doi.org/10.1016/j.ijproman.2017.01.010.

Myllärniemi, Jussi, Harri Laihonen, Henri Karppinen, and Kaisa Seppänen. 2012. "Knowledge Management Practices in Healthcare Services." *Measuring Business Excellence* 16 (4): 54–65. https://doi.org/10.1108/13683041211276447.

Nambisan Priya, and Satish Nambisan. 2009. "Models of Consumer Value Cocreation in Health Care." *Health Care Management Review* 34 (4): 344–54. https://doi.org/10.1097/HMR.0b013e3181abd528.

Nelson, Richard R, and Winter G. Sidney. 1982. *An Evolutionary Theory of Economic Change.* Cambridge: Belknap Press of Harvard University Press.

Nonaka, Ikujiro, and Hirotaka Takeuchi. 1995. *The Knowledge Creating Company.* New York: Oxford University Press.

Nonaka, Ikujiro. 1994. "A Dynamic Theory of Organisational Knowledge Creation." *Organisation Science* 5 (1): 14–37.

Nonaka, Ikujiro, Ryoko Toyama, and Noboru Konno. 2000. "SECI, Ba and Leadership: A Unified Model of Dynamic Knowledge Creation." *Long Range Planning* 33 (1): 5–34. https://doi.org/10.1016/S0024-6301(99)00115-6.

North, Klaus, and Tina Hornung. 2003. "The Benefits of Knowledge Management - Results of the German Award 'Knowledge Manager 2002." *Journal of Universal Computer Science* 9 (6): 463–71. https://doi.org/10.3217/jucs-009-06-0463.

Northouse, Peter Guy. 2008. *Liderstvo: teorija i praksa.* Beograd: Data Status.

Novaković, Pavle. (2012). *Perper crnogorski novac.* II izdanje. Cetinje: Antikva Montenegrina.

O'Reilly III, Charles, and Michael L. Tushman. 2004. "The Ambidextrous Organization." *Harvard Business Review* 82: 74–81.

Obel, Burton 1993." Strategi og Ledelse—Er der en sammenhæng? In *Strategi og Ledelse, Veje og Visioner mod ar 2000*, edited by S. Hildebrandt, 396–408. Herning, Systime (in Danish).

OCAI Online—Organizational Culture Assessment Instrument (2019). https://www.ocai-online.com.

Odendaal, Willem, Salla Atkins, and Simon Lewin. 2016. "Multiple and Mixed Methods in Formative Evaluation: Is More Better? Reflections from a South African Study." *BMC Medical Research Methodology* 16 (1): 1–12. https://doi.org/10.1186/s12874-016-0273-5.

OECD. 2018. *Health expenditure in relation to GDP in Health at a Glance: Europe 2018: State of Health in the EU Cycle*. OECD Publishing, Paris. https://doi.org/10.1787/health_glance_eur-2018-30-en.

Oh, Sang Yeob, Supratip Ghose, Chung Kyungyong, Joong Kyung Ryu, and Jung Soo Han. 2014. "Recent Trends in Convergence-Based Smart Healthcare Service." *Technology and Health Care* 22 (3): 303–7. https://doi.org/10.3233/THC-140822.

Olatokun, Wole, and Chinazom Irene Nwafor. 2012. "The Effect of Extrinsic and Intrinsic Motivation on Knowledge Sharing Intentions of Civil Servants in Ebonyi State, Nigeria." *Information Development* 28 (3): 216–34. https://doi.org/10.1177/0266666912438567.

Olubunmi, Funmilola. 2015. "Knowledge Management As an Important Tool in Organisational Management: A Review of Literature" *Library Philosophy and Practice* 4 (10): 1–23. http://digitalcommons.unl.edu/libphilprachttp://digitalcommons.unl.edu/libphilprac/1238.

Oluikpe, Paul. 2012. "Developing a Corporate Knowledge Management Strategy." *Journal of Knowledge Management* 16 (6): 862–78. https://doi.org/10.1108/13673271211276164.

Osei Frimpong, Kofi, Alan Wilson, and Owusu-Frimpong Nana. 2015. "Service Experiences and Dyadic Value Co-Creation in Healthcare Service Delivery: A CIT Approach." *Journal of Service Theory and Practice* 25 (4): 443–62. https://doi.org/10.1108/jstp-03-2014-0062.

Ostrom, Amy L., A. Parasuraman, David E. Bowen, Lia Patrício, and Christopher A. Voss. 2015. "Service Research Priorities in a Rapidly Changing Context." *Journal of Service Research* 18 (2): 127–59. https://doi.org/10.1177/1094670515576315.

Pečarič, Mirko, and Bojan Bugarič. 2011. *Javne službe*. Ljubljana: Faculty of Administration.

Peneder, Michael. 2002. "Intangible Investment and Human Resources." *Journal of Evolutionary Economics* 12 (1–2): 107–34. https://doi.org/10.1007/s00191-002-0103-2.

Pentland, Alex. 2014. *Social Physics: How Good Ideas Spread—The Lessons from a New Science*. New York: The Penguin Press.

Perc, Matjaž. 2019. "The Social Physics Collective." *Scientific Reports* 9 (1): 9–11. https://doi.org/10.1038/s41598-019-53300-4.

Pertusa-Ortega, Eva M., María D. López-Gamero, Jorge Pereira-Moliner, Juan José Tarí, and José F. Molina-Azorín. 2018. "Antecedents of Environmental Management: The Influence of Organizational Design and Its Mediating Role Between Quality Management and Environmental Management." *Organization and Environment* 31 (4): 425–43. https://doi.org/10.1177/1086026617718426.

Pertusa-Ortega, Eva M., Patrocinio Zaragoza-Sáez, and Enrique Claver-Cortés. 2010. "Can Formalization, Complexity, and Centralization Influence Knowledge Performance?" *Journal of Business Research* 63 (3): 310–20. https://doi.org/10.1016/j.jbusres.2009.03.015.

Peters, Linda D., Helge Löbler, Roderick J. Brodie, Christoph F. Breidbach, Linda D. Hollebeek, Sandra D. Smith, David Sörhammar, and Richard J. Varey. 2014. "Theorizing about Resource Integration through Service-Dominant Logic." *Marketing Theory* 14 (3): 249–68. https://doi.org/10.1177/1470593114534341.

Petition to increase doctors' salaries in Montenegro. 2019. https://www.peticije.online/peticija_za_povecanje_zarada_ljekara?fbclid=IwAR2Al4S3cToXooLfz-8pnZ-v7ehOGkib-6zq3GwNK7wYkUbsipVbJdFZV300.

Petković, Mirjana, and Jelena, Lukić. 2013. "Uticaj informacione tehnologije na dizajn organizacije: Primer organizacije u zdravstvu." *Sociologija* 55 (3): 439–60. https://doi.org/10.2298/SOC1303439P.

Philips, Marianne Ekman. 2004. "Action Research and Development Coalitions in Health Care." *Action Research* 2 (4): 349–70. https://doi.org/10.1177/1476750304047980.

Pilav, Aida, and Zaim Jatić. 2017. "The Impact of Organizational Culture on Patient Satisfaction." *Journal of Health Sciences* 7 (1): 9–14. https://doi.org/10.17532/jhsci.2017.411.

Pisano, Gary P. 1989. "Using Equity Participation to Support Exchange: Evidence from the Biotechnology Industry." *Journal of Law, Economics and Organization* 5: 109–26.

Polanyi, Michael. 1966. *The tacit dimension*. New York: Doubleday.

Polanyi, Michael. 1967. *The tacit dimension*. London: Routledge and Kegan Paul.

Ponzi, Leonard, and Michael Koenig 2002. "Knowledge management: Another management fad?" *Information Research* 8 (1). http://InformationR.net/ir/8-1/paper145.html.

Porter, Michael Eugene. 1990. *The Competitive Advantage of Nations*. London: Macmillan.

Porter, Michael Eugene. 2008. "The Five Competitive Forces that Shape Strategy." *Harvard Business Review* 86 (1): 78–93. USA.

Porter, Michael Eugene, and Mark Kramer. 2019. "Creating Shared Value." In *Managing Sustainable Business*, edited by Gilbert G. Lenssen and Craig N. Smith, 327–350. Dordrecht, The Netherlands: Springer

Porter, Noah. 1913. *Epistemology*. Springfield: Webster's Revised Unabridged Dictionary, G & C. Merriam Co.

Pouwels, Ivan, and Ferry Koster. 2017. "Inter-Organizational Cooperation & Organizational Innovativeness. A Comparative Study." *International Journal of Innovation Science* 9 (2): 184–204. https://doi.org/10.1108/IJIS-01-2017-0003.

Powell, Richardson. 1962. *Zen and reality*. New York: Taplinger Publishing.

Praag, Bernard, and Ada Ferrer-Carbonell. 2004. *Happiness Quantified: A Satisfaction Calculus Approach*. Oxford University Press. https://doi.org/10.1093/0198286546.001.0001.

Prahalad, Coimbatore Krisha, and Venkat Ramaswamy 2004. "Co-Creating Unique Value with Customers." *Strategy and Leadership* 32 (3): 4–9.

Prysmakova, Palina. 2016. "From Compliance to Commitment: Centralization and Public Service Motivation in Different Administrative Regimes." *International Journal of Manpower* 37 (5): 878–99. https://doi.org/10.1108/IJM-12-2014-0253.

Public Administration Reform Strategy of Montenegro 2002–2009. http://www.mup.gov.me/ResourceManager/FileDownload.aspx?rid=41581&rType=2&file=1197558453.pdf.

Public Administration Reform Strategy of Montenegro 2011–2016. http://www.mju.gov.me/ResourceManager/FileDownload.aspx?rId=268697&rType=2.

Puranam, Phanish. 2012. "A Future for the Science of Organization Design." *Journal of Organization Design* 1 (1): 18. https://doi.org/10.7146/jod.6337.

Pusić, Eugen. 1989. *Nauka o upravi.* Zagreb: Narodne Novine.

Quinn, Robert E., and John Rohrbaugh. 1983. "A Spatial Model of Effectiveness Criteria: Toward a Competing Values Approach to Organizational Analysis." *Management Science* 29: 363–377. http://dx.doi.org/10.1287/mnsc.29.3.363.

Rabiu, Mirae. 2009. "Knowledge Management in Nigeria Oil and Gas Industry: Theoretical Frameworks, Practical Challenges and Opportunities." *Petroleum Technology Development Journal* 1: 1–10.

Radević, Ivan, and Miro Haček. 2019. "Decentralisation Processes in Montenegrin Public Administration: Challenges of Health System." *Lex Localis - Journal of Local Self-Government* 17 (3): 471–93. https://doi.org/10.4335/17.3.471-493(2019).

Radević, Ivan. 2013. *Digitalna ekonomija i marketing menadžment.* Podgorica: Univerzitet Crne Gore—Ekonomski fakultet. ISBN 978-86-80133-65-2; COBISS.CG-ID 22752016.

Radević, Ivan. 2018. *Retorika u funkciji liderstva.* Podgorica: Fakultet za državne i evropske studije. ISBN 978-9940-537-14-2; COBISS.CG-ID 36606736.

Radonjić, Radovan. 2011. *Crnogorska retorika.* Podgorica: Dukljanska akademija nauka i umjetnosti.

Radonjić, Radovan. 2013a. *Retorika.* Podgorica: Fakultet za državne i evropske studije.

Radonjić, Radovan. 2013b. *Znameniti govori.* Podgorica: Fakultet za državne i evropske studije.

Rakočevič, Slobodan. 1994. *Državna uprava: vloga, položaj, organizacija, delovanje.* Ljubljana: Uradni list RS.

Rayner, Jennifer, Laura Muldoon, Imaan Bayoumi, Dale McMurchy, Kate Mulligan, and Wangari Tharao. 2018. "Delivering Primary Health Care as Envisioned: A Model of Health and Well-Being Guiding Community-Governed Primary Care Organizations." *Journal of Integrated Care* 26 (3): 231–41. https://doi.org/10.1108/JICA-02-2018-0014.

Reed, Darryl. 1999. "Stakeholder Management Theory: A Critical Theory Perspective." *Business Ethics Quarterly* 9 (3): 453–43. https://doi.org/10.2307/3857512.

Regmi, Krishna, Jennie Naidoo, Alan Greer, and Paul Pilkington. 2010. "Understanding the Effect of Decentralisation on Health Services: The Nepalese Experience."

Journal of Health, Organisation and Management 24 (4): 361–82. https://doi.org/10.1108/14777261011064986.

Resatsch, Florian, and Urlich Faisst. 2004. "Measuring the performance of knowledge management initiatives." *Proceedings of the 5th European Conference on Organizational Knowledge*. Innsbruck: Learning, and Capabilities.

Reynaud, Bénédicte. 2005. "The Void at the Heart of Rules: Routines in the Context of Rule-Following. The Case of the Paris Metro Workshop." *Industrial and Corporate Change* 14 (5): 847–71. https://doi.org/10.1093/icc/dth073.

Riege, Andreas. 2007. "Actions to Overcome Knowledge Transfer Barriers in MNCs." *Journal of Knowledge Management* 11 (1): 48–67. https://doi.org/10.1108/13673270710728231.

Rivero, Jean. 1971. *Droit administratif.* Paris: Dalloz.

Robertson, Maxine, and Jacky Swan. 2003. "'Control - What Control?' Culture and Ambiguity within a Knowledge Intensive Firm." *Journal of Management Studies* 40 (4): 831–58. https://doi.org/10.1111/1467-6486.00362.

Romer, Paul M. 1986. "Increasing Returns and Long-Run growth." *Journal of Political Economy* 94: 1002–37.

Rule, John, Roger Dunston, and Nicky Solomon. 2016. "Learning and change in the redesign of a primary health care initiative." *Journal of Workplace Learning* 28 (7), 451–67. https://doi.org/10.1108/JWL-09-2015-0069(2016).

Rulebook on more detailed instruction for monitoring and establishing the process of evaluation, with indicators and criteria to conduct monitoring and evaluation of the quality of health care (Official Gazzette of Montenegro 17/15).

Rumelt, Richard. 1974. *Strategy, Structure and Economic Performance*, Massachusetts, Graduate School of Business Administration, Harvard University. In *Organizacioni dizajn—pristupi, metode i modeli*, edited by Ondrej Jaško, Mladen Čudanov, Miloš, Jevtić, and Jovan Krivokapić (2017). Beograd: FON.

Rydenfält, Christofer, Per Odenrick, and Per Anders Larsson. 2017. "Organizing for Teamwork in Healthcare: An Alternative to Team Training?" *Journal of Health, Organisation and Management* 31 (3): 347–62. https://doi.org/10.1108/JHOM-12-2016-0233.

Sahoo, Debajani, and Tathagata Ghosh. 2016. "Healthscape Role towards Customer Satisfaction in Private Healthcare." *International Journal of Health Care Quality Assurance* 29 (6): 600–13. https://doi.org/10.1108/IJHCQA-05-2015-0068.

Santti, Ulla, Tuomo Eskelinen, Mervi Rajahonka, Kaija Villman, and Ari Happonen. 2017. "Effects of Business Model Development Projects on Organizational Culture: A Multiple Case Study of SMEs." *Technology Innovation Management Review* 7 (8): 15–26. https://doi.org/10.22215/timreview1096.

Saviano, Marialuisa, Ratri Parida, Francesco Caputo, and Saroj Kumar Datta. 2014. "Health Care as a Worldwide Concern. Insights on the Italian and Indian Health Care Systems and PPPs from a VSA Perspective." *EuroMed Journal of Business* 9 (2): 198–220. https://doi.org/10.1108/EMJB-10-2013-0050.

Sawhney, Mohanbir, and Emanuela Prandelli. 2000. "Communities of Creation: Managing Distributed Innovation in Turbulent Markets." *California Management Review* 42 (4): 24–54. https://doi.org/10.2307%2F41166052.

Scarbrough, Harry, and Jacky Swan. 2001. "Explaining the diffusion of knowledge management." *British Journal of Management* 12: 3–12.

Schedlitzki, Doris, and Gereth Edwards. 2018. *Studying Leadership—Tradicional and Critical Approaches*. Los Angeles: SAGE.

Schein, Edgar, H. 2004. *Organizational Culture and Leadership (Third Edition)*. San Francisco: Wiley.

Scholten, Gerard. R., and Ted Van Der Grinten. 1998. "Between Physician and Manager: New Co-Operation Models in Dutch Hospitals." *Journal of Management in Medicine* 12 (1): 33–43. https://doi.org/10.1108/02689239810225238.

Sciulli, Nick. 2008. "Public Private Partnerships: An Exploratory Study in Health Care." *Asian Review of Accounting* 16 (1): 21–38. https://doi.org/10.1108/13217340810872454.

Serenko, Alexander, Timothy Hardie, Nick Bontis, Lorne Booker, and Khaled Sadeddin. 2010. "A Scientometric Analysis of Knowledge Management and Intellectual Capital Academic Literature (1994–2008)." *Journal of Knowledge Management* 14 (1): 3–23. https://doi.org/10.1108/13673271011015534.

Shahzad, Khuram, Sami Ullah Bajwa, Ahmed Faisai Siddiqi, Ahmid, Fahran, and Ali Raza Sultani. 2016. "Integrating knowledge management (KM) strategies and processes to enhance organizational creativity and performance: An empirical investigation." *Journal of Modelling in Management* 11 (1): 154–79. https://doi.org/10.1108/JM2-07-2014-0061.

Sinisammal, Janne, Pekka Leviäkangas, Tommi Autio, and Elina Hyrkäs. 2016. "Entrepreneurs' Perspective on Public-Private Partnership in Health Care and Social Services." *Journal of Health Organization and Management* 30 (1): 174–91. https://doi.org/10.1108/JHOM-02-2014-0039(2016).

Snow, Charles C. 2015. "Organizing in the Age of Competition, Cooperation, and Collaboration." *Journal of Leadership and Organizational Studies* 22 (4): 433–42. https://doi.org/10.1177/1548051815585852.

Snow, Charles C. 2016. "Organizing in the Age of Competition, Cooperation, and Collaboration." *Journal of Leadership and Organizational Studies* 22 (4): 433–42. https://doi.org/10.1177/1548051815585852.

Snow, Charles C., Øystein D. Fjeldstad, Christopher Lettl, and Raymond E. Miles. 2010. "Introduction to the Special Issue." *Organizational Dynamics* 39 (2): 91–2. https://doi.org/10.1016/j.orgdyn.2010.01.011.

Sorrentino, Maddalena, and Massimo Simonetta. 2011. "Assessing Local Partnerships: An Organisational Perspective." *Transforming Government: People, Process and Policy* 5 (3): 207–24. https://doi.org/10.1108/17506161111157584.

Stanford, Naomi. 2007. *Guide to Organization Design*. London: *Profile Books*. In *Organizacioni dizajn—pristupi, metode i modeli*, edited by Ondrej Jaško, Mladen Čudanov, Miloš Jevtić, and Jovan Krivokapić (2017). Beograd*:* FON.

Stanišić, Milija. 2005. *Dubinski slojevi Trinaestojulskog ustanka u Crnoj Gori*. Podgorica: Istorijski institut Crne Gore.

Stanovich, Keith. E. 1996. *How to Think Straight About Psychology (5th ed.)*. Chicago: Scott Foresman.

Statistical Office of Montenegro—Monstat. 2020. https://www.monstat.org/cg/page.php?id=19&pageid=19.

Statistical Office of Montenegro—Monstat. 2019. https://www.monstat.org/cg/page.php?id=47.

Steiner, Reto, Claire Kaiser, Christopher Tapscott, and Carmen Navarro. 2018. "Is Local Always Better? Strengths and Limitations of Local Governance for Service Delivery." *International Journal of Public Sector Management* 31 (4): 394–409. https://doi.org/10.1108/IJPSM-05-2018-226.

Stogdill, Ralph, M. 1974. *Handbook of Leadership: A Survey of Theory and Research.* New York: Free Press.

Stoker, Gerry. 1991. *The Politics of Local Government.* Basingstoke: Palgrave Macmillan.

Strategy for Improvement of the Health Care Quality and Safety of Patients 2019–2023, with Action Plan 2019–2020 (2019). Ministry of Health of Montenegro. http://www.mzdravlja.gov.me/ResourceManager/FileDownload.aspx?rid=379784&rType=2&file=Strategija%20za%20pobolj%C5%A1anje%20kvaliteta%20zdravstvene%20za%C5%A1tite%202019-2023.pdf.

Strömgren, Marcus, Andrea Eriksson, Linda Ahlstrom, David Kristofer Bergman, and Lotta Dellve. 2017. "Leadership Quality: A Factor Important for Social Capital in Healthcare Organizations." *Journal of Health, Organisation and Management* 31 (2): 175–91. https://doi.org/10.1108/JHOM-12-2016-0246.

Subramani, Mani R., and Natarajan Venkatraman. 2003. "Safeguarding Investments in Asymmetric Interorganizational Relatiosnhips." *Academy of Management Journal* 46 (1): 46–61.

Šunje, Aziz. 2003. *Top-menadžer—vizionar i strateg.* Sarajevo: Tirada.

Sušanj, Zoran, Ana Jakopec, and Sanja Stamenković. 2013. "Uloga Stila Rukovođenja i Organizacijske Pravednosti u Identifikaciji Zaposlenika s Organizacijom." *Suvremena Psihologija* 16 (2): 185–201.

Swart, Juani, and Nicholas Kinnie. 2003. "Sharing knowledge in knowledge intensive firms." *Human Resource Management Journal* 13 (2): 60–75.

Swensen, Stephen, Grace Gorringe, John Caviness, and Dawn Peters. 2016. "Leadership by Design: Intentional Organization Development of Physician Leaders." *Journal of Management Development* 35 (4): 549–70. https://doi.org/10.1108/JMD-08-2014-0080.

Sydänmaanlakka, Pentti. 2002. *An Intelligent Organization: Integrating Performance, Competence and Knowledge Management.* Oxford: Capstone.

Teece, Davdi, F. Gerry Pisano, and Amy Shuen. 1997. "Dynamic capabilities and strategic management." *Strategic Management Journal* 18 (7): 509–33.

The Constitution of Montenegro. 2007. Official Gazette of Montenegro 01/07 and 38/13—Amendment I-XVI). http://www.skupstina.me/images/dokumenti/ustav-crne-gore.pdf.

The Law on Budget of Montenegro 2009 (Official Gazette of Montenegro 82/08, 31/09 and 51/09).

The Law on Budget of Montenegro 2010 (Official Gazette of Montenegro 87/09).

The Law on Budget of Montenegro 2011 (Official Gazette of Montenegro 78/10 and 28/11).
The Law on Budget of Montenegro 2012 (Official Gazette of Montenegro 66/11 and 29/12).
The Law on Budget of Montenegro 2013 (Official Gazette of Montenegro 66/12).
The Law on Budget of Montenegro 2014 (Official Gazette of Montenegro 61/13).
The Law on Budget of Montenegro 2015 (Official Gazette of Montenegro 59/14 and 47/15).
The Law on Budget of Montenegro 2016 (Official Gazette of Montenegro 79/15 and 73/16.
The Law on Budget of Montenegro 2017 (Official Gazette of Montenegro 83/16, 42/17 and 89/17).
The Law on Budget of Montenegro 2018 (Official Gazette of Montenegro 90/17, 17/18 and 55/18).
The Law on Budget of Montenegro 2019 (Official Gazette of Montenegro 87/18 and 45/19).
The Union of Municipalities of Montenegro (2019). http://uom.me/baze-podataka/opstinske-finansije.
Thurmond, Veronica A. 2001. "The Point of Triangulation." *Journal of Nursing Scholarship* 33 (3): 253–58. https://doi.org/10.1111/j.1547-5069.2001.00253.x.
Tisen, Rene, Daniel Andriesen, and Frank Lekan Depre. 2006. *Dividenda znanja: Stvaranje kompanija sa visokim učinkom kroz upravljanje znanjem kao vrednošću.* Novi Sad: Adižes.
Toni, Alberto F. de, Gianluca Biotto, and Cinzia Battistella. 2012. "Organizational Design Drivers to Enable Emergent Creativity in Web-Based Communities." *Learning Organization* 19 (4): 337–51. https://doi.org/10.1108/09696471211226699.
Treiblmaier, Horst 2018. "Optimal levels of (de)centralization for resilient supply chains." *The International Journal of Logistics Management* 29 (1): 435–55. https://doi.org/10.1108/IJLM-01-2017-0013(2018).
Union of Medical Doctors of Montenegro. 2019. https://www.sindikatdoktora.me/.
United Nations—Voluntary National Reviews at the High-Level Political Forum on Sustainable Development. 2020. https://sustainabledevelopment.un.org/member-states/montenegro.
Uribe, Diego F., Isabel Ortiz-Marcos, and Ángel Uruburu. 2018. "What Is Going on with Stakeholder Theory in Project Management Literature? A Symbiotic Relationship for Sustainability." *Sustainability (Switzerland)* 10 (4). https://doi.org/10.3390/su10041300.
Vanderstoep, Scot. W., and Deidre D. Johnston. 2009. *Research Methods for Everyday Life: Blending Qualitative and Quantitative Approaches.* San Francisco: Jossey-Bass—A Wiley Imprint.
Venkatraman, N., and Hüseyin Tanriverdi. 2004. "Reflecting 'Knowledge' in Strategy Research: Conceptual Issues and Methodological Challenges." *Research Methodology in Strategy and Management* 1: 33–65. https://doi.org/10.1016/S1479-8387(04)01102-6.

Vikkelsø, Signe, Peter Kjær, Haldor Byrkjeflot, and Simon Neby. 2008. "The End of the Decentralised Model of Healthcare Governance?: Comparing Developments in the Scandinavian Hospital Sectors." *Journal of Health Organization and Management* 22 (4): 331–49. https://doi.org/10.1108/14777260810893944.

Volberda, Henk W., Niels van der Weerdt, Ernst Verwaal, Marten Stienstra, and Antonio J. Verdu. 2012. "Contingency Fit, Institutional Fit, and Firm Performance: A Metafit Approach to Organization-Environment Relationships." *Organization Science* 23 (4): 1040–54. https://doi.org/10.1287/orsc.1110.0687.

Walker, Kenton B. 1993. "Centralized Information Systems Services: Managing the Transition to Decentralization." *Industrial Management & Data Systems* 93 (8): 8–12. https://doi.org/10.1108/EUM0000000001449.

Wang, Sheng, and Raymond A. Noe. 2010. "Knowledge Sharing: A Review and Directions for Future Research." *Human Resource Management Review* 20 (2): 115–31. https://doi.org/10.1016/j.hrmr.2009.10.001.

Wang, Xiaoying, and Yong Zeng. 2017. "Organizational Capability Model: Toward Improving Organizational Performance." *Journal of Integrated Design and Process Science* 21 (1): 5–24. https://doi.org/10.3233/jid-2017-0005.

Wang, Xiaoying, Yong Zeng, Aurilla Aurelie Arntzen, Kyoung Yun Kim, and Ying Liu. 2017. "Organizational Capability: Skills Related to Organizational Knowledge." *Journal of Integrated Design and Process Science* 21 (1): 1–3. https://doi.org/10.3233/jid-2017-0010.

Watcharasriroj, Budsakorn, and John C.S. Tang. 2004. "The Effects of Size and Information Technology on Hospital Efficiency." *Journal of High Technology Management Research* 15 (1): 1–16. https://doi.org/10.1016/j.hitech.2003.09.001.

Waterman, Robert H., Thomas J. Peters, and Julien R. Phillips. 1985. "Structure Is Not Organization." *Readings and Exercises in Organizational Behavior*: 151–61. https://doi.org/10.1016/b978-0-12-054752-4.50024-5.

Weilandt, Lisa. 2018. *How Can Supervision Contribute to Support Improvement in School, Health Care and Social Services?* Sweden: Swedish Health and Social Care Inspectorate—Inspektionen för vård och omsorg.

WHO—World Health Organization. 2018. *Global Health Expenditure Database.* https://apps.who.int/nha/database.

Wickramasinghe, Nilmini 2010. "Perspectives of Knowledge Management in Urban Health." *Healthcare Delivery in the Information Age* 1: 21–39. https://doi.org/10.1007/978-1-4419-5644-6.

Wikström, Ewa, and Lotta Dellve. 2009. "Contemporary Leadership in Healthcare Organizations: Fragmented or Concurrent Leadership." *Journal of Health, Organisation and Management* 23 (4): 411–28. https://doi.org/10.1108/14777260910979308.

World Bank. 2019. https://data.worldbank.org/indicator/SH.XPD.CHEX.GD.ZS & https://data.worldbank.org/indicator/SE.XPD.TOTL.GD.ZS.

World Economic Forum. 2019. *Study Shows That Relationships Have the Biggest Effect on Health.* https://www.weforum.org/agenda/2019/10/according-doctor-biggest-contributor-health.

World Health Organization—Helsinki Statement—Framework for Country Action—Health in all Policies. http://apps.who.int/iris/bitstream/handle/10665/112636/9789241506908_eng.pdf;jsessionid=902FBC3F3751FCAEF029700F206F7388?sequence=.

World Health Organization—Regional Office for Europe—European health policy framework—Health 2020. http://www.euro.who.int/__data/assets/pdf_file/0011/199532/Health2020-Long.pdf, 1. 1. 2019.

Worldometers—Provider of Global COVID-19 Statistics. 2021. https://www.worldometers.info/coronavirus.

Xinhua—Chinese State Agency. http://www.xinhuanet.com/english/2019-10/17/c_138479441.htm.

Xu, Ke, Agnes Soucat, Joseph Kutzin, Callum Brindley, Nathalie Vande Maele, Hapsatou Touré, Maria Aranguren Garcia, Dongxue Li, Helene Barroy, Gabriela Flores, Tomas Roubal, Chandika Indikadahena, Veneta Cherilova. 2018. *Public Spending on Health: A Closer Look at Global Trends.* WHO—World Health Organization. Global Report: http://apps.who.int/bookorders.

Young, Ronald. 2010. *Knowledge Management Tools and Techniques Manual.* Tokyo: Asian Productivity Organization. ISBN: 92-833-7093-7. www.apo-tokyo.org.

Zavyalova, Anastasya, Michael D. Pfarrer, Rhonda K. Reger, and Debra L. Shapiro. 2012. "Managing the Message: The Effects of Firm Actions and Industry Spillovers on Media Coverage Following Wrongdoing." *Academy of Management Journal* 55 (5): 1079–1101.

Zhao, Jing, Tao Wang, and Xiucheng Fan. 2015. "Patient Value Co-Creation in Online Health Communities: Social Identity Effects on Customer Knowledge Contributions and Membership Continuance Intentions in Online Health Communities." *Journal of Service Management* 26 (1): 72–96. https://doi.org/10.1108/JOSM-12-2013-0344.

Ziaee Bigdeli, Alinaghi, Muhammad Kamal, and Sergio de Cesare. 2013. *Information Sharing through Inter-organisational Systems in Local Government. Transforming Government: People, Process and Policy* 7. https://doi.org/10.1108/17506161311325341.

Index

Page references for figures are italicized.

About the Author

Ivan Radević works for the Faculty of Economics, the University of Montenegro in Podgorica—Department of Management and Organization. He is engaged in the following courses: Fundamentals of Management, Organization Design, Business Economics, Management of Small and Medium-sized Enterprises, Leadership and Change Management. Also, since 2019, Ivan has been engaged at the Faculty of Electrical Engineering, University of Montenegro on courses of Management in ICT and Basics of Business Administration.

Before that, Ivan was a manager of the Faculty of Administrative and European Studies in Podgorica, and an associate at the Department of Economics (2010–2015). Ivan is engaged as a lecturer in the Human Resources Management Authority of Montenegro, as well as in the School of Rhetoric in Podgorica. He is a licensed state examiner in the field of informatics and certified ECDL lecturer and examiner. For more than twenty-five years, Ivan has been active in his family's business—the printing house "Grafo Press" Podgorica. He is one of the founders of the Sports and Recreational Association "Ekomen."

Ivan obtained a master's degree in economics and in public administration legal studies. He defended his doctoral thesis in the field of management and organization—*Knowledge Management and Organizational Design as Quality Factors of Health Organizations' Services*.

He published two books, *Digital Economy and Marketing Management* (2013) and *Rhetoric in the Function of Leadership* (2018), as well as many scientific papers.

Ivan attended many educational programs and participated in a number of seminars and conferences on different topics in the field of economics, in the country and abroad. He participated in the development of many projects and studies that are being implemented by the Government of Montenegro, Faculty of Economics in Podgorica, and Faculty of Administrative and European Studies, or were carried out in the past.

Ivan is a member of the global professional association of scientists in the field of management and organization *Academy of Management* and of *Mensa of Montenegro*.

For more details about the author visit: www.ivan.me.

www.ingramcontent.com/pod-product-compliance
Ingram Content Group UK Ltd.
Pitfield, Milton Keynes, MK11 3LW, UK
UKHW020841290926
15470UKWH00004B/1485

9 781793 64102